Coaching
with Spirit

Coaching *with* Spirit

Allowing Success to Emerge

Teri-E Belf

JOSSEY-BASS/PFEIFFER
A Wiley Company
www.pfeiffer.com

Published by

JOSSEY-BASS/PFEIFFER
A Wiley Company
989 Market Street
San Francisco, CA 94103-1741
415.433.1740; Fax 415.433.0499
800.274.4434; Fax 800.569.0443

www.pfeiffer.com

ISBN: 0-7879-6048-9

Library of Congress Cataloging-in-Publication Data

Belf, Teri-E.
    Coaching with spirit : allowing success to emerge / Teri-E Belf.
      p. cm.
    Includes bibliographical references and index.
    ISBN 0-7879-6048-9 (alk. paper)
    1. Leadership. 2. Success. I. Title.
HD57.7 .B4476 2002
658.4'092—dc21

                                                                          2002001146

Printed in the United States of America

We at Jossey-Bass strive to use the most environmentally sensitive paper stocks available to us. Our publications are printed on acid-free recycled stock whenever possible, and our paper always meets or exceeds minimum GPO and EPA requirements.

Jossey-Bass/Pfeiffer also publishes its books in a variety of electronic formats. Some content that appears in print may not be available in electronic books.

Acquiring Editor: Matthew Davies
Director of Development: Kathleen Dolan Davies
Developmental Editor: Susan Rachmeler
Editor: Rebecca Taff
Senior Production Editor: Dawn Kilgore
Manufacturing Supervisor: Becky Carreño
Interior and Cover Design: Bruce Lundquist
Front Cover Photo: Kim Allen Williams

Printing   10   9   8   7   6   5   4   3   2   1

DEDICATION

This book began in Spirit, evolved with Spirit,
and is dedicated to Spirit—the Spirit of and in coaches.

Ode to Spirit

We are the light, we know,
Shining from within, we glow.
Honoring what is unique
in our clients, we seek
to
Purposefully share our best,
with coachly passion and zest.
Whether we "be" or "do,"
we allow
Spirit to shine through.

Contents

Foreword xi

Preface xvii

Acknowledgments xxi

Introduction 1

Chapter 1 The Relationship Between Coaching and Spirituality 11
Coaching 12
Spirituality 15
Coaching and Spirituality 16
The Path to Coaching with Spirit 22
The Three Grounded Principles of Coaching with Spirit 25

Chapter 2 Connection with Self 27
Seven Magic Words and the Wizard's Belief 29
Do to Be and Do to Do 30
Three-Step Approach 38

The Voice of Spirit Is Intuition 42

Encompassing Me and My Shadow 49

Chapter 3   Connection with the Client 51

Encompassment 55

The Question 62

Summary 71

Chapter 4   Connection with the Whole 73

Synchronicity Is Purpose Behind Circumstances 74

Cycles, Circles, and the Dip 77

Metaphors Facilitate Connection 86

Spirit in the Environment 91

Summary 95

Chapter 5   The Present Moment 97

Making a Different Difference 99

Spirit's Physiological Presence 102

Expectancy 106

Using Humor 108

Neutrality 110

Embodied Spirit 113

Chapter 6   Responsibility 121

Thoughts and Beliefs 122

Action 142

For Managers Only 148

Summary 150

Chapter 7   Marketing Coaching with Spiritual Fluidity 151

Four Ways Spirituality Enhances Marketing Effectiveness 152

The Toughest Coaching Choices 158

The Six Steps to Fluidly Market Coaching with Spirit 161

Summary 168

Chapter 8   Executive Coaching with Spirit 169

Personal Purposefulness 170

Acknowledgment 175

Executives Talk About Feelings 176

Connection 177

Executives Have It All 179

Competencies Used to Coach Executives 195

Summary 197

Chapter 9   International Coaching with Spirit 199

Stories from Five Countries 199

Summary 212

Chapter 10   Coach Leader Perspectives on Coaching with Spirit 213

Fourteen Coach Leaders' Viewpoints 214

Coaching Pointers 227

Summary 229

Chapter 11   Fanning the Embers of Client Transformation 231

Ten Examples 231

Summary 241

Chapter 12   Stoking the Fire: Coaching with Spirit Learning Communities 243

Coaching Learning Communities 244

The Newfield Network 244

Professional Coaches and Mentors Association (PCMA) 248

Success Unlimited Network (SUN) 250
Turn Down the Heat 252

Epilogue   What's Next? The Space for Coaching 253

Appendix   Coaching with Spirit Assessment 257

Bibliography 267

About the Author 271

About the Contributors 273

Index 287

Foreword

We are not human beings having a Spiritual experience.
We are Spiritual beings having a human experience.

Pierre Teilhard de Chardin

THE BOOK YOU ARE NOW HOLDING is a gift from Spirit combined with the talents of many contributors. *Coaching with Spirit: Allowing Success to Emerge* will invite you to reflect on and perhaps resonate with its profound message long after you have finished reading the words. I read many books. Some entertain and some enlighten; a few books, like this one, both enlighten and entertain. As you read *Coaching with Spirit,* I predict you will smile with delight and recognition; you will ponder; you will recall your own experiences with Spirit; and you will seek out others to share what you have discovered.

After reading *Coaching with Spirit,* you will no longer need to just wait for Spirit to arrive. You will know how to set the stage appropriately for its appearance, recognizing and accepting Spirit through the myriad ways it makes its presence known.

Personal and Professional Coaches

It behooves all personal and professional coaches to read *Coaching with Spirit* because it is written by coaches and for coaches, making it especially relevant and valuable to the coaching profession. I am enthusiastic about how this book connects coaching with Spirit in a way that is both practical and subtle.

In addition, I endorse *Coaching with Spirit* for a larger audience. I believe every coach will recommend it to clients, friends, family, and significant others; and those people, in turn, will find it of value and pass it on to others—especially those involved in business and sports, where bottom-line performance matters.

I recommend this book so highly because I *know* coaching. I'm a full-time personal and professional coach—both to individuals and to groups—and I also serve as a youth soccer coach. My preparation includes practical experience, academic achievements, and graduation from two International Coaching Federation accredited (ICF) coach training programs—Success Unlimited Network and New Ventures West. Additionally, I volunteer many hours with ICF and leaders in the coaching profession as we work with defining coaching, continuing education, and credentialing.

I know our profession will continue to expand, with or without this book, but I also know that a coach who is comfortable and confident when Spirit emerges is a more effective coach. In the words of Sir Thomas Aquinas, "All that is true, by whomsoever it has been said, has its origin in the Spirit" (Boldt, 1993, p. 69).

Having coached many adults through work performance as well as young athletes in sports performance, I err whenever my attachment to a particular outcome seduces me into trying to manage Spirit. When I'm wise enough to step aside or, better yet, step into the "flow," I succeed beyond my expectations.

Executives, Managers, and Supervisors

If you manage others, this book can increase your management effectiveness. If you are open to experiencing Spirit's presence—if you can move out of your own way and enter into the flow when Spirit shows up—then your work group can reach unexpected performance results.

For example, I recall one experience at work when Spirit showed up. Overwhelmed by the urgency and the expanse of a project assigned to a professional work group that I was a member of, we met, tentatively discussed, and cautiously planned our next action steps. From cautiousness, one person spoke to our intention rather than to our task. From that moment, Spirit emerged and we merged as a group, performing in an extraordinary manner. We spoke few words, yet each knew what the other was doing and planning. We collectively moved smoothly through the bureaucracy, and upper management accepted our proposals without question. We did not notice the unusual dynamics of our experience until we completed the task. The policies and procedures developed by that work group some fifteen years ago still remain in effect, and our story remains in the folklore of that organization.

People Who Play and Coach Sports

In sports, players and coaches spend hours, days, and years in preparing for and concentrating on achieving excellence. The thrill of victory is a powerful motivator, but it is not enough. At best, victory only comes to half of the participants in an athletic competition. I do not think they play to win or lose. I believe they play to have the opportunity to experience "being in the zone"—that connection with Spirit that makes all the effort meaningful. For players, coaches, and spectators, being in the zone is a spiritual experience of unparalleled joy and extraordinary achievement. The experience can be so awesome that we want to repeat it again and again. Spirit is what brings us back to the game. Let me tell you about one of my sports experiences.

Standing on the sideline of a competitive youth soccer match, I could feel something shift before I could see the evidence. As the soccer coach, I knew my team could perform well but not great, and the opposing team on that momentous day was exceptionally talented. My team and I had moderate expectations—play well and walk off the field after the match knowing we had offered our best effort. Little did we know Spirit would be in attendance.

The game stands out in the memories of those who were fortunate to have observed the match. It was one of those golden moments in sports. Everyone present that day was touched by Spirit. Both teams played magically—the individual performances, invisible, and the play of each team, incredible. The young men moved about the field as if connected physically to every shirt of the same color. Possession of the ball seemed to lift one team just above the ground so that players moved with a grace not often seen in teenage males.

When the collective and connected efforts of determined opposition took its toll and the other team gained possession, the ever-present grace of movement shifted to that team. Back and forth the teams played while coaches and spectators were strangely silent—no commands and no cheers, just awe. Each team scored goals and allowed goals. At the end of the match, it was a draw. The players of both teams lingered on the field, conversing, congratulating, and absorbing every last moment of that very special game.

Why You Should Read This Book

The essence of *Coaching with Spirit* enables us to be more aware of our spiritual being and more likely to recognize and enjoy such moments in business, in sports, or anywhere where we can observe Spirit in action.

For most of us, Spirit remains mystical or magical and not often present in our everyday lives. Often the literature about and the language of Spirit leaves us feeling awed but removed, rather than aware and open. We read stories of Spirit's presence and we are intrigued, perhaps even inspired, but often unable to take action to increase or enrich our own spiritual experiences. To facilitate our awareness of the many ways Spirit can be invited into our lives, *Coaching with Spirit* provides many excellent and motivating stories of Spirit emerging during coaching meetings. It also provides the language and practices that can enable each of us to "see" and "speak" Spirit in everyday life. Imagine the life we each could lead if Spirit is our usual experience rather than an extraordinary event!

In *Coaching with Spirit*, author Teri-E Belf demonstrates that we can welcome Spirit into coaching and into our lives with both lightness and depth. Her easy-to-understand language reveals that spiritual experiences are not a mystery known only to a select minority but are a joy that we all can experience in daily life. Belf presents familiar spiritual concepts—*connection, present moment,* and *responsibility*—with the intriguing added value of combining practical how-to steps with the anecdotes of Spirit in action. Through the reflection experiences offered in each chapter, Belf encourages you to develop your own language for Spirit. True to coaching form, you may end with more questions than answers, but our profession will know more about Spirit's involvement as a result of this seminal contribution to the field.

Belf is *the* coach to write this book, and I have a distinct advantage in making this claim. I have experienced the material over the past several years in the presence of the author. Belf speaks the language of Spirit—not sometimes, not often, but *always*. For Belf, coaching with Spirit is a natural, comfortable, confident way to be with people, and her practical side makes the material on how to connect with Spirit accessible to all.

In addition, Belf, with all the credentials, experience, and wisdom you expect from a renowned leader in the coaching profession, is also the coach to write this book for at least three other reasons.

1. "Where the Spirit does not work with the hand, there is no art," said the famous Italian Renaissance artist and sculptor Leonardo da Vinci (Boldt, 1993, p. 1). By da Vinci's standards, Belf is an artist. Spirit works with her hand.

Coaching with Spirit demands that you go beyond your discipline into your artistry. She has the courage of an artist, stepping beyond her formal training and giving herself over to the magical process of Spirit. Belf walks the talk. No prescriptions or shoulds, this book is an expression of her Spirit.

2. During the past fifteen years, Belf has a successful track record of attracting spiritually based persons to the coaching profession. She personally and individually develops her coach-trainees to integrate spirituality into their lives and into their coaching business. This book is your opportunity to partner with Teri-E Belf.

3. Attracting collaborators, a special talent of the author, has enabled her to serve as a magnet for many gifted individuals who contribute to *Coaching with Spirit*. She attracts people who have a deep appreciation for human and spiritual experiences. You hold in your hands their gift. In the pages that follow, you will find an incredible opportunity to tap into these experiences and learn from these Spirit-filled coaches. Allow yourself to receive; their gifts will stay with you.

And, finally, as you read *Coaching with Spirit,* know that you will spend some delightful time in "conversations" with Belf. Spirit will show up in your view of the world, in your explanations of the world, in your self-talk, and in your conversations with others. A new focal point, a new perspective, and, perhaps, a brand new you will emerge.

Travis Twomey
ICF Master Credentialled Coach
SUN Coach Trainer

Preface

How This Book Came to Be Written

During several consecutive meditations, I learned that this book was to emerge in a particular way. Spirit spoke to me: "Let go of preconceived notions. Pay attention to when I am present during your coaching and write down what is happening. How do you know I am present? Be fully aware and conscious of Spirit." Feeling energized by my instructions and challenge, I proceeded, eagerly awaiting client meetings and additional messages through daily meditation.

A year later, Spirit suggested I selectively invite colleagues to collaborate. Over the past sixteen years, I have been fortunate to have thousands of coaches pass through my life. How would I know whom to ask?

In the past I would have

1. Identified criteria for inclusion;

2. Drafted a long list of people who might be possibilities;

3. Tracked down current phone numbers and email addresses;

4. Prioritized the list and scheduled time to make contact; and

5. Set this game plan in motion.

Planning Versus Flow

My past method of operating would mean a lot of planning and effort for my researcher, organizer, and list-maker personas. Through the process of writing this book,

I discovered another path, equally productive and a lot easier! I learned that when I let go of control and allow Spirit to lead, miracles happen. I find that this process lives with a pulse of its own.

Two parts of me merged in writing this book—the researcher and the coach. Under the microscope, the motivations of each turn out to be the same. Coaches and researchers both thrive on curiosity; both pursue learning to add to a colossal body of information; both seek to advance understanding of our choices for living as well as our surroundings, personally and collectively.

Although I have not engaged in any formal research to studiously track and record coaching interactions, I am acutely aware of patterns, inconsistencies, and trends— and some statistics I do keep, such as percentage of results achieved and well-being.

The Purpose of This Book

The dual purpose of *Coaching with Spirit* is to increase coaches' awareness of the part Spirit plays in their interactions with clients and to enhance coaching effectiveness by welcoming and integrating Spirit into coaching meetings. Submissions by and interviews with coaching leaders reveal a plethora of perspectives relative to how Spirit manifests.

This book was not intended to teach spirituality or the application of spirituality in daily living. These stories may suggest personal growth and development avenues and may motivate you, although this is not the purpose for which they were collected. Because the material is organized around anecdotal stories and offers exercises and questions for reflection, readers who prefer this learning mode will likely take away the greatest value.

The Audience

This book is about coaching, for coaches, and written by coaches and clients. Represented here are thoughts, insights, stories, and experiences from coaches who coach in person, over the telephone, or over the Internet; coaches who are leaders with decades of experience and novice coaches; coaches who have extensive training or coaches without training; coaches who operate in clients' business or personal lives or both; and coaches who work individually or in groups. This book is for seasoned coaches, personal coaches, professional and executive coaches, managers in the process of adding a coaching component to their jobs, coaches internal and external to organizations, life coaches, and sports coaches from soccer moms to professionals. Because managers do not always assume the coaching role, the use of coaching skills is not always appropriate. The manager's job description lists numerous management skills, called forth as required by the situation: directing, motivating, orienting, training, interviewing, monitoring, and evaluating performance, to name a few. When a manager needs to direct an employee's work effort, the position of allowing success to emerge appears quite contrary to what is typically called for. The most effective manager has multiple behaviors at his or her command and can flexibly and nimbly switch gears to call forth the suitable skill. Adding the "allowing" aspect of coaching to one's repertoire merely adds to the manager's cornucopia of available options.

Coaching with Spirit will also interest people exploring coaching as a new career or adding an adjunct skill set to an existing career. Those in the process of becoming coaches, whether or not enrolled in one of the myriad coach training schools or academic programs for coaches, will find this material useful.

Finally, this book will be of particular relevance to individuals in fields most closely aligned to coaching, such as social work, training and development, therapy, pastoral counseling, neuro-linguistic programming (NLP), career development and management, personal training, teaching (all levels), and organization development. Because the focus is on connection and communication, anyone wishing to improve or enhance personal or professional relationships might be intrigued with the perspective, material, and exercises offered. Managers can use this book to coach supervisors and employees to experience work as more meaningful, be better problem solvers and team players, and experience more balance. Most importantly, anyone working at any level within an organization can learn life purpose through coaching and can assess how he or she fits into the mission of the organization as a significant and necessary part of the entire operation.

Selection of Contributors

The choice of contributors happened with Spirit guiding me. I did not know the criteria used for selection. "*Sometimes you do not need to know*," I was gently reminded. "*Just trust.*" I marveled at who would show up and the perfection of sequence and timing. Quite often I heard, "I was thinking about writing on your topic—your timing, your call is perfect now." On the one hand, I hypothesized Spirit would be revealed in many different forms and expressions. On the other hand, I sensed I might tap into a commonality shared by all. Both theories turned out to be true. In spite of contributors' requests to preview what I had written as a way to establish context, I took care to ensure no contributor read another's submissions in order to avoid influence or bias. I believe this editorial decision further validates the recurrence of themes I received.

About two-thirds into the writing process, I chose to abandon a survey of the literature because I believed that interviews with coaching leaders would supply the most current thinking available, given that other books about coaching with Spirit have not yet been published.

Anonymity

All the stories presented here really happened, although some names were changed, and sometimes several clients were merged into composite characters to protect anonymity. Contributors have been named for stories submitted; all other material emanates from the author.

Acknowledgments

I APPLAUD ALL COACHES willing to explore the process of coaching with Spirit and support the integrity and evolution of our transformational process. Deep love and appreciation to my kind husband, Phil, for his unbelievable support. A big thank you to my inspiring son, Kim, who generously shares laughter, poetry, and photos through which his loving and creative Spirit emerges. Special heart gratitude to my dear friend, agent, editor, and PJ buddy, Pam Leigh, for transforming my words into the third dimension, perhaps even the fourth.

Introduction

Setting the Stage

When asked about the essence of the Success Unlimited Network® (SUN) coaching approach, I describe how we integrate spirituality into our work and prefer to train people willing to do the same. The next question usually is, "How do you define spirituality?" After I share the key principles you will read about in this book, I can count the number of replies on two hands:

- "That is not far out; that is common sense."

- "I am interested in your program because it mentions spirituality."

- "I have been trying to find a profession where I can offer all of myself."

- "I wonder why your program is one of the very few that uses the word spiritual."

- "Oh, now I understand; I am glad you are not one of those new age programs."

- "I am delighted it is not a religious program."

- "That describes my spiritual perspective too."

- "I am a very religious person and I can relate to that."

- "The word spirituality attracted me on your website."

A sampling of these daily requests from all around the world reinforces my assumption that the timing is right for coaches to bring their spiritual base into coaching. It does not take statistical analysis to understand this message.

Addressing the Topic of Coaching and Spirit

What is really going on backstage, and what beckons us to proclaim our spiritual truth now? The answer requires a peek into our evolution and current state of affairs. The following article explores why the partnership between coaching and spirit does come at the perfect time.

The Zeitgeist Is Ready for Coaching
Phil Nelson, Ph.D., C.S.C.

Zeitgeist means spirit of the times. The spirit of our times, our evolution, continues to move toward interrelatedness and complexity. Coaching emerges at the perfect time in our history.

Accelerating Evolution

For three-quarters of the time living organisms have existed on earth, life was composed of simple one-cell animals. The speed of evolution accelerated rapidly with the development of multi-cell animals—to vertebrates, to social non-human colonies, to humanity. Even though complexity increases, we must remain connected or we risk perishing. Coaching connects us to our purpose and to our spirituality within the universe.

Each millennium brings a quickening pace and with it a new dominant spirit and culture. The last millennium shift arrived with the dawn of the Information Age, the speeding up of the Spiritual Age, and an unprecedented rate of change that is still accelerating. Supported by the higher order of synergy, we appear ready to cross the threshold to a higher order of interrelatedness as evidenced by the World Wide Web, global commerce, and the germination of global unity. We are being called on to evolve our ability to adapt and respond to this increasingly complex world. Which profession has surfaced to support us to respond nimbly, survive, and, better yet, thrive, during this massive and tumultuous transition? Coaching.

Androgynous Power

Each of us is being called on by our emerging culture to become more balanced and whole, more highly developed both in sensitivity and in androgynous power. Becoming a more integrated human being will enable us to live in this higher order. This leap in evolution supports a cultural revolution characterized by synergy, cooperation, teamwork, and community—all predominantly feminine characteristics. Our male leaders, managers, and supervisors are being summoned to draw on and develop their feminine sides. We will all need to become aware of and develop our latent capacities. Developing increasing awareness of these multi-faceted capacities is one of the key reasons for coaching

Why is the timing right for the coaching profession to emerge *now*? Coaching is an excellent vehicle to guide us in identifying and developing our unattended parts. Holistic perspectives and integrated choices constitute the bedrock of the coach's work.

The Wisdom of the Question

Each age is built upon successes of the prior age. The best evidence of wisdom to catapult us forward appears to be a question. Questions enable challenge to the old, exploration of the new, progress, and . . . yet another question. The coaching process is based on inquiry, starting with the basic questions surviving all human generations: *Who Am I?* and *Why Do I Exist?* History documents transitions from one century to another, bringing a surge of questioning seekers. Surrounded by media raising our consciousness about our past, bombarded by visionaries and psychics predicting our future, we wonder, "Why am I here now? What is the meaning of my life, of life in general?"

Because the zeitgeist is ready, the profession of coaching emerges ready to guide purposeful discovery and eager to facilitate our individual and collective adventures into uncharted territory.

Lessons to Learn

Attendance in this earth classroom requires lessons to be learned. With both the Information and Spiritual Ages upon us simultaneously, we have a particular mandate for human evolution on our chalkboard. Our assignment today is to learn how to manage an overload of information. Whirlpools of information feel like Class V rapids on a white-water rafting adventure. If we do not exercise some of the following skills, we become pulled under at the mercy of the power of the swirling vortex of energy.

- Ask for help, so we do not have to manage alone;
- Prioritize and make choices to focus our attention on selected options;
- Create external systems and structures for support; and
- Be still, allowing all options to become clear.

The last skill taps into the essence of Spirit. When we take care to select consistent with our purpose and values, we can *trust* necessary information to be available at our beckoning. Our minds can be open and free to connect with internal information (Source and intuition) and be fully present. The ability to live in the moment is a key Spiritual Age lesson for both client *and* coach.

A Rose Is a Rose Is a Rose and Spirituality Is . . .?

Why have we been and are we still clandestine about our spirituality relative to coaching? Both coaching and the Spiritual Age have blossomed in the past decade with undeniable profusion. Why has no book yet been written solely on the topic of exploring the relationship between coaching and spirituality? Perhaps because spirituality is similar to the concept of love in that it means so many different things, has so many interpretations, and has so many interpreters. With a jaded interpretation, we might lose forward momentum or muddy the potential waters of the profession. Perhaps the "S" word has been stuffed in the back of the closet long enough!

The Structure of This Book

Wind beneath my sails, I often find myself on the leading edge of new attitudes, sparking challenges, igniting curiosities, sprinkling possibilities, and unearthing insights. Coaching with Spirit is a natural process. Energized by the correspondence between nature and coaching, I offer the four elements—earth, water, fire, and air—as metaphors to enrich the meaning of certain chapters.

Chapter 1. The Relationship Between Coaching and Spirituality

By defining the relationship between coaching and spirituality, we set the stage. The beginning of any coaching process must be life purpose. Uncovering one's reason for existence presupposes any effort to explore new intellectual domains or make different behavioral choices. With clarity of purpose, one carries intention to be (and do) the best one can be (and do). Within the context of purposefulness, choices become supportive of one's journey rather than detrimental. When life meaning is established, one is more likely to test and tweak old habits and risk moving out of autopilot into new and fertile grounds. For the past twenty years of spiritual exploration—studying metaphysics and quantum physics, religion, personal growth and development, and having my share of spiritual experiences—I have come to identify three basic principles: connection, the present moment, and responsibility (CPR) and I have chosen them to organize the concepts and examples in Chapters 2 through 6.

Chapter 2. Connection with Self

The first of the three grounded principles of coaching with Spirit is being present within oneself, aware of the life and lessons of the intellect, the emotions, and the body. I explore the relationship between doing and being and the personal qualities supporting connection with self. Techniques reveal how to attain the highest vertical and horizontal perspective for a wide-ranging connection with self as well as how to prepare to partner with Spirit.

Chapter 3. Connection with the Client

The relationship in coaching is paramount to success. Factors such as transformational listening, a sacred silent space brimming with curiosity and respect, the speech of silence, encompassment, and the process of questioning all play a vital role in a successful client, coach, and Spirit partnership.

Chapter 4. Connection with the Whole

Our spiritual paths lead us to integration and wholeness. Synchronicity, rituals, metaphors, and coaching patterns such as cycles, circles, and dips provide clues to assist coaches in opening the gateway to the broadest perspective available. I also convey how the coach's holistic attitude and the coaching environment influence the process.

Chapter 5. The Present Moment

The best place to live is in the present. We do this by attending to our emotional, mental, and physical capacities. Because the physical resides in the present at all times, it provides a rich source of data for our learning. Discussing the embodied spirit; pronouncing feelings; assessing well-being; creating expectancy, humor, and neutrality; and accessing long-term memory offer insights into the richness of data available to the coach open to Spirit in the moment. One exercise reveals how to ascertain the client's physical place of purpose. We also explore Spirit as an omnipresent inner coach.

Chapter 6. Responsibility

Each of us is responsible (able to respond) for our choices expressed through our body, mind, and emotions. This chapter addresses both beliefs and actions, because choice begins with thoughts, is expressed through words, and converts into actions. Responsibility will be examined from the point of view of beliefs, language, and action choices and also from the angle of supporting clients to be responsible for their choices. At the end of this chapter is a section, For Managers Only, with ten common managerial challenges and possible coaching with Spirit approaches.

Chapter 7. Marketing Coaching with Spiritual Fluidity

Taking a holistic view plunges us into other aspects of the business of coaching outside the process of client meetings. Marketing has a stream of spiritual principles that, when consciously allowed and used, facilitate coaches to be in the flow, attract more clients, and, therefore, do more coaching. Marketing does not turn on and off like a faucet; it can be a seamlessly fluid process. Hence the metaphor of water enhances the message of this chapter. Clients in hand, we flow into applying the CPR principles to subsets of the population: executives, different cultures, and coach leaders.

Chapter 8. Executive Coaching with Spirit

An intriguing question from many people centers on whether executives need a different form of coaching than others do. Prevalent is the myth that executives are not ready or not willing to acknowledge Spirit in their work lives. This chapter reports stories from the experience of nine executive coaches and the extent to which Spirit shows up in their coaching.

Chapter 9. International Coaching with Spirit

Several coaches who have coached internationally or are coaching internationally share perspectives on coaching with Spirit. I wondered whether the experiences would be any different from those of coaches in the United States. Although not representative of the whole world, anecdotes from the United Kingdom, Indonesia, Netherlands, Canada, and France give interesting glimpses into the homogeneity of the coaching experience.

Chapter 10. Coach Leader Perspectives

What do coaching leaders have to say when asked, "What does coaching with Spirit mean to you?" Master Coach Diane Hetherington interviewed fourteen coaching leaders about the role Spirit plays in their coaching business and consolidates thirty-five pointers coaching leaders offer to help increase the ability to coach with Spirit.

Chapter 11. Fanning the Embers of Client Transformation

This book would offer a lopsided view of coaching with Spirit if it presented only coaches' stories. Clients' points of view ignite a more complete picture of this professional partnership. People who are considering coaching as a profession or who are adding coaching as a skill will delight to learn that clients openly welcome the integration of spirituality into the coaching process. In this chapter, ten clients relate their experiences of being coached by coaches who actively endorse Spirit as part of the process. One might refer to coaching with Spirit as a spontaneous combustion of two souls passionately living on purpose—so fire became the appropriate metaphor.

Chapter 12. Stoking the Fire: Coaching with Spirit Learning Communities

How do coaches stay "hot"? To do and be a coach with continual spark demands support. Because coaches value relationships, it is predictable that coaching learning communities are lighting the way for support. More interesting is that spirituality appears to fuel each of the three communities—The Newfield Network, Professional Coaches and Mentors Association (PCMA), and Success Unlimited Network (SUN)—described with behind-the-scenes anecdotes.

Epilogue. What's Next? The Space for Coaching

Running with the wind, I hang glide in my imagination using the coaching wind to cross-fertilize many venues of life with coaching community circles. My vision soars with the potential beyond transforming personal clients and corporate settings. The future of coaching is created by our ability to *allow* the transformation.

How to Gain Maximum Value from This Book

For maximum benefit, read this book with ease (E's): envision, examine, experiment, expand, evaluate, engage, and evolve.

- *Envision yourself engaged in the scenarios as you read the examples.* Pay attention to what feels *un*comfortable or is outside your comfort zone. Perhaps the greatest growth lies in these moments of uneasiness. Revel in the similarities; seize on oddities to open new learning gates.

- *Examine your thoughts and behavior.* What would you have done in these situations? How flexible are you when it comes to trying something different? Please remember, coaching with Spirit does *not* substitute for coaching competency or skill. To the contrary, coaching with Spirit complements them.

- *Experiment with new and alternative ways.* Questions for reflection are offered at the end of most key points. Take time to ponder them. Several exercises throughout Chapters 3 through 7 provide detailed instructions more elaborate than reflections, beckoning you to try out new behaviors. Experiment with the exercises and bring a new twist to your coaching and other communications. Design your own research project with *you* as the subject. Go further—create your own unique behavioral offshoot matched to your circumstances and personality.

- *Expand your perspective by inviting Spirit to participate.* What does Spirit mean to you? How can you entertain Spirit as a coaching partner? To what extent are you comfortable mentioning Spirit in your coaching meetings?

- *Evaluate the results.* To do this presumes you know the desired results and have some measurement to determine success. At the beginning of selected chapters, you will find an assessment instrument to help you evaluate the degree to which you already coach with Spirit. Assess your thoughts and actions prior to reading the material and then read the stories and principles and use the reflections to experience new mindsets and behaviors. After six to twelve months, revisit the entire Coaching with Spirit Assessment that appears in the Appendix. Taking this approach mirrors how the coaching process operates. We help clients assess where they are, where they want to go, and how to get there.

- *Engage colleagues in discussion.* Create a coaching circle so you and your colleagues can collaboratively discuss applications and implications of your coaching with Spirit experiences. Consider the success of this new behavior. Did you achieve the outcome you intended? Was it more ecologically efficient and effective than your old way? How did you feel during the experiment? Afterward? What did you do well? What might you do differently next time? What happened differently as a result of your experiment? What additional questions does it raise for you? Develop and use your coaching support systems.

- *Evolve to a new level of coaching.* Spirit is holographic, so enjoy jumping around this book as your eye flits to just the perfect place to begin. Stay as long as you wish, then dance to the next place that grabs your passion and curiosity. Let your doubts dangle. Learning dollops abound; trust and enjoy the process of free-falling into pages of relevance.

CHAPTER 1

The Relationship Between Coaching and Spirituality

ASSESSMENT

Please rate yourself on the extent to which you coach with Spirit.

0 = never; 1 = rarely; 2 = sometimes; 3 = often; 4 = most of the time;
5 = almost always

To what extent do I . . .

0 1 2 3 4 5   believe spirituality is a natural part of who we are?

0 1 2 3 4 5   believe Spirit can partner with me in coaching?

0 1 2 3 4 5   believe that people can learn their life's purpose?

0 1 2 3 4 5   continually ask myself, "How can I be of service now?"

0 1 2 3 4 5   guide clients' awareness to the purposefulness
of circumstances?

0 1 2 3 4 5   believe growth can come from challenges and problems?

0 1 2 3 4 5   know what my life lessons are?

Coaching

My official definition of coaching, derived from the British training I received in 1987, is an inquiry process of helping people master the ability to consistently obtain the results they want in all life areas with a sense of well-being. The longer I coach, the more I realize coaching extends far beyond realms I ever imagined.

The greatest tool coaches have is the question. Questions come from a yearning to know more about ourselves, others, and the whole. The source of questions can be our intellect, our emotions, and our spiritual meaningfulness.

Intellect

Curiosity motivates intellectual inquiry; we coach because we are curious about what makes people tick, curious about why people succeed and fail, curious about human nature. Self-directed questions keep us on the leading edge of our own wisdom. We want to know, to gain more knowledge. Coaching at the intellectual level spawns conversations about strategic planning, knowledge and fact gathering, and coaching for achievement. For example: "What blocked you from obtaining that result? What might you do differently next time?"

Emotions

The emotional cousin of curiosity is deep caring, acceptance, or love. When the motivation for coaching becomes emotionally based, the question, any question, becomes a legitimate excuse to connect with another human being. Coaching questions that have their source in affect tend to center on the "being" side of experience, typically on increasing joy, peace, and happiness. For example: "How might you have experienced that situation differently? What choice would bring greater peacefulness?"

Spiritual Meaningfulness

Broader than intellectual curiosity and emotional caring is the search for meaningful connection with the whole—the transformational reason for coaching. Coaching dialogues address belonging and purposefulness—the most expansive forms of context conceivable. Questions in this domain invite ruminations: "Why do you think these things have happened to you now? How does this relate to your highest way of contributing in the universe?"

My Definition of Coaching

This prelude leads to my unofficial and nowadays preferred definition of coaching—bringing us closer to coaching with Spirit.

> When a coach takes the initiative to create a space of unconditional acceptance or love (as well as a coach, a human being, can), then, for a time period of at least four months and for as long as the coaching partnership lasts, the client can *just be* whom he or she truly is.

The Difference Between Coaching and Therapy

In the past eighty years, psychotherapy has played a vital role in helping people understand their dysfunctional and emotional selves, ready to move beyond an unhealthy past to heal psychologically destructive patterns and relationships. When one feels emotionally healthy, hopeful, and optimistic, future plans take a different shape than when one feels stuck. The natural sequence is to clean up old garbage, then build success on a new platform. Coaching picks up where traditional therapy leaves off, moving people to integrate their therapeutic insights into practical everyday living. As therapy draws to a conclusion, clients ask "Now what? Now that I have probed and cleared my past, how can I create my life with the new me?" Enter coaching!

Someone once told me the difference between therapy and coaching: Therapy takes bad things and chunks them smaller while coaching takes good things and chunks them bigger. People seeking coaching appear ready to chunk bigger.

Preparing to Coach with Spirit

Coaching with Spirit brings a different perspective to the fore. For those considering becoming coaches, take time to reflect on your answers to the following ten questions. The more you know yourself, the more effective you will be as a coach.

1. How strong is my sense of self?

2. Do I know my values?

3. How do I acknowledge myself?

4. What role does service play in my life?

5. How do I cope with stresses within relationships?

6. How much am I willing to share my vulnerabilities?

7. How strong is my sense of purposefulness?

8. To what extent do I trust?

9. How important is my growth and development?

10. How authentic am I?

Why Unconditional Acceptance Is Transformational

I have boldly claimed coaching with Spirit involves unconditional acceptance or love. Have you ever tried to accept unconditionally a client who is an incessantly loquacious talker—a "motor mouth"—burdened with the inability to stop? If yes, you may have encountered someone like my client Milena. Or have you worked with clients defeated by procrastination, intensely under pressure from all corners to "get on the stick" and take action? If so, you may have coached someone like my client Ethan.

If you fell prey to the tendency to try to help the Milenas or Ethans eliminate their unwelcome behaviors, you may have missed the boat. Garrulousness could be a sign of fear. Consider what happens when the talking stops; the connection might be severed and lost. Keep spewing utterances of any sort and your listener remains in captivity, close at hand. Chances are people in Milena's ring of connection, such as her acquaintances, family, and colleagues, have chastised her for her annoying way of relating. Imagine instead loving her just the way she is. I did. You might witness what I call a coaching miracle. Milena began to honor moments of silence, connecting through energy instead of with her words. These short moments stretched out long enough for her boss to commend her for learning listening skills from her coach. Interestingly, I had no game plan to teach her listening skills.

Harvesting the learning from Milena and eager to carbon copy my new knowledge, I embarked on showering love on Ethan. Once again something remarkable and, from my vantage point, unexplainable occurred. In both cases, when our connection reached a level of certainty, Milena and Ethan moved into a place of choice *and* chose the opposite behavior. Ethan sprinted into action, causing his wife to thank me for helping him overcome procrastination. The "cave" (his garage) was finally getting cleaned out. But I did not work on helping Ethan overcome procrastination. So what catalyzed these outcomes? I believe it was unconditional acceptance.

Perhaps we experience miracles when we envelop clients with love and acceptance, respecting them just as they are, whether they choose to change or not. Encouraging someone to be at choice is more important than eradicating unwanted habits. I know my clients and I have learned and relearned that choice resides in the space of acceptance.

Spirituality

Spiritual Handicaps

Spirituality is often equated with religion. Throughout history, millions of people have been killed in the name of sundry religions trying to demonstrate superiority over one another. Not exactly evidence of one of the fundamental spiritual principles of this book: We are all connected.

Cults commit suicide to honor "spiritual" gurus. Terrorists and murderers claim that spiritual voices told them to perform heinous acts. Masses follow spiritual leaders without awareness of the personal power they relinquish. No wonder we shrink from proclaiming our spirituality publicly. I, too, experienced moments of disconnection during the widespread spiritual mania that swept the United States in the late 1980s.

A Personal Story. I invite you down memory lane to August 11, 1988, a day referred to as the Harmonic Convergence. Broadcast in the media as the day for planetary spiritual awakening, events to honor this day occurred across the globe. My son and I meandered down to the Washington Monument to see what the capital of the United States had planned. We arrived to find a circle of thirty people, all clothed in white from head to toe. As we inched closer, we alarmed someone from the inner circle, who quickly approached us and said firmly, "Don't come any nearer. You are not wearing white." Dumbfounded, we retreated, surprised that spirituality was defined as the color of attire. What happened to spiritual awakening and the principle of encompassment? This true story epitomizes how spirituality can be misinterpreted. No wonder many refrain from mentioning spirituality or relegate it to the back burner of their lives, only exposed on specific days when "sanctioned" religious observances occur.

This event led me to ponder what spirituality meant to me, and in time I came up with the following definition: Spirituality is the quality of evolving toward greater wholeness and integration while experiencing multilevel connections (to self, to another, and to the whole); being in the present attending to emotional, mental, and physical needs; and responding purposefully.

What aspects of spirituality bring us together instead of separate us? And what does this have to do with coaching?

Coaching and Spirituality

Spirit, our essence, is omnipresent with every coach and every client. When we coach with Spirit, we encompass all that is available. Let us refer to all that is available as Source. If we do not include Source, something is missing. Because Source is always present, what is missing in this word so_ _ce? You are (soURce). Coaching with Spirit suggests *you* can welcome, reveal, and understand this Spirit. When we coach with purposefulness—relegating what is not purposeful to the background; deleting attachment to results; trusting what happens is for the highest good of ourselves, our clients, and all concerned; being in the present moment, available, connected to ourselves, one another, and the whole; choosing our responses, in a state of wonder and curiosity; being of service and being grateful for all of this—then, we coach with Spirit.

Questions a Coach Asks Self While Coaching with Spirit

- How can I be of service now?
- How is this purposeful for me?
- Is this issue my "stuff" or my client's?
- What action is for the highest good of all concerned?
- What is the best way to connect? for each of us? for both of us?

Life Purpose

The ultimate spiritual question throughout the ages has been "Who am I?" or "Why do I exist?" and this is where coaching begins. After identifying the trail of purposefulness, the next hurdle is to become aware of when one is off track and to learn how to jump back on. Some become sidetracked for moments; others veer off course for years.

Coaches assist people to recognize purposelessness, as well as help clients resume purposefulness *if* they choose that track. It is a choice! When we choose our actions, we feel empowered; when we feel as if others hold the reins, we feel victimized. Even though the victim state erodes our Spirit's solidarity, it still remains a choice. When we choose purposefully, we experience greater satisfaction, fulfillment, and meaningfulness. Coaches do not attempt to influence an outcome; we facilitate awareness to bring clients to their choices. When clients appear to create obtuse detours, seemingly far off purpose, the coach's role is to remember patiently that we all create opportunities and experiences from which to learn. Acknowledge clients for making choices, whether you agree with the choice or not.

Sometimes we become sidetracked and lured by external trappings and wrappings. I became aware of this conundrum at the impressionable age of seventeen. Seated on a luxurious boat, soaking up the sun during a college break, I leaned over to an adult whom I knew to be in an internationally prestigious and influential position and naïvely commented, "Oh, you have it all; you must be so happy." His face fell, his brows furled for an instant, and he responded, "I'd rather be a carpenter." Shocked by his reply and his willingness to share it, I bit my tongue. To this day I recall that moment whenever a client has the courage to admit that something in life is missing. We all seek meaningfulness. I have never heard anyone admit to choosing to live a life without meaning.

In *Learning from the Inside Out,* the coaching book by Bianco-Mathis, Nabors, and Roman, the authors acknowledge the role of personal purposefulness in the organizational setting: "An organization that is built on the basis of a coaching mindset is able to capture the human spirit—and it is this ingredient that aligns personal and organizational goals and results in high performance" (Bianco-Mathis, Nabors, & Roman, 2002).

Spirit as a Partner

The following examples describe when I recognized Spirit as a partner in coaching.

Example

 During the first coaching meeting in which we uncover life purpose, I ask clients to recall and share times when they have experienced meaningful moments. I take notes and then studiously craft samples of life purpose statements using my notes.

Once, as I proceeded to create a statement, a magical event occurred. In real time it took but three seconds, yet I felt whisked into timelessness. Compelled to enter silence, I closed my eyes, looked up, and in the blink of an eye expressed gratitude for being allowed to do this work, affirmed that whatever happened was for the highest good of myself, my client, and all others concerned, acknowledged how blessed I felt to be part of the process enabling another person to understand connection to Source, and released any expectation of the correct answer.

Suddenly, I went mentally blank. When I opened my eyes, I began writing purely through sensation, oblivious to any cerebral processing. As different iterations emerged beneath my pen, my client grabbed his pen and created a life purpose statement that suited him to a T.

Spirit's Involvement Is an Honor. Since this incident from 1987 until the present day, the depth of increasing connection I feel with Spirit has been profound. Having had this experience thousands of times in many different coaching situations, I now feel Spirit's involvement as an honor instead of an oddity. I welcome and integrate these moments into my coaching, not just in the introductory or life purpose meeting but at any other time as well. When I feel stuck or unclear how to proceed, I deliberately close my eyes, allowing silence to speak. Answers always come when I allow space for Spirit.

Example

Helping clients to determine which career best suits their purpose is common to my business. When I contracted with Randy, he wanted a coach to help him think bigger than he could alone. "Bigger" turned out to be a handsomely paid leader in his field in an executive position. However, using Randy's life purpose statement as a guide, "bigger" also had to include a job that tapped into his passion and desire to contribute something meaningful.

As is often the case, coaches work with clients to clarify pieces of a puzzle and might not hang around to see the puzzle finished. We can help people clarify dreams; *they* still need to take action. Randy chose not to pay attention to *all* aspects of his purpose, convinced that if he made enough money and had enough power he would feel as if he was making a meaningful contribution.

Randy phoned back several years later, proud of his success but claiming something was missing. His executive position paid royally, offered panoramic visibility, and fulfilled his materialistic wishes, *but* did not feel fulfilling.

Randy learned one cannot be partially purposeful. A full commitment is needed! Revisiting his purpose statement, we wrote a job description including visibility, power, money, *and* contribution. A year later, Randy, well-established in his new job, feels more spiritually integrated and honors his entire being.

Spiritual Integrity Is Not Part of the Equation—It Is the Entire Equation. Hold up your mirror. If you do not coach with Spirit, your whole being may not be shining through. The profession of coaching, one of the most meaningful ones I have encountered (do you hear *my* purpose shining through?), requires complete integrity and authenticity.

Example

Christopher, a high-ranking military officer, wanted a coach to help him plan retirement. In his life purpose meeting, the word "peaceful" popped up over and over again, ending up as a key word in his purpose statement. At the moment of this discovery, Christopher's energy quivered. I verbally and nonverbally assured him it was acceptable to be authentic in my presence. He began softly crying, admitting he never had cried in front of anyone before. His two sides had collided—that mendacious part committed to thirty career years leading fighters and that part he later referred to as "the peacemaker." Ideas for his retirement game plan prior to coaching became diametrically opposed to the one he set out to design after acknowledging his truth.

"As soon as you trust yourself, you will know how to live," German philosopher and poet Johann Wolfgang Von Goethe wisely stated. Indeed, the life purpose meeting served to surface Christopher's inner truth.

One might conclude that spirituality in coaching is no more than validation, and in one sense that is so. However, learning life purpose is just the first step. The coaching process continues by guiding clients to develop the habit of using purpose to make choices and the habit of examining obstacles that hinder purposefulness. Having a coach while awakening and experimenting with your genuine self supports and eases the transition to more consistent purposeful living.

Example

Coach Debbie Call received this testimonial from one of her clients, Susan B. Crew, a personal coach and management consultant herself, lauding the importance of coaching with the spirit of purposefulness:

> The primary benefit for me was your ability to guide me to connect with my central essence and to connect with guiding forces larger than myself. This new perspective has increased my creativity, willingness to take risks, ability to pay attention to and enjoy my loved ones; has given me an expanded sense of what is possible in my work; and has resulted in more work (business) of the kind I want. Some of what helped this process was your gentleness, your ability to respond to my concerns by creating a safe space, your willingness to share some of your own experiences when this facilitated my journey, your practicing what you teach, and your connectedness to your own Spirit forces (Susan's Story, 2001).

When an event occurs that appears to derail clients from a purposeful trajectory, coaches can guide clients' awareness to the purpose behind every circumstance. Coach Peter Vajda uses the symbol of the spiral to explain how this works.

The "X" Spot of the Spiral
By Peter Vajda

When clients become discouraged during coaching, coaches can provide support without judgment or subjectivity by explaining discouragement or frustration using the spiritual metaphor of the spiral. The spiral represents the essence of the universal plan—reflecting that each of us is in a continual process of growth and development as we seek to align our personal consciousness with universal consciousness. When the former (evidenced by beliefs, thoughts, feelings, and actions) aligns with universal consciousness, we experience an innate sense of joy and well-being that holds steady even in the face of the initiating cycle of the new spiral, sensed as a downward movement.

Most clients understand that the spiral has downward cycles. Many clients need to realize no spiral ends on a downward cycle; life is in a continual upward spiral flow. In fact, every spiral ends on an upward swing. This means we continue to move forward in a positive direction, even when we feel as if we are sliding backward.

The repetitive point where the spiral moves horizontally may be perceived as a place of stasis, an absence of movement. Feelings of helplessness, being stuck, and going nowhere abound. We can refer to this experience as "the X spot" (see Figure 1.1), the point in the cycle where it looks and feels as if one is repeating old patterns, reminiscent of experiences.

Figure 1.1. The "X" Spot of the Spiral

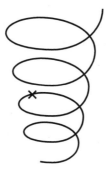

The "X" spot creates the opportunity for purpose to become a driving factor in conjunction with will and an understanding of the growth process. Trust and faith become supportive allies. On a spiritual plane, the "X" spot presents a challenge. Clients and coaches can use this doorway of opportunity to cross the threshold of fear and doubt by saying "No" to familiar sabotaging and disabling thoughts and feelings. Working to support clients to understand and persevere while acknowledging and experiencing the "X" spot often results in tremendous spiritual growth and emotional freedom and the ultimate prize—purposeful action.

The Path to Coaching with Spirit

Much happens before we become more purposeful. Our path of learning takes us from the quagmire of the pits and the problems into predetermined patterns of roadmaps, the dead end of polarization, paradoxes, preparation, construction zones of possibilities, and finally to the straightaway of purposefulness to partner with Spirit.

Many levels of learning happen as we journey up the spiritual path toward perfection. Perfection on the human plane is not possible because, if we experienced perfection all the time, we would have nothing to learn. The very reason for human existence is learning, and the path I metaphorically refer to represents advancement—the process of evolution. "The frontiers are not east or west, north or south, but wherever a man *fronts* a fact" (Thoreau, 1971, p. 30).

The Pits and Problems

At the entrance to the path to perfection exist problems and "the pits." If we stay in the pits, we yield to complacency or negativity and deny ourselves the option of resolution, growth, or a way out. Problems and obstacles ironically could be nicknamed "growing buddies" because they keep us in discovery mode. Without movement or change, no new brain synapses can be jumped, no new convolutions built, no learning can occur. In order for us to adapt to constant fluctuations in our vibrational environment, we, too, must keep vibrating or changing.

Invite problems in because they offer grist for learning. Snags, snafus, and glitches induce us to detach from the danger of the smug status quo. Certainly you do not need to seek out problems, but when they knock, allow them entrance.

Patterns

The easiest way to remain stuck is to develop patterns or habits—unconscious routines that keep us on autopilot, shielding us from the requirement to be fully present to what is at hand. When instinctive or autonomic behavior rules, choice is removed. If we do not have to think, we do not have to learn. It appears to be almost humanly impossible to operate 100 percent out of habit. Shifting external environments keep us on a delicate fulcrum between habit and choice. Paradoxical creatures that we are, we resist change with a vengeance, yet crave learning and insight to enable further evolution.

Polarization

Polarization separates, creates extremes, and denies the reality of the continuum. Familiar polarizations such as yes or no, black or white, always or never, and all or nothing diminish options, thereby sheltering the subtleties of life. For a moment, think about the weather forecast and assume the evening news reported bad weather racing your way. Without further information, you would make very different plans if you knew it to be a light sprinkle, heavy snowstorm, rain, sweltering heat, thunderstorms, or gusty winds. The more information you have, the more choices you have, the better judgment you can make.

Continuum thinking and subtlety expand the menu of options; polarization creates myopia. *Always* and *never* miss the possibility of *sometimes* and *periodically; yes* and *no* deny the existence of *perhaps* or *maybe; black* and *white* preclude shades of *gray.* The absolutist lives in a simplistic world devoid of complexity. The more complex and interrelational our worldview, the greater the number of responses available to us, the more learning is possible, and the higher the probability of adaptability and evolution.

Paradoxes

A paradox—a statement that is seemingly contradictory or opposed to common sense and yet is perhaps true—creates confusion and therefore a delightful launching pad into a space for learning. Contrary to the calm in the center of a hurricane, we cannot rest comfortably in the center of a paradox. Restless, we grapple with the conflict until some resolution becomes apparent, some logical sense regained. In the midst of this mental wrestling match, the fruit of discovery blossoms. Anyone who has attempted to resolve a paradox at the level at which it was created has experienced a frustrating dead end. Abstract thinking, creativity, and higher forms of cognitive ability such as synthesis and evaluation enable us to move beyond the paradox—processes replete with learning. With a twist of humor, the ultimate coaching paradox might be: I have the answers as to how to coach with Spirit. Perchance another paradox forms as we begin to explore how to prepare to be more fully in the present.

Preparation

All of these steps along the path, the problems, patterns, polarizations, and paradoxes intervene in our moment-by-moment experience to catalyze learning. When we exhibit certain qualities of being, our chances of learning increase. Curiosity, playfulness, attention to process instead of outcome, and being in a state of wonder serve as allies allowing us to relax into a new unknown.

Preparation means getting ready. At any given moment, how quickly can we respond? Travelers pack a necessity bag filled with essentials like shampoo, shaving cream, a toothbrush, and so forth. Those who travel frequently keep their kits stocked and packed, ready to go with them at a moment's notice. What do we find in our coaching with Spirit bag? What do we deem essential to do coaching, to be the coach? Many who have contributed to this book cite their spiritual work as the preparation enabling them to be the best coaches they can be.

Possibilities

Learning, the formulation of cerebral pathways, happens in the present moment because of our power to choose. Coaches often feel as if they operate on trial and error. I suggest we rename it "trial and trial" to honor all that is learning and growth. There are no errors! The "here and now" contains all possibilities, every option, in an infinitesimal intangible worldwide web. Remaining constantly in the present moment challenges most of us; yet we strive to increase those moments. We make every effort, even though we cannot succeed, for that would be perfection, and with perfection, learning disappears. Humans have more choices than other living beings and also the gift to exercise the power to choose. How can we remain open to all possibilities while at the same time select those that bring the greatest learning for all?

Purposefulness

Purposefulness comes with clear intention, focused energy, and integrated alignment for the good of all. Exercising choices consistent with one's purpose brings meaningfulness and discovery at the most subtle and ubiquitous levels. Every person's purpose is unique, a magnificent personal signature claimable and ascertainable by any seeker interested in the pursuit. Living on purpose magnetizes us to our greatest individualistic learning. The purpose of life is to learn; the purpose of learning is to live more purposefully.

Partnership

The most a coach can aim for is to be in partnership with Spirit, preparing for and cocreating a life full of learning—using every problem, unconscious pattern, polarization, and paradox that springs forth to guide us on our unique journey. This best describes the path to coaching with Spirit.

☙ R E F L E C T I O N

1. Would you be willing to risk exposing your Spirit at work if it meant an increase in your management effectiveness and ease of relating with colleagues at all levels in your organization?

2. Do you know your life purpose and how it relates to your company mission statement?

3. As a manager, how can you manifest your Spirit when coaching?

4. How might you introduce the "X" spot of the spiral to your employees? Colleagues? Work team?

The Three Grounded Principles of Coaching with Spirit

Three staples form the backbone of coaching with Spirit. Just as emergency medical technicians catapult into action fully prepared to resuscitate a breathless patient, coaches must be ready to infuse their spirit into the life of coaching. Keeping spirituality alive requires CPR: C = Connection, P = Present moment, and R = Responsibility.

Coaching examples and anecdotes from different venues of coaching illustrate varied applications—excavating life and giving meaning to each. Finally, harvesting the questions for reflection enables readers to assess, increase, and keep the ability to coach with Spirit alive and well. The metaphor of earth weaves throughout these chapters, reminding us how grounded spirituality can sprout down-to-earth transformation.

The next chapter, the first of the triad exploring connection, begins with an examination of the importance of connection with oneself.

Connection with Self

ASSESSMENT

Please rate yourself on the extent to which you coach with Spirit.

0 = never; 1 = rarely; 2 = sometimes; 3 = often; 4 = most of the time;
5= almost always

To what extent do I . . .

0 1 2 3 4 5   remember to return to my center when thrown off track?

0 1 2 3 4 5   believe I have the inherent ability to learn life lessons?

0 1 2 3 4 5   deal with the issue bigger than the one in the moment?

0 1 2 3 4 5   detach from my client's outcomes and results?

0 1 2 3 4 5   know with certainty that my clients have their own answers?

0 1 2 3 4 5   prepare myself spiritually before meeting a client?

0 1 2 3 4 5   begin meetings with a moment of silence, centering,
                   or stillness?

0 1 2 3 4 5   have techniques to calm my mind?

0 1 2 3 4 5   honor my own needs during a meeting?

0   1   2   3   4   5   keep perspective on the balance between doing and being?

0   1   2   3   4   5   look to see where I am negatively charged when I encounter negativity?

0   1   2   3   4   5   check my internal physical state for information during coaching?

0   1   2   3   4   5   check my emotional state for information during coaching?

0   1   2   3   4   5   hold up a mirror and reflect where I relate to my clients' issues?

0   1   2   3   4   5   take time afterward to assess how I experienced each client meeting?

0   1   2   3   4   5   take time to check my intuition?

0   1   2   3   4   5   recognize when I hear the voice of Spirit through my intuition?

0   1   2   3   4   5   trust my intuition?

0   1   2   3   4   5   act on my intuition?

0   1   2   3   4   5   appropriately let go of plans and expectations during a meeting?

WITH A BEMUSED LOOK and a satirical expression, comedienne Lily Tomlin quips, "Just remember, we're all in this alone." In contrast, we have heard, "No man is an island." These two opposite sides of an interesting tug-of-war philosophy blaze our trail into the topic of connection. Three aspects of connection will be explored: connection with *self*, connection with *another*, and connection with *the whole*.

This chapter delves into different facets of connection with self. At the intellectual level, connection translates into beliefs such as being of service, understanding the importance of integrating doing and being, allowing Spirit to source responses, and honoring the gifts received. When we link emotions and energy to the activities at hand, we connect even more with who we are. Certain personal qualities (humility, gratitude, patience, and openness) facilitate connection. To welcome Spirit into the coaching partnership requires preparation, intention, and letting go of expectation and attachment. You must be prepared to allow space, emptiness, a void, or silence for Spirit to emerge.

Seven Magic Words and the Wizard's Belief

Words: How can I be of service now?
Belief: When in doubt, let the client figure it out.

Coaching does not mean changing lives; it means changing the questions we ask and being open to what happens; it means replacing arrogance with humility.

Throughout this book you will find reference to one gold mine—a particular question containing seven words: "How can I be of service now?" I call these "magic words" because of their potency. When I ask this question internally to myself or aloud to my clients, I am humbly reminded to dismount my arrogant ego horse and transfer the power of wisdom to my client. The answer to this question is the "wizard's belief": "When in doubt, let the client figure it out."

The dictionary defines magic as a way to produce a desired effect or result that presumably assures human control over secret or mysterious knowledge. In this case, the desired effect becomes the client's increasing awareness, and the secret or mysterious knowledge is that clients already possess internal wisdom and their *own* answers. Magic subsumes the extraordinary power of influence, and we can and must guide our clients to remember *they* already know it all. This is our coaching mission.

Spirit Is a Super Coach Trainer. From the first time in 1987 when I experienced the magic of my heart and my "third eye" merging until today, I have intentionally welcomed and allowed this into all facets of my coaching. Having had this experience thousands of times in my coaching career, I recognize and honor Spirit's involvement as my number one coach trainer. When I feel stuck or unclear about how to proceed, I close my eyes, look up, and silently ask, "How can I be of service now?" Answers always come when I allow a question and space to coexist. I must confess, even after fifteen years coaching, it still feels like magic every time I ask the seven magic words, honor the wizard's belief, and rediscover that my client knows the answer.

We would do well to adopt the role of "Wizard Coach." Etymologically the word "wizard" stems from the philosopher or sage. Wizards have power, wise power. Our power is to allow clients to plow into *their* power to resolve their situations.

Every time a coach in training asks, "What should I do?" I reply, "When in doubt, let the client figure it out." Each time I feel thwarted, unclear, uncertain, foggy, muddy, incompetent, stymied, confused, and so on, I remind myself: "When in doubt, let the client figure it out." Then I remember this is how I can be of highest service now.

Sometimes, after you introduce coaching to a potential client, the person concludes with a thank you and a comment that the timing is not right to begin now. Trust people to know and honor their sense of timing. Avoid burrowing into their rationale. Also, if a client, for whatever reason, feels like terminating your agreement, trust the client again to know the timing is right to stop. Never argue or try to convince him or her otherwise. All you can ask is to unearth any learning to make you a better coach. And for this opportunity be deeply grateful.

Do to Be and Do to Do

"Being and doingness are like a triangle where each side supports the others. They are not in conflict with each other. They all exist simultaneously" (Gawain, 1995, p. 35).*

Connecting to oneself is a critical aspect of coaching with Spirit and must be examined from the "being" angle as well as from the "doing" angle. Because coaching deals with the whole person and spirituality by definition involves the whole person, we cannot coach just the "doing" part of a client or we would not be coaching with

---

*Reprinted from *Creative Visualization,* 1995, with permission of the publisher, Entourage.

Spirit. Those who focus exclusively on doing (achieving external goals, living hyperattentively to outward manifestations of success) are in the "do-do" business, not coaching. The coaching profession is committed to assisting clients to master the ability to produce results *with* a sense of well-being. Let us continue this analysis of connection to self with a look at the doing and being realms of coaching.

Centering

Both coaches and clients who discuss coaching with Spirit discover they engage in some form of centering activity to preserve their ability to be open and present with Spirit. These centering methods can be experienced as either "being" or "doing" activities. For example, walking is usually viewed as a *doing* activity. However, when I walked a peace labyrinth on the Millennium New Year's Eve, my experience was entirely in the *being* domain. As author of the best-selling *Inner Game* series of books, Gallwey eloquently states, "Building this bridge between inner and outer can bear much fruit in every game we play" (1998, p. xvii).

Because an activity can be experienced either or both ways, I began to wonder about my tendency to interpret clients' activities as doing when they might be perceiving them as being. I certainly ought not assume that I know which is which for a client. (When in doubt, let the client figure it out.) The following common coaching example portrays an individual who needed to have permission to just be.

Example

 Fast-paced, assertive, and continually busy, Natasha hoped that coaching would bring her into balance. I asked, "What would it look like if you were to experience balance?" She identified ten things she could do on a daily basis that would remind her to regain equilibrium and proudly emailed them to me. Some of her examples were to stop and take deep breaths, chew slowly, get up and stretch every fifteen minutes when working at the computer, take a short walk twice a day, and so on. Just reading the list exhausted me!

When we met again I asked about her experience of balance. She reported no change as a result of adding all those doing things and did not understand why she had not achieved the balance she craved. I asked her why doing more, albeit different things, did not bring her balance. In that moment Natasha realized she was exacerbating her problem by adding activities to her already drowning daily list.

Her new journey began. She refashioned her old way of conceiving balance, that is, just doing *different* things, and now allows herself to stretch her times of being (doing nothing). With amusement she told me she now "goes faster by going slower" and the balance she desires comes forth.

✿ REFLECTION

1. Think about a client who is overly focused on doing. How can you increase his or her awareness about being?

2. In visualizing accomplishing a result prior to any action, ask:
   - How would you need to be in order to obtain that result?
   - What feeling would support you?

3. After a client reports that a desired result has not been achieved, ask:
   - How would you need to have been to have obtained that result?
   - What feelings would have supported you?

4. Log times when you experience ten minutes of clock time as being and it feels like you have just engaged in thirty minutes of accelerated productivity.

5. Name three things that you define as "doing" things. Name three that are "being."

6. Ask several people whether they consider your choices as "doing" or "being."

The preceding example looked at internal connection related to doing and being. The next example illustrates the "Piggyback Principle," where external connection can bring internal integration.

The Piggyback Principle

External connections can trigger internal integration. Sometimes I find it appropriate to intentionally put two things together in the external world to give my client relational perspective. I call this the "Piggyback Principle of Coaching" because it reminds me when my Dad carried me piggyback on his shoulders and I gleefully caught his view of the living room from a towering height.

Many opportunities exist within our multifaceted lives that offer challenges for increased integration; these occasions can give us an edge toward sensing greater connection. The following example shows how Daniel used piggybacking to integrate two elements of his life.

Example

Daniel, fully engaged in the process of dumping incomplete projects and actions out of his brain and onto paper, left our coaching meeting committed to continuing this homework assignment. At the next meeting Daniel reported no progress because he left the list in his coaching notebook, which he did not open daily. Whenever he did remember to do the assignment, his coaching notebook was elsewhere. Aware that his time management system never left his sight, he realized he needed to integrate these two systems. He revamped his time management system to include his coaching homework.

True, Daniel had not accomplished his homework. However, Daniel learned a valuable lesson by recognizing that he had the power to "piggyback" by creating one system for all of his commitments. Piggybacking produced integration, and integration is a lifelong organizing principle.

I encounter opportunities to introduce piggybacking frequently in coaching. The principle involves taking new and useful thoughts, tools, techniques, processes, or actions and piggybacking (connecting) them with effective systems already in place. Piggybacking encourages broadened awareness of how everything of value connects.

✿ R E F L E C T I O N

1. Identify three ways you piggyback or could piggyback.

2. In what areas of your coaching life can you imagine further piggyback integration?

3. Ask your clients to brainstorm ways to piggyback new behaviors with ones that already serve them.

Bigger Than the Issue of the Moment

Every interaction, however seemingly insignificant, creates opportunity for guiding awareness to a long-term sustainable mindset. Micro-learning anchors to a specific event; macro-learning generalizes to many settings or areas of life and is sustainable beyond the timeframes of coaching partnership. When we leave the micro level and move to the largest whole, we offer a more complete coaching service. Because transferability and sustainability are desirable outcomes, coaches who engage clients in both levels of learning offer more to clients than those who remain at the micro level.

Coach Cindy Loughran, who has great sensitivity to this phenomenon, delightfully refers to this perspective as "bigger than the issue of the moment."

Example

Coach Marcy had just completed forty-five minutes of an hour-long telecoaching meeting. She asked the client how she could best be of service and heard back, "I'd love to get off the phone and go back to work." Marcy felt shot down, feelings of unworthiness creeping in. During our next meeting, she shared how deflated she felt when her client clearly ranked her as second priority. I explained that an even bigger issue was demanding attention and helped Marcy retrench by examining alternative options for responding and feeling. Tending to take things personally, Marcy had lost sight of one of the reasons for coaching, which is to acknowledge clients for making priority choices. When Marcy realized she could have acknowledged her client for being clear about her priorities and speaking her truth, she tapped into a bigger issue—authenticity. Authenticity takes courage! I honored Marcy for being authentic, and she in turn honored her client.

Sometimes coach training helps expand our repertoire; other times Spirit enters when least expected and most welcomed to offer a gift of perspective. Keep your learning caps on while you read how Spirit partnered with a coach to help Joe tweak his perspective to "balloon" beyond the presenting issue.

Example

Joe, a sixty-year-old Vietnam veteran with a horrific war experience, had been forced to declare bankruptcy a decade earlier and had just learned his wife of thirty-five years wanted a divorce. Three major life blows left him feeling bitter, angry, and carrying an impenetrable metal box around his heart. He arrived at our meeting bursting to dump his complaint, feeling victimized because he had to pay $500 monthly alimony for five years. Tired of a heavy heart, he wished he could come from a place of love instead.

I was unsure what to do next so I mentally asked myself the seven magic words: "How can I be of service now?" An idea came to mind immediately and I posed these three scenarios for Joe's consideration:

Scenario 1. "If I knew about a weekend workshop that could make all your anger go away and guarantee you will return loving yourself, and it costs $250, might you be interested?" "Oh yes", Joe quickly answered.

Scenario 2. "If I could refer you to a therapist specializing in helping patients move through intense rage and anger in just six to nine months guaranteed, and your total fee would not exceed $4,500, would you want to be referred?" After hesitating, Joe broke his reflective silence with an affirmative reply.

Scenario 3. "If I could create a game in which you would be guaranteed to soften your heart, and the rules of this game required you to pay $500 per month for five years, would you be willing to pay the $30,000? How much are you willing to pay to learn this lesson?"

Joe was quiet, eyes traversing left and right as he processed my hypothetical proposition. Finally a *yes but* formed on his lips: "How can I get the guarantee?" I shared my spiritual understanding about how life works, affirming that when life gives us a lesson of any magnitude, even a whopper, we always have the knowledge and ability to handle it. If Joe did not learn it this time, his stakes would likely increase again.

No coach training prepared me to proceed down this path with Joe. My facilitation began with active listening, letting go of all my familiar coaching techniques, opening to the space of Spirit, and trusting that I had the skill to coach this. Quite honestly, I was just as surprised as Joe when the three scenarios poured from my mouth, almost sounding as if I had prepared and rehearsed them to perfection.

I wish you could have experienced Joe's loving heart as he thanked me and left.

Why Is That Important?

One of the easiest ways I have found to open perspective to the biggest issue is to simply ask, "Why is that important?" several times in a row, instructing the client to use the answer received when answering the question the next time. In the example above, coach Marcy could have asked, "Why is that important for you to get back to work now?" Possible reply, "Because I have a deadline to meet." Coach continues, "And why is that important to meet the deadline?" Client: "So I can do a good job and receive a bonus at my next evaluation." Coach: "Why is a bonus important?" Client: "A bonus makes me feel acknowledged." Coach: "And why is it important that you feel acknowledged?" Client: "When I feel acknowledged, I sense the meaningfulness of my contribution to the company." Coach: "Why is it important to you to experience meaningfulness?" Client: "My self-esteem soars and I am a better role model for my kids."

Look at the distance covered in this hypothetical example, beginning with the need to get back to work and ending with having unearthed the importance of being a good role model. You can trace any action or thought to its top line (largest component) in contrast to its bottom line by using just four simple words: "*Why is that important?*" Using this technique enables you and your clients to go from pebble to boulder thinking, remaining connected to the biggest picture.

ℛ E F L E C T I O N

1. Do you know your life lessons?

2. Have you detected an increase in intensity with each recurring event?

3. Have you noticed you have the ability to handle your lessons?

4. What do you think are some of your clients' lessons?

5. Identify something rather unimportant that happened to you today. Use the above technique to ascertain its significance to you.

6. Do you ask clients how they can take what they learned back into their community, their family, their business life?

7. When clients have insights or learning in one area, do you ask, "How can this be applied to another area of your life?"

I can conclude unequivocally that the coach's best preparation for a client meeting is to do whatever it takes to remain open to Spirit.

Letting Go of Attachment

In an attempt to downsize and simplify, people question possession of and attachment to an excess of material things. As the years go by, we gather so much stuff reminding us of our life journey. At some point we risk bursting at the seams like an earthquake and, in desperation, cave in to simplification.

A coach can support a client's ambition to streamline by asking, "What do you choose to own and what is merely passing through your life?" This question effectively invites exploration of why we sometimes connect more strongly to external belongings than to our true belonging within. The following example provides some insights using a down-to-earth approach.

Example

Carlos loved books and obsessively bought every new professional book recommended. His ratio of purchase to reading was 7:1. However, his purchase to retention ratio was 1:1. His library, double-stacked on wall-to-wall shelves, was packed tightly to the brim. Finding anything was a nightmare and always required extra time to move and relocate books during the search. In coaching, Carlos began to realize that his books represented an external security blanket, and he hung onto them to compensate for his lack of internal security. As his feelings of safety increased, his hoarding relationship with his books began to shift. His internal connection propagated a new connection to the external environment.

Eventually he was able to let go of his attachment to save all books. More space was created, new books came in, and some merely passed through. His library looked more balanced and functional.

When connection to self is out of balance, the natural flow interrupts. For the cycle of life to keep flowing, space needs to be available for the new to enter. This concept is poetically captured by Ruth E. Rhodes as a double entendre in the last sentence of her poem, *Emptiness:* "I must clean my house, cluttered with the debris of life's decades . . . Open the doors so the wind can blow away the must. My house . . . is empty . . . but filled with Sunshine."

✣ R E F L E C T I O N

Examine your life, your coaching office, and your relationship with clients.

1. Have you any spaces or areas out of alignment?

2. Do you hoard resources? If yes, what one step can you take to release something to return to your natural state of balance?

3. Do you feel attached to your clients?

4. Are you attached to your clients obtaining results with you as the coach?

5. Are you attached to certain ways of coaching? Certain techniques? Certain forms?

6. Do you feel attached to clients feeling good about the work you do together?

7. What steps can you take to detach from any of the above?

8. How will you know when you have succeeded?

We have looked at how coaches guide clients to enhance internal connection and internal to external connections. The remainder of this chapter offers a three-step approach that coaches can use to increase self-connection in order to be more prepared to co-create with Spirit. The contributors share effective coaching examples illustrating this co-creative process.

Three-Step Approach

When one is mentally quiet, emotionally neutral, and physically relaxed, one increases the possibility of letting go of attachment and accessing the morphogenetic field—the fertile land of universal thought. Elmer and Alyce Green from their studies at the Menninger Clinic offer greater physiological understanding of this phenomenon (Green & Green, 1977).

1. *Mental: Quiet the Mind.* If a coach is mentally trying to figure out the best question to ask next, the emphasis will be on the intellectual thought process to the exclusion of the emotional and physical realms.

2. *Emotional: Neutralize the Emotions.* Feeling proud and successful for facilitating a good client discussion or, to the contrary, feeling confused or anxious about how to proceed with a client brings undue attention to the emotional realm. Learn to experience neutrality.

3. *Physical: Relax.* Keep your body tuned up, just like your car. Take a few deep breaths or use any other method you have found to relax. Doing so opens your physical channel. From this space, allow whatever emerges to come forth.

Practice

The key to successful passage into the universal field is practice. How often do you sit with a client in silence and allow whatever is present to emerge without preconceived expectations or attachment to outcome? The voice of Spirit lives in the unknown. Because we live mostly in the known, we fail to hear it. My experience with training coaches has shown me that those who coach with Spirit more comfortably live in silence than those who do not. For a beginner feeling challenged to offer something of value, silence might often be self-perceived as ignorance, uncertainty, or lacking worth. It takes practice to move from the known to the unknown. Although any sport could have been selected to illustrate one sequence for moving from the known to the unknown, I chose the game of golf.

Golf Analogy

Step 1. Sight where you want the ball to go.

Step 2. Let go of where you want the ball to go.

Step 3. Empty your mind.

Step 4. Neutralize your emotions.

Step 5. Relax.

Step 6. Trust some part of you knows where the ball needs to go.

Step 7. Swing as you return your attention to the ball while following through.

Note: When you begin the swing, the ball is in your peripheral vision, if at all. Not until after the club passes the ball does your attention move toward the goal. Imagine swinging while you rivet your attention on the goal instead of the ball. Challenging to hit the ball?

Practice this seven-step process daily in any setting, such as selecting your wardrobe, creating your staff meeting agenda, preparing a performance review, and so on. Vital for success is your comfort with the sixth step, letting go and trusting.

Adapting the Golf Analogy to Coaching with Spirit

Establish Purpose

> **T**arget your goal;   let go of attachmen**T**
> **R**elax   your   body   so   it   feels   calme**R**
> Ne**U**tralize emotions;   diff**U**se feelings
> **S**ettle the mind;   experience mental emptines**S**
> **T**ackle what is under your nose;   be presen**T**

✿ R E F L E C T I O N

1. Practice.

2. Practice.

3. Practice.

Keep your focus on what is in front of you with an empty mind, neutral emotions, and a relaxed body and you can be a co-creative partner with Spirit. With spiritual preparation you can trust your desires to lead you to express your authentic self.

Ken Blanchard (2001), chief spiritual officer of the Ken Blanchard Companies, a widely respected global business leader and teacher, focused his keynote address before the fifth Professional Coaches and Mentors Association conference in Costa Mesa, California, on a back-to-basics message. Challenging the three hundred coaches and mentors in the audience, Blanchard asked us to examine our top-of-the-morning habits that support us in being masterful professionals. What have we created to set ourselves up for our day as an integrated spiritual person? If we do not engage in habits that support us, yet still expect this from our clients, then we operate without coaching integrity.

Coach Julia Walz takes us inside precious moments when she knew Spirit prepared her to participate in coaching.

Spiritual Preparation
By Julia A. Walz

Preparation comes in many forms: mental preparation (reviewing client files and history), emotional preparation (feeling positive, centered, and anticipatory), and physical preparation (one last visit to the restroom or turning the kettle on for tea).

What Can We Do to Prepare Spiritually?

My mentor coach taught me to imagine an interconnected ring of light around my client and myself as I open the door to invite the client in. During this moment I feel my feet planted firmly on the ground and my heart open.

How Does Spirituality Play a Role in My Coaching?

I rely on connection to something greater than myself and the client, something encompassing both of us.

Before any meeting with a client, I turn within to become quiet and to enter a steady and calm space. We meet in a room filled with light streaming through the skylights and from the porch looking out on trees and a pond with a fountain. During a meeting, soft instrumental music plays in the background to further add to the relaxing, calming environment.

I focus on maintaining an inner state in which I see the highest potential in clients and feel love and compassion for their current situations. The more I am focused and fully present during a meeting, the more I can listen to the client's communication through words, facial expressions, and body language. I access a wealth of information when I am clear and open to receiving from the client.

Intuition

In addition to listening to a client, I also listen to the information provided by my intuition. Intuition for me is accessing information on a more subtle level beyond words. These insights get to the heart of any issue or challenge and provide the opportunity to reach a new level of awareness. I apply these insights to support the client in gaining further clarity and understanding by empowering the client to discover answers from within, answers not considered previously.

Unfolding for the Highest Good

When I am open to the process unfolding for the highest good of my clients, the greatest growth occurs. Over and over again, my clients expand their understanding and their hearts to fully experience gratitude and love. They connect to something greater than themselves that allows them to continue going deeper within their hearts to their inner truth. For me, this deeper connection in my coaching with Spirit nurtures my clients' well-being.

What options do I have for my growth when encountering a negatively energetic client? I can:

- Leave the person's space;
- Create a white light bubble around me and my client;
- Chunk up, that is, reflect on the purpose for our connection; and/or
- Look inside to see where I am negatively charged.

I choose the last one. Whenever a negative client appears, I now hold up a mirror and reflect where in *my* life I relate to my client's stuff. The more I open to the similarities between my clients and myself, the more I feel in touch with the subtleties of living. I firmly believe every client comes into my life to teach me something and I remain intrigued with what I am to discover with each new one.

Awareness of spiritual, physical, and emotional space is relevant prior to the client meeting, during the meeting, and afterward as well. For instance, if *you,* the coach, begin to feel tired after discussing office organization, take care of yourself. Take a break. Drink water. Go to the bathroom. Stand up. If you feel tired, the likelihood is your client also feels tired. In case your client feels fine, it is still important for you to honor your own needs. So be a role model.

When a client leaves, focus your attention on how you feel: Energized? Drained? Confused? Pleased? Bet your client shares your experience!

෴

The Voice of Spirit Is Intuition

Dr. Elaine Gagné, an executive coach, explains the role of Spirit in her coaching by offering us a clear differentiation between intuition and Spirit—concepts often used interchangeably. An example follows her explanation.

The brilliant part of me is the best coach . . . It is always with me, always alert and on the job. My job is to listen and interpret accurately. It is always right; I am not always right in "hearing." What I am learning more and more is to give it a chance, to voice what I think it is saying, and to check it out with my clients. This brilliant part of me, the part that never sleeps, is Spirit; the voice of Spirit is intuition.

What a gift to me and to my clients when I realized the power of intuition. So I now listen and voice what it is saying to clients. I let them tell me if it sounds "on" or not. Sometimes a client will not want to hear what that voice says. And that is OK. If it is accurate, some part of them *does* hear and important work is being done at deep levels to emerge later, when the time is right.

My greatest realization is that this brilliant part of me *is* me; that the voice of intuition *is* mine; that the context of coaching that the client and I create is the perfect medium to magnify the gift of Spirit and intuition.

Example

I was talking with a client recently. His words said one thing, but something else was happening in the spaces between the words that conveyed something entirely different. My inner voice said, "You can't say what you are thinking; you'll get fired!" But suddenly, the interchange became more about my client hearing what I was thinking—for what it was worth to him—than it was about me not getting fired. I shared my thoughts. He gave a big sigh, thanked me, and we proceeded down an entirely different path that soon got him to where he wanted to be. So what made the difference? *Spirit!*

﹏ R E F L E C T I O N

1. How often do you hold up a mirror and reflect where in your life you relate to your client's issues?

2. What ways do you have to remind yourself to use the mirror?

3. Take time after each client to assess how you experienced the meeting.

4. How do you know when you hear the voice of Spirit through your intuition?

5. How might you track the accuracy of your intuition?

Coaches report Spirit nudges them in different ways, visually with pictures, auditorily with words, and sometimes through sensations or feelings. Coach Mary Ann Robbat first describes how she coaches with Spirit and then shares what happened when she followed the voice of Spirit with her client Selina.

Honoring the Voice of Spirit
By Mary Ann Robbat

The first thing I do prior to a coaching meeting is create an outline of what we should cover based on what the client wants to achieve and our work in previous meetings. Then I ask my guides, Spirit and God, to assist me in giving my client exactly what he or she needs. During this process, I set aside any preconceived ideas of what should happen. As I visualize sitting with my client and letting the positive energy of the universe and my guides flow through me to my client, I visualize my client smiling and acknowledging he or she received exactly what was needed from our meeting.

This preparation enables me to create a totally present space for myself wherein I can respond to clients' needs or wants. The following example of coaching Selina demonstrates my process and an amazing outcome.

Recently Selina had many challenging experiences, and she felt overwhelmed in her roles as a senior vice president, mother, community leader, and an individual with her own wants and needs. During coaching Selina talked about her seventy-plus hour workweek. Even with all the hours she put into her work, she still felt behind. A "juggling act" described her life because in addition to work, she took care of four active and involved children. Her coaching goal was to simplify her life, be less distracted and run down, and feel more in control. As I listened to her story, I determined I could coach her to learn to delegate, to use her resources in her organization, to prioritize work, and to communicate her expectations—simple, focused, and proven management methods to increase job effectiveness.

My Spirit Guides Assist. Being in this open space with my Spirit guides assisting, I received these words: control, belief, and fear. The message to me was that the issue was not to increase Selina's skills with control tactics, but the issue was learning how to live *out of control.* I would never have approached the conversation from the perspective of living out of control. I heard this little voice in my head saying: "Ask her the question, how do you live when you are out of control?" So I did.

We discussed her need to control every aspect of her own life as well as the lives of those revolving around her. Truly a monumental task! Through questioning, she discovered she feared not knowing what was next and lacked confidence at handling the unexpected. This explained why she managed at 120 percent beyond what was needed to make sure everything would line up just the way it should. As a result of her fear of the unexpected, she controlled her life so strictly she never left room to be surprised, to give people opportunities to grow in ways unknown, and to enjoy spontaneity.

The voice in my head continued: "Take the next twenty minutes and do whatever you want." I verbalized this idea aloud. We can talk, walk, eat, just sit and smile at each other, or close our eyes. You can imagine Selina's initial reaction when I left it up to her to choose whatever she wanted to do for twenty minutes. "We can't take twenty minutes," she exclaimed and rattled off her list of what she wanted to accomplish in our meeting. I asked her to trust me, assuring her we could take the time and also accomplish what she wanted. In truth I did not know how we were going to achieve everything if we took that much time out. However, when I coach from intuition and Spirit, I always trust the process.

Trusting the Process. After a few uncomfortable moments, she decided she would love something to eat. We went upstairs to my kitchen, and while I made tuna fish sandwiches, she played with my young triplets. I heard her laughing over their antics and having fun playing with the toys they gave her. I glanced over to see her on the floor, skirt hiked up to her knees, jacket off, and laughing. I allowed her to continue for the full twenty minutes before we went back downstairs.

Selina appeared relaxed, admitting with a smile it had been some time since she had a good "play meeting," laughed out loud, or been totally absorbed in the moment. I asked her to tell me about her experience of the unexpected, the previous unplanned minutes during which she had not controlled her time, while she was just present, playing with my kids. She replied, "Fantastic!" I reminded her that she did not pre-plan the events that had just occurred; to the contrary, she just sampled what it felt like to live out of control. By the end of the meeting, she was much more relaxed and our work together flowed.

Outcome. Selina learned it was fun not to have every minute accounted for; it was enjoyable not knowing what to expect next, just letting life happen. About a month later, I learned her daily impromptu time would sometimes span an hour. More importantly, she no longer felt tense when something arose unexpectedly because she realized she now knew how to handle the unexpected.

❦

❦ REFLECTION

1. What percentage of the time do you follow your plans for client meetings? What percentage do you end up with unexpected events or discussions?

2. Create some quiet space and listen for words that surprise you because it feels as if you would not have thought of those words yourself.

Spirit speaks in many ways to different people. Similar to Walz, Byers also speaks of Spirit showing up without warning to move the awareness process along.

Victory in the Void
By Ken Byers

Connection to Spirit often does not come as a long process. In fact, I believe that Spirit only exists as an instantaneous union with the universal consciousness. Anything over a split second gives ego a chance to jump in and devalue the experience and mind a chance to rationalize away the gift. One of the difficulties in coaching men is that generally it is difficult for them to drop into the feminine energy channel that allows this connection to happen easily.

As a man, the struggle to define, accept, and live within my feminine has been a decades-long awareness. Although Spirit recognizes and favors no gender, it is through the feminine that Spirit moves most easily. As a coach, I use the energy provided by my feminine to grease the skids, ease the flow, and provide access to the intuition through which, I believe, a coach must work to be effective.

Example

 I worked with a client who had been in great emotional upheaval in the aftermath of a long, tumultuous marriage and depressing divorce. He moved a substantial distance from his boyhood and family home, left his three teenage children with their mother, and embarked on a new career. These are three of the most difficult things a person can do separately, but together they make up a plan based in self-sabotage and denial and destined for trouble. He also could not find the right apartment, roommate, job, or friends.

When I met him, he was considering becoming a coach and asked me to coach him through his decision-making process. He had joined a Catholic church and was preparing to convert through catechism classes. He had joined Parents Without Partners (PWP) and wanted to give lectures but could not come up with a program. One evening during our weekly phone meeting, he was decrying the trouble he was having getting people at PWP to give him a chance to do a workshop, belittling the church and priest for not supporting him into becoming a Catholic fast enough, and complaining about the lack of affordable rents in the area where he wanted to live. His inner turmoil had obviously reached the boiling point. I asked him to take a deep breath and try to quiet down. In that moment I really had no idea where I was going to take him and used those few moments to just drop into my own relaxed state and ask Spirit to intervene as it saw fit, as this was a man in obvious pain.

These moments can be terrifying to a coach. Trusting in the coaching process is key to effective coaching, but my internal gremlins began telling me there is supposed to be talk going on. After all, he was paying me what was, for him, a lot of money, and we only had thirty minutes a week together. It took a moment for me to get through my mind talk and settle into the same state I was asking my client to move into. Given my awareness of my own gremlins talking, I became appreciative of what my client must have been experiencing. I gently asked him to put his gremlins aside and just be—to allow his listening to move to a higher level. We waited a few more timeless minutes and I got nothing. Suddenly, just as my gremlins were starting up again, my client started to sob and told me he just realized that everything he had been doing was aimed at filling a terrifying loneliness to feel needed and appreciated.

He recognized a great guilt and deep sorrow about not being able to see his kids and admitted all his other activities were simply ways to meet new women. This man is a successful professional with no lack of intelligence and experience. He realized immediately he had received a gift with much value in his recognition.

Spirit had moved through me, not even bothering to let me know about it, and passed through to him with a great opening. I allowed him to stay with that feeling and ended the call, asking him to just meditate on what he might do to start healing the wounds. We hung up and I realized I was totally drained of energy. I sat and tried to recompose myself, knowing at that point something wonderful had happened that I could not fully appreciate in the moment.

The following week he called and announced in his opening volley that he had given notice to his landlord and was moving back home at the end of the month. He had called his ex-wife and told her he wanted to come back to see the children and she offered him the house with the kids, saying she wanted to move out to be on her own. Other family dynamics aside, the decision made sense to both of us. Spirit had not stopped with him but had also opened a door for his wife that had been too long stuck.

He realized taking on this responsibility was a great risk—perhaps the greatest risk of his life, but it was also the greatest growth opportunity he had ever faced. His roadblocks started almost immediately but his intention was strong and it came from a powerful place. Gremlins are everywhere in our humanity—their job is to keep us comfortable without regard to what we need for our growth. Spirit is the age-old nemesis of the gremlin and is indeed a powerful force. Once touched by it, it is difficult to deny. The battle goes on and will be difficult for this courageous man, but he has a new ally that will stay with him only for the asking.

✢

Did you catch how Ken used the wizard's belief at a critical moment when it would have been so easy to talk and abandon the trust essential to the silence?

✤ REFLECTION

1. What is your experience of the void?
2. How much silence can you comfortably tolerate?
3. Do you or does your client first break silence?

The previous two stories offer evidence of coaching effectiveness when coaches access the quiet unencumbered space of the eternal being.

Encompassing Me and My Shadow

A discussion of connection with self would be incomplete without referencing our shadow, those parts in the dark, unknown, or unconscious. One way to become aware of the shadow side is to cull key life purpose words and values and identify their opposite. For example, "inspire" is one word in my purpose statement. For me, the opposite of inspire is bored. (*Note:* It is important for the client to select language for the shadow side; it may not be the dictionary antonym.) Certainly, over the years I have chosen to keep my life extremely busy to avoid boredom. As I grow in awareness, I learn to encompass or embrace this shadow aspect of me and learn to befriend it. By beginning to befriend it, it transforms into a different experience, that of peaceful centeredness.

Shadow Side and Coaching. In this book I just mention the shadow side; to do it justice would require another whole book. What becomes relevant to our discussion is the necessity for coaches to be aware there is a shadow side and it does come into play during coaching. Following the stream of thought above and using my own purpose words or personal qualities as shadow sides of me, I created the following example to show how the two could conceivably conspire to handicap my coaching ability.

Example

 In coaching Anita, I became aware of feeling impatient (versus patient) because she procrastinated in doing her homework to create a system (versus chaos) to streamline her life. I had introduced the tools and could not fathom why she did not proceed. My buttons pushed, I realized I had become self-absorbed in my issue and regressed to my shadow side, "knowing" what was best for her. Quite annoyed, although not expressing it overtly, I meekly tried to coerce her to "play my game." Furthermore, when I inquired why she did not accomplish what we together had agreed, I learned she chose to relax after work and watch TV instead (versus boredom). Once I established awareness of my interference, I followed it to realize I had no idea how to proceed with Anita. Another form of my shadow side loomed forth. Losing my confidence as a coach, I activated negative self-talk spiraling myself down into a pit of pitiful incompetence.

Just by becoming aware of my shadow I elevated it to a place where I *might* have choice of thought and behavior. This awareness happens in an eye blink, and as quickly as I enter this rut I can dig out with our seven magic words: "How can I be of service now?"

Although connection with Spirit is a theme throughout this book, thus far, the focus has been on connection with oneself. Common to almost every scenario presented so far is the need for space as the welcoming atmosphere for spiritual connection with self. Harold Kushner (2001) in his book, *Living a Life That Matters,* relates that "When Martin Buber, the Jewish philosopher and theologian, was asked 'Where is God?' he answered that God is found in relationships . . . *between* people. When you and I are truly attuned to each other, God comes down and fills the space between us so that we are connected. . . ." The chapter that follows opens the drawbridge to exploring the space, the connection between the client and the coach.

CHAPTER 3

Connection with the Client

ASSESSMENT

Please rate yourself on the extent to which you coach with Spirit.

0 = never; 1 = rarely; 2 = sometimes; 3 = often; 4 = most of the time;
5 = almost always

To what extent do I . . .

0 1 2 3 4 5   avoid seeking acceptance from my clients?

0 1 2 3 4 5   consider it unimportant to "make a difference" in my clients' lives?

0 1 2 3 4 5   automatically relate to my clients' highest potential?

0 1 2 3 4 5   allow myself to go into the void during a meeting?

0 1 2 3 4 5   trust that what emerges is perfect?

0 1 2 3 4 5   comfortably admit that I do not know something?

0 1 2 3 4 5   allow ample silence after I ask a question?

0 1 2 3 4 5   learn from my clients?

0 1 2 3 4 5   find the value in what a client says?

0 1 2 3 4 5   feel comfortable with silence?

0 1 2 3 4 5   use silence as a form of encouraging connection?

0 1 2 3 4 5   feel authentic in my expression of who I am while coaching?

0 1 2 3 4 5   listen more than I speak?

0 1 2 3 4 5   know what issues block me from being the best coach I can be?

0 1 2 3 4 5   draw parallels between my clients' issues and my own?

0 1 2 3 4 5   acknowledge I expand my self-awareness the more I coach?

0 1 2 3 4 5   encompass my client's experience as a way of maintaining rapport?

0 1 2 3 4 5   perceive Spirit as real?

0 1 2 3 4 5   think both coaching competence and spiritual discipline are necessary?

0 1 2 3 4 5   habitually ask questions instead of giving answers?

0 1 2 3 4 5   knock myself off the pedestal when clients put me up?

0 1 2 3 4 5   avoid embedding recommendations within questions?

0 1 2 3 4 5   ask questions that lead to client awareness?

0 1 2 3 4 5   use questions to foster rapport with clients?

0 1 2 3 4 5   operate from a paradigm of spiritual inquisitiveness?

0 1 2 3 4 5   fully and unconditionally accept my clients?

0 1 2 3 4 5   trust that what emerges is perfect?

0 1 2 3 4 5   feel neutral in my heart instead of successful?

0 1 2 3 4 5   approach a challenging situation with neutrality?

0 1 2 3 4 5   know when my shadow side emerges?

CONNECTION WITH SELF is just the first step; however, without this critical piece, the second step cannot happen. When one feels grounded in one's physical, emotional, and mental bodies, ripples of positive, centered energy become available to encircle the client. This is the birth of partnership—the relationship between the two people co-creating a field of caring and possibility wherein "magic" happens. In the amazing photo in Figure 3.1, we can see that, even at the cellular level, we do not exist alone. Like us, neurons want to thrive and live and can do so only through connection with each other.

Figure 3.1. Neurons in a Culture Dish

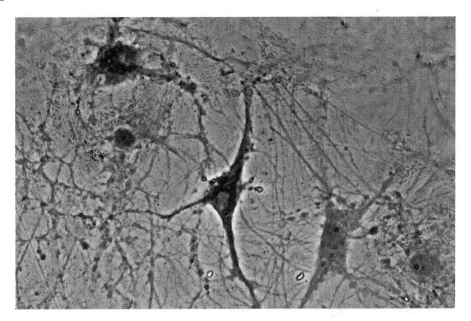

Source: Joan King, coach; speaker; president of Women in Neuroscience; professor emeritus, Tufts University School of Medicine; author of *Cellular Wisdom,* to be published by The Crossing Press in Santa Cruz, California, in 2002; and principal of Beyond Success shares one of her photos of neurons growing in a culture dish and reaching outward, which is inherent to neurons. This photo clearly shows how neurons extend toward each other to make connections. Single neurons are completely ineffective in inducing action in the body. Chains of neurons are vital.

This look at the principle of connection takes us into the mirror of indistinguishable separation where interrelationship envelops coach and client with respect. Mandatory is an encompassing attitude, qualities of trust and curiosity, and an atmosphere of silence. Clients do indeed change in the safe space created by the coach-client partnership—and so do the coaches. The co-created space of connection serves as a platform for shared personal discovery and is highly welcomed by coaches; we are as eager to grow and to learn about ourselves as are our clients. Every coaching opportunity becomes a two-way street for both coach and client to increase awareness. Terrie Lupberger shares her perspective from the coach's point of view.

Coach You, Heal Me
By Terrie Lupberger

After coaching for many years, I am still in awe of the profound ways I am changed when I work with clients. You would think it would be the other way around!

It has repeatedly been my experience that my clients' issues are my own, confirming the old saying in reverse—when the teacher is ready (to learn), the student appears. For me coaching is so much more than helping someone reach a particular goal; it is ultimately as much a healing of my soul as the soul of my client.

A recent coaching experience of mine is an example of this principle at work. A successful salesman, Sam, hired me to help him work smarter, that is, to work fewer hours and produce more income. We initially conversed about strategies for time management, marketing, how to make more effective requests, and so on. Shortly after beginning our work, Sam uncovered a deep-rooted belief that he was not really competent to take his business to a new level even though he had all the trappings of success and no evidence to support that belief.

What makes this a special experience is that Sam appeared in my life at the exact same time I too experienced self-doubt despite all the trappings of my success. Our conversations and practices were not only for him but for me as well.

In retrospect, I know we came together to go through a journey. We had remarkably similar stories, backgrounds, goals, and limitations and, after interviewing several coaches, Sam chose me. Coincidence? Maybe. But that is not my experience. For me, coaching creates space or clearing for Spirit to show up for both the coach and the client.

&⚹

⚘ R E F L E C T I O N

1. Name an instance when you sensed timely perfection for your own growth in the presence of a particular client.

2. Name your two key issues as a coach. Examine the key issues of your current clients. Any similarities?

3. Have you noticed the issues of your clients changing? Do these issues parallel your changes?

Encompassment

Encompassment is the practice of going with emergent energy instead of denying or resisting. The word compass, representing the whole circle, lies within en*compass*ment. In coaching, encompassment means drawing a circle around you and the client so both reside in the same circle. When you encompass a client, rapport and respect strengthen.

Follow this exchange as the first coaching meeting begins.

Coach: Ready to learn your life purpose?
Client: I'm a bit nervous. This is a big deal. I've been trying to find it for years.
Coach: Anxiety is energy moving. I'm glad you have this energy; otherwise you might be lackadaisical or disinterested. Let us use it to get started.

Notice how the coach simply used all that was available in the moment, in this case the client's nervous state, to keep the coaching process moving forward. This is encompassment. Listen carefully for ways you can encompass your client's words and feelings. It is more fun to play the connection game instead of the disconnected one!

⚘ R E F L E C T I O N

1. Listen carefully to yourself during your next three coaching meetings. Become aware when you use the word "no" or the phrase "not exactly" as a way of politely

differentiating what you mean in contrast to what was said. Reflect how you might be able to use encompassment language instead.

2. List three ways in which you *differ* from a close friend. Pretend you are introducing yourself and your friend to a stranger. Present these three differences using encompassment language.

Encompassment can happen through verbal language, physical gestures, or the sounds of silence as indicated by the next exercise.

The Power of Silent Speech

I have used the following exercise for years in numerous skills practices when I train coaches. Its purpose is to increase the skill of silent speaking. The comments that follow disclose how coaches experienced this coaching with Spirit process.

Exercise

Wait thirty seconds before you would typically respond to your client. Either mentally consider every possible response or be internally silent during this time. Process your experience afterward. What was it like? How did you feel? What were you thinking? Were you aware of any physical sensations? What did you guess the client was thinking? Were you correct? What did you learn?

Allow plenty of time to think. In the space of silence your client will also think. The unspoken invitation unleashes creative space. *You* need to take the initiative to allow it. Enjoy the miracles that result.

Following are rich comments made by coaches and coaches role playing clients who experienced the magic of space spawned by silent speech.

Coaches' Insights

- I felt the client's feelings and, because I couldn't speak them, I was surprised to hear her say them right after I felt them.
- I realized what a strong urge I had to fill in the empty space.

- I felt more deeply the client's struggle because I wasn't wondering about what I would say next.

- When I did not respond, the client went deeper into her emotions.

- When I felt OK about being in the empty space, the client felt safe to go deeper too.

- I felt inauthentic as a coach when maintaining silence. I realized how uncomfortable I feel with silence.

- What I thought I would ask became unimportant as my silence continued and the client took charge of the process.

- We felt the chaos of creation. I wondered how I could best be of service now.

- I felt the client looking for me to respond. When I didn't, the client solved his dilemma.

- I feel powerful for being willing to be silent.

- I never realized how silence could be such a useful tool.

Clients' Insights

- When my coach didn't reply, I felt more determined to do something about my situation.

- I moved with my thoughts myself.

- I began to reveal deeper things, layer by layer.

- I pulled myself out instead of expecting my coach to pull me out.

- This was a quiet supportive space. We were totally together.

- I wondered who was accountable for this process, my coach or me. Having no answer, I made myself accountable.

- I felt supported and validated.

Our language includes both words and space between words. Master Coach Lee Salmon guides us into further reflection on this phenomenon by drawing on concepts and theories extrapolated from selected writings. Note the parallels between "silent speech" and "transformational listening."

Coaching and Transformational Listening
By G. Lee Salmon

At times in a coaching relationship, the client and coach experience a deep listening that creates a powerful sense of trust. During these times, clients are often able to make a breakthrough in understanding and their ability to see the world or themselves in a new way. The experience is powerful and transformative, both for the coach and for the client.

What is it that creates this empowering situation? What has happened to allow trust to reach a point that the pair is able to open to a new paradigm or have profound insights that can lead to transformation? What is the role of listening and what characterizes it? Some people speak of this as listening to the soul; others describe the experience as a spiritual encounter. Is it possible for the coach, through intention, to create the conditions whereby a transformational experience has a greater probability of occurring? I would like to explore these questions and suggest a model that may be useful in bringing further understanding to experiences at the heart of coaching.

The Importance of Intention. Coaching begins with building a relationship between the coach and the client. Without relationship, there is no coaching. The strength of relationship depends on establishing trust between the partners. Coaches set the tone by their intention and the way they see and regard their partners. Intention relates to the high esteem coaches hold in their heart for their clients. It also relates to the positive, affirming vision coaches hold of their clients and the way these people are seen in all their power and beauty. Intention becomes a powerful template upon which relationship is built.

The Safety Net. Through the relationship, the coach seeks to construct a container, a place of safety in which clients feel secure and where they need not fear judgment or condemnation for who they are, what they think, or what they feel. This is a place where the client can relax and the coach can receive, as social psychologist Michael Broom says, "Any and all of the person's energy with compassion, appreciation, and curiosity" (Broom & Klein, 1999, p. 168). It is in this container that transforming experiences of empowerment can occur. Clients can choose to be influenced by the coach or not, depending on the level of trust present. Ultimately, it is not the coach who changes the client, but the client who chooses to be open to changing him- or herself.

The Coach's Authenticity. There are other factors affecting the level of trust and the strength of the container. The first is the extent to which the coach accepts the client without judgment, conditions, or expectation. Master Coach Julio Olalla says, "Coaching happens in the experience of being accepted, respected, and heard. Actual words matter less . . . . A coach is tireless in her pursuit of acceptance" (1998b, pp. 121, 247).

In the same way, coaches must accept themselves and be authentic in their conversations with clients. Kevin Cashman, founder and CEO of Leader-Source, a leadership and executive coaching consultancy firm, defines authenticity as "the core of relationships around which synergy and trust grow . . . the life force of relationships" (1998, p. 120).

As all the factors of intention, compassion, appreciation, curiosity, and authenticity come together, the container is crafted to hold the energy of transformation present that can increase through the power of conversation and listening.

Julio Olalla (1998a) emphasizes in his class, *Living in the Mystery of Coaching*, "You need three essential ingredients in coaching: listening, listening, and listening."

Listening to More Than the Words. We hear words, but rarely do we listen. We hear words, but do we also hear the emotions, the fears, and underlying concerns? When a coach listens authentically, he or she pays attention to managing the internal distractions and interpretations that can get in the way of hearing what the client is saying. Cashman notes that authentic listening is "centered in compassion and in a concern for the other person which goes beyond our self-centered needs. . . . Authentic listening is about being open to purpose and learning coming to us through the other person" (1998, p. 121).

Most of the time we appear to be focused on our internal dialogue and noise and do not pay attention to the speaker. Listening occurs only in the present moment, and the power of listening is in silence. It is in the spaces between words that we can begin to hear what is not spoken. Listening sets the stage for building relationship, connection, and trust that is essential. The coach listens to the client on multiple levels:

1. The level within (what is going on inside the coach). The coach pays attention to what comes up in consciousness and is guided by intuition.

2. The level of what the client is saying, the story. Often what the client is not saying can be more important than what is said.

3. The meta level—listening for collective shared meaning or patterns that can reveal points of leverage and openings for change.

4. The coach also pays attention to what is going on within him- or herself and the client from the domains of the body, the emotions, and language.

The Energy Field Builds. As the coach lets listening guide the conversation, the energy field between the coach and client builds. The coach directs energy through the use of powerful, probing questions. With the guidance of the coach, the client's resistance to change can decrease and new possibilities can be discovered—new choices that can be profound and radically change the client's paradigm of the world. Moments of deep transformation and empowerment come when trust reaches the point where the client feels truly heard.

As coaches we can consciously create this ritual space, this vibrational container, in which the transformative experience of empowerment can emerge and be given birth with coaches serving as midwives. Through our intention, our compassionate, artful, and affirming listening and conversation, we help life emerge and let it have its way. Listening and silence are the twins of being; they create and maintain this ritual space. Silence is so rich with possibilities; it is where we can meet, connect, and dance with life.

❧

Ontological coach Susan Belchamber contributes a wonderful personal example of transformational listening.

An Awakening of Inner Knowing
By Susan Belchamber

Many enter the coaching profession because the energy flow just seems different; coaching involves seeing the coachee not so much as needing a therapeutic "fix" as already spiritually whole.

The whole self of the ontological coach (one who focuses on the nature of existence or being) is brought into service, not just listening and analytic skills, but all of our ways of "knowing"—the great wisdom of our intuition, emotions, and body, in addition to cognitive reasoning. By opening this door to "inner knowing," we essentially tap into a larger, transpersonal space— we enter "the flow"—a space where energy is released versus sucked dry. From this space it is possible to witness a coachee's "story" from another level. This wider view opens vast new possibilities for being in the world and redefining personal "reality."

My spiritual guidance does not seem to come from angelic voices as much as from listening to my own mental, emotional, and physical "hunches." Often we begin a coaching session by taking three deep breaths together— an extremely simple yet profound way for both of us to slow down and create intimacy. Then I generally ask to set an intention for opening to whatever wants to manifest for that particular coachee. This seems to help generate a creative space for conversation. I also try to model that I am not afraid to make "mistakes," my observations and questions coming from an attitude of exploration rather than certainty. I offer a variety of possible new steps to the dance, but the coachee decides which to choose. Together we create sacred space where it is safe for the coachee's "real self" to show up and be truly seen.

My Awakening

I was not always comfortable with my intuitive self; in fact, it genuinely scared me at first. My "reality" had involved years of psychotherapeutic training that set up definite barriers to being spontaneous, let alone being intuitive. In this "reality," mind was considered the sole source of wisdom—Spirit and body virtually did not exist. But I found myself wanting more.

I attribute a good deal of my awakening to my training with the Newfield Network and their commitment to exploring all forms of "knowing." One day in particular stands out for me. It was one of my final days of training just prior to my certification as a coach. As part of the coaching program, we were led through a powerful exercise in which we listened to ways we might know and serve the client without relying so much on our intellect or rationalism. We were asked to partner with someone else in the room. As this had been a large class, Jan, my partner, and I had not had the chance to get to know each other, but I had prayed for guidance. As part of this exercise, we were supposed to focus on a word. When I said the word that came to me was "joy," Jan just glowed. It had been the exact word she had been holding in her mind's eye.

We proceeded to have one of the most moving coaching sessions either of us had ever experienced. We both knew we were accessing a different level of communication. Jan said she felt held and "known," while I felt I had entered "the flow" where a higher Source was augmenting my limited skills as a coach. Since then, my trust in my spiritually inspired moments of intuition has grown. When I free up my sense of what's "real" to include Spirit, I find I can go places with a client that I could never have gone to alone.

୭ଧ୍ୟ

Spirit and Inquiry: A Partnership

In creating a relationship with a client, the coach's key internal asset is Spirit and the coach's primary external tool is the inquiry process. To sow the seeds of connection, ask a question. Coaches who deem the question as the most important aspect of the process miss the potential of the Spirit and inquiry partnership. Remember, the primary purpose of coaching is to coach the client, not to use the meeting to demonstrate external competence. Encompass your precious questions in an atmosphere of unconditional acceptance, thereby ensuring that *the client* receives value on *all* three of the following fronts:

1. Has the client moved closer to obtaining the desired result?

2. Has the client learned something through a new perspective or awareness?

3. Has the client experienced a deep caring connection?

The Question

We have read how coaches can get out of the box, the shadow box, with a question. We also know coaches make it possible for clients to step outside of their boxes to gain perspective by asking questions. Beginning coaches often wonder how to identify the "right" questions, much like the mosquito in a nudist colony—so many opportunities yet not knowing where to begin.

Habitual creatures that we are, we tend to lazily ask the same questions repeatedly. I do not include the magic question ("How can I be of service now?") in this collection because this is one question we want to continue to ask any time and every time we feel stuck or uncertain how to proceed. Indeed, this one question brings us quickly to the space of Spirit. However, when we want to have other questions at our fingertips, from which garden do we pluck? Atypical questions open new horizons; new perspectives open up unexpected connections. To facilitate clients' paradigm shifts, use any one or any combination of the twelve templates listed below.

Template 1. Past, Present, Future

- What resources have you assembled in the past to handle this?
- What resources can you access now to handle this?
- What resources can you create in the future to handle this?

Template 2. Visual, Auditory, Kinesthetic

- What would it look like if you succeeded?
- What might it sound like if you succeeded?
- What would it feel like to succeed?

Template 3. Physical, Emotional, Mental, Spiritual

- How can your sensations give clues?
- What emotions would support your effort?
- What thoughts/beliefs might bring greater results?
- What outcome would bring the greatest good?

Template 4. Doing, Being

- What would you do to be successful?
- How will you feel when you are successful?

Template 5. Process, Outcome

- How might you go about getting the result?
- What would happen if you did succeed?

Template 6. Shift from Either/Or to Both/And

- Instead of looking at this situation as an either/or situation, how might you see it from a both/and perspective?

Template 7. Logical, Creative

- If you approached this systematically, how would you proceed?
- If you approached this creatively, what might you turn up?

Template 8. Life Areas (Home, Career, Relationships, Money, Fun, and So On)

- What would the effect on your home front be?
- How might your career be affected?
- What would happen to your relationships?
- What financial resources can you access?
- What would happen if you made this fun?

Template 9. Where, When, Why, Who, What, How

- Where will this take place?
- When will you commit?
- Why do you want to approach it this way?
- Whose support can you count on?
- What might happen?
- How will you go about that?

Template 10. You, Others, the Whole

- How will this action affect you?
- How will this action affect others, your family, your colleagues, your team?
- How will this action affect your group or department?
- How will this action affect your community or organization?
- How will this action affect society or the planet?

Template 11. Need, Want, Choose, Deserve, Have

- What do you need to succeed?

- What do you want to have happen?

- What choices will enable success?

- What do you feel you deserve?

- What do you have to succeed?

Template 12. What If? (Taken to the Absurd Extreme)

- What if you could only succeed?

- What if you could create it the way you want?

- What if the rules changed?

As you can see, the combinations and permutations of just one dozen templates have endless possibilities for generating questions. Two examples from coaching meetings elucidate how a coach can use the templates; for ease of reference, the specific template is noted. Consider each of these questions as another way to establish connection.

Example

 Your client has difficulty relating to his son. He tends to give his son advice instead of listening, and the son unequivocally rejects the advice. To help your client gain perspective, you might ask:

- What happened when you gave advice in the past? (Template 1. Past)

- What might happen if you continue to give advice to your son in the future? (Template 1. Future)

- What reaction did you see from your son? (Template 2. Visual)

- How did you feel when you gave advice? (Template 3. Emotional)

- What other options did you have instead of giving advice? (Template 7. Creative)

- What is the benefit of giving advice? (Template 9. What?)

- What did you choose by giving advice? (Template 11. Choose)

- What might happen if you were prohibited from giving advice? (Template 12. What If?)

Example

 Coaches need to be alert to being placed on a pedestal by a client. If you feel this happening, have a talk with your client to bring the relationship back to a partnership.

- What in my behavior suggests I am superior? (Template 3. Physical)

- What spiritual reason do you think brought us together? (Template 3. Spiritual)

- Can I be both your coach and partner at the same time? (Template 6. Both/And)

- What do I need to do to change this situation? (Template 11. Need?)

Armed with these basic connecting tools, coaches can generate a myriad of questions and enable clients to open the keg of learning dynamite ready to explode into new perspectives. Contrast the inquiry process of coaching to this ancient Chinese proverb:

To be prosperous for one year, grow rice. (These coaches answer clients' questions.)

To be prosperous for ten years, grow trees. (These coaches answer clients' questions and help them apply the information to other life areas.)

To be prosperous for 100 years, grow people. (These coaches ask clients questions.)

⊗ R E F L E C T I O N

1. Next time you ask a client a question, think about which template you used. Imagine what the outcome might have been if you had used a different question.

2. Do you tend to ask the same questions repeatedly?

3. Select an atypical question for your style and use it this next week a few times.

4. When you ask a question, do you accept whatever answer the client gives?

5. Do you wish to focus on rice, trees, or people?

Pick a Few Good Questions

Slowly begin to expand your repertoire to include different questions. Feel yourself grow-ing and expanding with the ability to facilitate new viewpoints. At the same time, be aware that the goal of the questioning process is for *the client* to learn the questions and adopt the habit of asking them, not for the coach to look smart. This means avoid asking loads of different questions and stick with a few preferred ones so the client can learn to use them through role modeling. "A well-designed question becomes a self-correcting life map" (Zink, 1991, p. 246). A few well-defined questions are better than too many.

Are Some Questions Better Than Others?

Beginning coaches crave questions, any question, because they have learned the ques-tion is their greatest tool. As a beginning coach, I amassed dozens of questions and cat-egorized them using a system from my dissertation. However, the more questions I gathered and used, the more I realized it did not matter which question I asked. Any question, hop scotching holographically in a playground of questions, could keep the client's process of self-discovery flowing. Ultimately, questions gift us with the spirit of connection to another human being.

After years of coaching, you will likely come to the same conclusion: When you coach with Spirit, the right question manifests at your silent beckoning.

Follow a Question with Silence

When I allow space, I send a message that I honor clients and what they have to offer. I will never forget being in the presence of the Native American director of the Taos nation in New Mexico. For three hours I sat, riveted, listening to him relay a story about a frog falling off a log. Three sentences long, the story had many, many minutes of silence. After a while, shedding my impatience, I began to understand that much of the story took place in between the words—an amazingly powerful experience.

In David Abram's (1996) visionary book *The Spell of the Sensuous,* he reminds us, "A living language [is] woven out of silence by those who speak. . . . And this silence is that of our wordless participations, of our perceptual immersion in the depths of an animate, expressive world" (p. 84).

The Ultimate Question: Why Question?

What does questioning have to do with Spirit? After reading the above templates, perhaps our spiritual, holistic selves can be heard screaming: Stop compartmentalizing! Too many categories! Too rigid! To better understand how to use questions maximally, let us unearth the motives, frame of reference, and timing and sequence behind the practice of questioning.

Motives. Obvious at first glance, we question to obtain information. Paradoxically, we also inquire to give information. However, imparting information as a query turns out to be nothing more than concealed advice embedded in a question, usually intended to protect self from the possibility of criticism or rejection. If a client sought data about a potential company for employment, the coach could conceivably ask, "Could you look it up in a library?" Not a pure question at all because the answer "look it up in the library" is given.

Questions can also be asked to make oneself look good, such as when coaching an employment recruiter, executive search consultant, or career manager: "Do you think it might be more useful to help your client create a career vision before deciding which job would be a better fit?" By asking that question, I unacceptably behave as "Ms. Know-It-All." If I ask a question to preserve my feelings of security or the status quo, I reveal lack of self-confidence and position myself on a pedestal, which is a long way from the partnership I hope to establish with clients.

Frame of Reference. The questioner's frame of reference might provide some clues about the motive. If a client suspects that a question comes from a coach's ulterior motive, such as a self-centered wish to know, the learning space might diminish and Spirit space retreat. If the question is for the client's benefit, the space for Spiritual connection blossoms.

Coaches motivated to facilitate learning environments ask questions inviting clients to increase awareness, to learn, to explore freely, to discover, and to unearth something new and interesting. These types of questions serve as the linking pin to coaching with Spirit.

Remember my preferred definition of coaching—the creation of a space of unconditional deep acceptance wherein a client can just be authentic? This space is packed full with respect. When one's motive for questioning begins with honor and respect, open space becomes available. The question constructs this space—but not just any haphazardly posed question. The frame of reference and the motivation must stem from genuine intention for clients to discover their truth.

Timing and Sequencing. When one coaches from Spirit, one will find the timing of a question to be as important as the sequencing of questions. Asking the right question at the wrong time is no better than asking the wrong question at the right time.

✍ R E F L E C T I O N

1. What motives do you have for your questions?
2. What if the main reason for the question is to create this space of honor between two people and only secondarily to learn?

One who questions possesses strong qualities of curiosity, wonder, and, perhaps, even naiveté. While you read the following poem, ask yourself whether you feel like a puppet following preprogrammed moves (asking the "right" question because you learned it), or if you are able to enter the place of unknowing or innocence and ask the question sourced from Spirit?

From Innocence to Ignorance
By Kim Allen Williams

> Babies. Innocent and pure,
> Perfectly healthy with no need for cure.
> Do we learn or do we forget
> or do we turn into someone's puppet?
> So long we try to achieve perfection
> when all we have gained is protection
> from our innocence.

An amusing yet clever role model for this "innocent" personality is the fictional TV detective Columbo. Read in the next section how donning your "Columbo Persona" enhances your ability to coach with spiritual inquisitiveness.

The Columbo Persona

Columbo, skilled at extracting information, can magically unearth anything from anybody by pretending (or is it a pretense?) to be curious. By coming from wonder and awe, we encourage clients to reveal and share nuggets that open up awareness. Using the Columbo persona helps the coach keep client meetings light and fun, which in turn supports flexible thinking, creative problem solving, energetic exchanges, learning retention, and self-discovery.

Example

 Listen to clients who say "*you*" when referring to themselves. It might mean an unwillingness or inability to take responsibility for their actions. This is only one clue. To be sure, use other evidence as well.

For example, if I tell you I am looking for a birthday present for my father and I switch into the "you" mode, I might say, "I went to the local mall and *you* know how it is, *you* can never find a parking space. Y*ou*'ve got to drive around. *You* get so frustrated."

To handle this in a light way, pretend with surprise that you thought the client actually meant you. Rewind this scenario, only this time use the Columbo Persona.

Imagine you just finished hearing this piece of the description: "I went to the local mall and you know how it is, you can never find a parking space."

Interrupt, playing Columbo: *"I* can't? You mean *me?"*

Client stops and reassesses: "No, I mean *I* can't" and continues, "You've got to drive around."

"I've got to drive around?"

"No, *I* drive around."

After a few rounds, your clients will likely pick up the message to claim ownership of their actions, and their language will fall into congruence. Of course you also could have turned this into a mini-lecture and sounded like a high school English teacher. If both avenues lead to the same result, why not choose the friendlier, fun way to surface awareness?

Example

 Otto fears not making enough money to support himself and pay bills during his transition to becoming a coach. You ask about his worst fear. Otto replies, "If I don't get clients, I will walk the streets and be homeless."

As a wide-eyed Columbo, say: "Really? That's awful! You, walking the streets!"

    Otto: "Not really. I probably could get some kind of job."

    Coach: "Like what?"

    Otto: "Going back to my earlier career as a sales associate or, worst case, working in a retail store."

After several Columbo interruptions, clients hear the pattern and you can gently ask for permission to bring this language to their attention. I have found the Columbo Persona to fruitfully increase clients' awareness of choosing accurate and empowered language for assuming personal responsibility.

✒ R E F L E C T I O N

1. Listen for "you" when the speaker refers to self.

2. When you hear yourself thinking or speaking "you" when you really mean "I," ask yourself, "Why I am using words that avoid taking full responsibility?"

Summary

In Chapter 3, we broadened our perspective from connection with self to connection with another by looking at the space between the client and the coach. In this magical vacuum is housed the possibility for creating authenticity *if* caring, respect, curiosity, and silence exist. The sheltered space serves coach and client as a mutual haven for healing—both encompassed within the transformational circle at the beckoning of a question.

Now let us expand further out to the most panoramic connection possible—connection with the whole. The best place to begin discussion about wholeness is with the notion of synchronicity described next.

Connection with the Whole

ASSESSMENT

Please rate yourself on the extent to which you coach with Spirit.

0 = never; 1 = rarely; 2 = sometimes; 3 = often; 4 = most of the time;
5 = almost always

To what extent do I . . .

0 1 2 3 4 5   accept the present moment as perfect?

0 1 2 3 4 5   access the morphogenetic field?

0 1 2 3 4 5   allow myself to go into the void during a meeting?

0 1 2 3 4 5   acknowledge we are part of a much larger universal force?

0 1 2 3 4 5   appropriately share my spiritual learning with clients?

0 1 2 3 4 5   note synchronicities in my life?

0 1 2 3 4 5   bring synchronicities to clients' awareness?

0 1 2 3 4 5   refer to the cycles of nature while coaching?

0 1 2 3 4 5   honor all phases of the coaching cycle, the upswings, and the dips?

0	1	2	3	4	5	use metaphors to guide clients' awareness?
0	1	2	3	4	5	mirror my spiritual values in my coaching environment?
0	1	2	3	4	5	recognize that Spirit is always around?
0	1	2	3	4	5	intentionally welcome Spirit into my coaching life?
0	1	2	3	4	5	feel myself surrender to Spirit while coaching?

WE ARE A PART OF SOMETHING BIGGER, much bigger than our awareness has the capacity to grasp. Einstein's theories, the field of quantum physics, and metaphysical philosophies offer clues to the vastness of universal consciousness and connectedness. On the research front, scientists have learned that the part of the brain differentiating self from others switches off during times of deep meditation, enabling the meditator to experience a sense of oneness and unity with the universe. If in the laboratory we rapidly move toward weaving our scientific hypotheses into the same fabric as our spiritual experiences, why not in coaching? Meandering through the realms of connection takes us into exploring synchronicities, cycles, metaphors, and holistic attitudes as portholes to the whole—the home of Spirit. Speaking of home, we also do justice to the physical environment in which coaching takes place, seeking ambiance to enhance spiritual connection. When all elements synergistically fall into place, a flow experience becomes apparent, confirming coaching with Spirit is taking place.

So think big—*bigger* and *bigger*—and sport your holographic shoes to step into the world of synchronicity.

Synchronicity Is Purpose Behind Circumstances

If no purpose is discovered, we say the event is just random or accidental. Quantum physics revitalized the premise that each event is a signature, a hologram of the complete whole (Talbot, 1988). By examining larger events, we gain greater and greater perspective until the entire picture comes into view.

Take a moment to look at your coaching patterns. First, survey your client load. Reflect on your current clients. What themes do you note? Why do you think these particular people chanced into your life now? Recall clients you coached three years ago. Any similarities with those you have now? Any differences?

A common pattern for me is the pattern I nicknamed "cosmic triplets." Over the past fifteen years I noticed things repeatedly happened in threes. For instance, during the same season I coached three significantly overweight women. Three black professional men signed up to be coached in the same week. Single parents came in threes. Clients had birthdays in the same month. As I write this, I note I now have three "recovering" lawyers as clients.

Furthermore, I discovered that client issues and presenting problems also appeared in threes. Three professional executive women worked on minimizing perfectionist behavior. Three clients described challenges with ailing parents. Three young women complained of fatigue. Three men wanted to learn about intuitive business decision making. Three clients paid for the program in advance.

Stepping back as far as I could imagine, I realized my situation revealed a microcosmic mirror of what also occurs with my colleagues. Unveiled before me was a planetary slice. I opened to the possibility that by being alert to these synchronicities, I would somehow increase the success of my clients, my coaching, and myself. Often an exploration of synchronicities becomes a pivotal portal in opening awareness to Spirit's presence in coaching. As Wayne Dyer says, "You will taste the fruits of synchronicity wherein you are in collaboration with fate to manage the coincidences of your life (2001, p. 130). The worksheet in Exhibit 4.1 may facilitate your discoveries; please use it with clients, too.

✿ R E F L E C T I O N

1. What is common among the three events noted on your Synchronicities Worksheet?

2. What can you learn from this? About yourself? Your clients? Your colleagues?

3. What can you learn from this about your profession? About the impact on the world?

4. How can you use this information to improve your coaching?

Both past analyses (externally initiated) and future intentioning (internally sparked) illustrate how to maximize connection through synchronicities. In the next section we

Exhibit 4.1. Synchronicities Worksheet

Identify three events that happened to you in your coaching business in a recent week.

1.
2.
3.

Ask yourself the following questions about each of the three events:

- What do you know about how this came into your life?

- What beliefs and thoughts were present?

- What emotions played a role?

- What physiology or physical actions were involved?

- What was the outcome?

shift the frame of reference from synchronicities to repetitions. Which signature coaching events magnify snapshots of the coaching process as a whole?

Cycles, Circles, and the Dip

The image of a circle and the concept of cycles have frequently been used to illustrate repetitive processes. Yet in any process, there is likely to be a moment of confusion or indecision, hence "the dip." To better understand these three predictable phenomena and their relevance to coaching, I invite you to visit the third and fifth principles embedded in *The Kybalion,* the study of the Hermetic philosophy of ancient Egypt and Greece (Three Initiates, 1940).

Cycles

The Fifth Hermetic Principle—the Principle of Rhythm—embodies the truth that "in everything there is manifested a measured motion; a to-and-from movement; a flow and inflow; a swing forward and backward" (Three Initiates, 1940, p. 159).

Have you ever reflected on the ebb and flow of ocean waves? Do you pause to consider the significance of squirrels collecting nuts in the fall? When was the last time you appreciated the regularity of a waxing or waning moon? These examples represent nature's cycles—phases that together comprise a complete picture. It seems easier (and less threatening) to contemplate nature's big picture than it is to look at ourselves and see our patterns. Nature reveals more clearly the existence of a grand plan. Think of the word we have chosen to describe our earth, a *plan*et. Perhaps *all* we have to do is tune into the plan that already exists.

The following example of how cycles operate in our daily life, some more obvious than others, helps us apply wisdom from ancient spiritual philosophy to our current day. A good place to begin is with one of the most common issues for clients—the cycle of regaining life balance.

Example

 Action-oriented Felicia complained of feeling tired. She has just expended two months of intense effort accomplishing a makeover of her entire house and she enlisted me in her plea to regain energy as soon as possible. It would have been tempting to be seduced into helping her explore ways to move back into action. Instead, I wondered whether she had entered a selective splice of a larger cycle and, if so, which cycle was operating.

I remembered reading a musing by Eileen Caddy, one of the founders of the Findhorn community in Scotland: "I watched a rosebud going through its various stages of unfoldment until it reached maturity. I heard the words, 'Let go. Do not try to interfere but let the plan unfold in true perfection.'" What if Felicia's current experience was part of a divine plan? My inclination is often to fix a problem at face value. I often forget to step back; yet when I do, I realize I have other choices.

So I stepped back and examined the larger perspective, the context for this issue. Using my cyclical context, I invited discussion with the following questions:

- What do you think about people who feel tired?
- Can you accept "downtime" as part of a cycle?
- Do you find it unusual to be tired after three months of intense effort?
- If being tired was a gift for you, what might the gift be?
- What has happened now that might not have happened if you had maintained your usual level of activity?

Felicia left the meeting no longer resenting her lethargy; to the contrary, she gave herself permission to feel tired, affirming it to be part of her healthy cycle. Her entrance into a life of balance was a refreshing breather, ending a long season of exhaustion.

✧ REFLECTION

1. What are the natural parts of the coaching cycle?
2. Which phases of the coaching process do we overlook? Pay attention to?
3. How do you know when it is time to rest? For how long?
4. Do you know your 1–2–3 formula for balance? Alone time (1); with one other person (2); in a group with three or more people (3).
5. Do you have a formula for breaks? Daily? Weekly? Monthly? Annually?

The Grand Finale in Coaching

One of the most sacred segments of the coaching relationship is the ending of the partnership, the finale—a guaranteed part of every client-coach relationship. By this time the client has learned, grown, changed, or progressed in the direction laid out when the coaching agreement began. Almost to be treated like a rite of passage, the conclusion of a coaching relationship simultaneously symbolizes an ending and a new beginning. For both partners, a new passage opens.

The Role of Ritual. If coaching was successful, the client has tools and supports in place to sustain the new thoughts, beliefs, and behaviors without the coach. Tools and techniques lie in the external realm of doing. Yet the important internal relationship—the strong bond based on trust and respect—must also change. Anthropologists and sociologists tell us that whenever transitions of significance are at hand, societies create rituals to facilitate changeover to the new state. Rituals honor process and progress and create space for emergence. Perhaps it is not by accident that the word ritual is embedded in the word *spiritual.* Think about a birthday ritual, complete with song, balloons, cake, presents wrapped in papers and bows, cards, and candles. An entire kinesthetic, visual, auditory gala designed to celebrate another year.

My coach understood the value of ritual and upon my "graduation" as a client, I received a touching, heart-felt poem that I treasure to this day. Upon completion of my coaching certification program, my coach presented me with a dozen long-stemmed red roses, marking my entrance as a colleague in the world of coaching professionals.

I chose to continue the custom of gift giving in addition to several other elements to help my clients *and me* feel complete. The client and I together review the process and results and determine the percentage of success. Reflecting on memories of our special time together, we also revisit the insights we call "Guidelines for Winning" (Belf & Ward, 1997, p. 71), the lessons learned. I also ensure that both the client and I feel complete, internally and externally.

From a spiritual perspective, the coaching partnership never ceases. The client takes away learning; the coach gains wisdom. Both have a piece of the other and carry that influence into future transactions. Because we are all connected, we might even say our very existence is comprised of little bits of learning and influence from all we have encountered thus far and will continue to be molded from all those we encounter in the future. Thus "complete" becomes redefined as transformed and changed, not finite.

Finishing Touches. I give my clients a final appraisal form and a follow-up agreement with two questions for them to consider within two to three months following our completion: (1) What am I doing differently or how am I being differently as a result of the coaching? and (2) How will I know if what I am doing or being works? Finally, my favorite part: I acknowledge how much I have enjoyed the relationship and the commitment to self-discovery I have been privileged to witness.

✿ REFLECTION

1. What rituals do you already have in your coaching?

2. What rituals can you create at key crossroads during the coaching process?

3. What rituals can we devise to help clients feel complete, both internally and externally?

4. What do we do for ourselves as coaches to feel complete internally and externally?

Circles

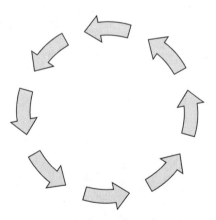

The great Third Hermetic Principle—the Principle of Vibration—embodies the truth that "motion is manifest in everything in the Universe—that nothing is at rest—that everything moves, vibrates, and circles" (Three Initiates, 1940, p. 137). Let us examine the circle, as a subset of cycles, and its relevance to coaching.

When we spin in a circle, we go nowhere; we return to the same spot. Taking the habitual route activates our autopilot. However, spinning our wheels has some advantages. When we spin, we have the freedom to focus on something other than spinning. Centrifugal force generates momentum. When we do not focus on external realities, our fully conscious mind can retire backstage so our attention can be freed for brain activities such as meandering daydreams and imaginative explorations. We cannot engage in these musings when faced with making new choices because something new requires deliberate focus and attention.

A Familiar Example. Think about shampooing your hair. Note if you always begin by touching your scalp in the same place with the same hand. Notice your habit. I recall that when I had a bandage on my head, most of my thoughts dealt with the logistics of how to shower to keep my bandage dry. No room for my usual mental aerobics or spontaneous singing. However, when I operate automatically my thoughts wander and wonder with the luxury of weaving imaginative fabrics. This explains the frequency of insights and problem solving occurring while I shower.

Allow your clients (and yourself) to spin wheels. It is a natural and necessary part of our cycle of creativity.

When spinning too long causes dizziness, how can one exit the loop? One way is to move from the insignificant to the significant. Many clients come to coaching with immediate concerns, and these are addressed. After five months of coaching, however, these concerns seem to become less important because spiritual life lessons can come into focus. Moving perspective from microscopic to macroscopic itself is a cycle, repeatable every time another issue appears. In the following piece, Butch Farley explains how we all benefit long-term from the process of talking *about* our spiritual journey. Sharing spiritual learning makes it possible for everyone involved to leave a repetitive loop and evolve to a higher level.

Lasting Revolution
By Butch Farley

Spirituality, difficult to define, invisible, not something to touch, but so enormously powerful it can spark a revolution.

You cannot "see" it, but you can see evidence by how it "appears"—you can see results. You cannot touch it, but you can feel its presence. It makes no sound as it goes about its work but can be heard in the softness of a kind voice. And to me, it is most obvious when not present.

Can you "teach" someone to be spiritual? I have discovered I cannot, but

I can teach someone *about* spirituality. And doing so can help start an internal revolution. As a coach, I work with an assortment of individuals and organizations that come for a variety of reasons—many in transition, some to improve the bottom line, and others to get oriented. Although the motives differ, one thing I have noticed: Each comes to me to find something that is missing.

The presenting situation might start with a client claiming to need more "time" but end up with needing more space. Or, coaching might begin with someone needing more money but end up with needing fewer "things." Almost always coaching meetings begin with a focus on something unnecessary and end with something essential.

Recently I concluded a relationship with a client who initially came to me after a layoff from a high-tech firm. In actuality he was relieved at the layoff, so instead of talking about it we spent considerable time reorienting to his passions. This was important for him because he had come to me spiritually "dead," lacking energy and meaning, depressed, and unenthusiastic. As a result of coaching, he discovered a new life in which he defined professional and personal success in terms of meaningfulness.

Sharing My Spiritual Journey

When he identified a goal to become more "spiritual," I had him try some of the things that work for me. For example, when clients want more peace and calm I recommend meditation. Why it works I do not know, but it is part of *my* calming formula, and when I feel calm, my life just seems to flow. I did not actually teach him how to meditate; I told him of my experiences and the benefits I received.

We talked about taking time alone and time with loved ones and the difference between the two. We mused about working with passion. We touched on topics of happiness and love and how their meaningfulness and permanence come from within. I suggested he take a leadership role in a divorce group with which he had just become associated—an opportunity to give and receive.

Work on Yourself First

As I become wiser, I realize the best thing I can do for others is to work spiritually on myself. When I embrace all the things I can do, I create a more balanced and peaceful life. I become mindful. I take time. I create space. I love. I smile and learn compassion. I give. I am kind. All of these represent tangible signs of a spiritual life and the ingredients of revolution. The best thing I can do is to hold the light so others, seeing my shadow, will venture forward.

৵৵

✿ REFLECTION

1. Which aspects of your spirituality are you comfortable sharing with clients? Which are you not? Any difference between the two?

2. What might happen, positively and negatively, if you took a risk and shared more?

The Dip

> *"Every change looks like a failure in the middle."*
>
> Elizabeth Kubler-Ross

> *"The order of sequence is necessary, the order of time is not."*
>
> Zink, 1991, p. 36

Within the coaching cycle, one phenomenon is guaranteed—what I call the "dip." All coaches and coach trainers should be alerted to expect it. After learning life purpose and having high expectations about possibilities for success, clients reach a point, typically midway (about two to three months into a five- to six-month coaching process) when thoughts shift to the future.

Evidence of the Dip

- Clients begin to fear coaching will not work and results will not be produced.
- Everything seems up in the air.
- Internal beliefs and external habits have been challenged and called into question.
- Incongruence between current life and desired life becomes obvious.
- Clients see no way for "miracles" to occur in the second half; the path to success is foggy.

I know clients experience the "dip" when I read the following on the clients' midpoint coaching appraisal forms:

"This isn't working."

"This costs too much money."

Or I hear on the answering machine:
  "I can't come to the next appointment because I haven't done anything."

Or I hear in person:
  "I guess coaching isn't for me."

  "I will need more than five months to make this happen."

All Clients Go Through the Dip. It is an essential part of the coaching cycle. We can come to welcome this phenomenon because it enables a particular effect. Earlier you read Vajda's account of the illusionary backward trip of the upward spiral. The dip in the context of the entire coaching program translates into major backward slides. Upheavals in careers, relationships, and health often trigger the dip experience—an unpleasant jolt in our status quo circuitry. Is there life after the dip? You bet!

After the dip, something magical happens; clients move more intentionally and quickly to obtain results. As if overnight, clients realize achievement of results will only happen if *they* produce them—a triumph for the coach committed to helping clients learn that success is a personal responsibility. (We will explore personal responsibility in greater detail in Chapter 6.) The "dip" offers fertile ground for new thoughts and behaviors to germinate. Coaches can appreciate the dip and trust the client has encountered the phase where transition and transformation become possible. By the completion of the coaching process, clients typically soar past the entry point, having achieved success and greater well-being.

Zero in on the following perfect example of encountering the dip.

My Path Is Perfect
By Tim Hodge

My challenge was to remain centered and clearly see all experiences moving me on my life purpose.

I lost my job at a new technology startup company that promised employees riches when the company went to market with its product. On the eve of the company's success, I was informed my skills no longer fit, I was overpaid, and I had to leave. I felt my life was over. This company would have provided so much financial opportunity that I had already envisioned living in a new house with enough money for three kids to attend the college of their choice.

In the weeks that followed, I interviewed at many different companies. Several reasonable offers were made, each slightly below my current salary. Seeking something better than the position I left, I held out, waiting for a company that wanted me for all my fifteen years of acquired skills.

During these interviews, I realized I had not been using my fullest potential in my former position and came to believe they did me a favor by asking me to leave. The perfect job came—the monetary benefits tremendous: my compensation increased 50 percent. I never believed this was possible.

What seemed like the biggest disaster of my life turned out to be the biggest opportunity. All along my coach asked how each part of the process was purposeful. From this experience I learned that events that happen to me are neither good nor bad, just opportunities to adjust my path to be more in tune with my life purpose. The good news is I expect many more opportunities to practice this lesson.

✒

✿ REFLECTION

1. Can you recall a big client dip? How did you handle it?

2. Which of your clients seem in the dip now? Pre-dip? Post-dip?

3. Have you noticed several clients in the dip at the same time?

The Dip Shows Up for Coaches Too. The coaches I train encounter the dip approximately halfway into their certification process. How do I know? I hear:

- I doubt I can become a successful coach.

- I will never learn to stop giving answers and ask questions instead.

- I made a mistake thinking I can be good at this.

- My coaching is not worth my fee.

I remind them about the dip. Why should clients experience it and not coaches? We are both in the same learning process—letting go of old ineffective patterns and integrating new effective ones. So next time, celebrate when you reach the dip phase and remember to remain open to trusting it as a natural part of the learning cycle.

❧ *R E F L E C T I O N*

1. When you began your coaching business, did you too encounter the dip? What did it look like? After the initial flurry of success, did you say to yourself things like, "I am having difficulty attracting clients." "I thought asking questions would be easy." "How do I know if I am giving clients value?"

2. Do you explain the dip to your clients? If yes, how?

3. In what ways have you seen the dip manifest? Recall a recent personal setback. Did you experience the dip? How did you know? Have you moved beyond seeing it as a setback? How did you get from there to here?

I concocted the dip as a metaphor to explain a phenomenon I observed over and over again. Metaphors serve me in many ways in coaching with Spirit.

Metaphors Facilitate Connection

"The greatest thing by far is to be the master of the metaphor," said Aristotle. Metaphors reveal connection. Because everything is connected, metaphors facilitate the process of discovering the bridge leading to connections.

The Game of Spirit

The best metaphor I have found to increase clients' awareness is the "game." According to *Webster's Encyclopedic Unabridged Dictionary of the English Language,* 1994 edition, game has several distinct meanings: the first out of twenty-three definitions and most familiar is "organized amusement or pastime." The fifteenth definition caught my eye— "having the required spirit." Game and Spirit linked, I proceeded to play with the idea of coaching as an organized game of Spirit with Spirit as the creator. I became curious about the rules of the game; the qualities one needs to play a good game; what winning means; who creates the game; how does one feel before, during, and after the game is played. I asked my coaching community to mind map game using a radiant thinking model taught at one of our retreats. Mind mapping is a right-brain technique where thoughts quickly convert to words or pictures without time for thought or judgment. After the first level dumps out of the brain, another round forms a second tier. This part is known as radiant thinking. My intention was to discover any parallels if we interpret coaching as a game with Spirit. Little did I realize the value we would all obtain from this simple, fun exercise!

Try this for yourself, then read what others generated.

Exercise

Step 1. Write the word "game" or draw an icon representing game in the middle of a blank sheet of paper.

Step 2. Draw ten spokes off the center, like rays of the sun.

Step 3. Along each ray, write a word or phrase that occurs to you as you free-associate to the word game.

Step 4. Draw at the end of each ray two more rays like a "V."

Step 5. Free-associate two different things on each of the rays of the "V" based on your reflection of the main ray.

Step 6. Compare your words to your understanding of the coaching process. Note similarities and differences.

An example is shown in Figure 4.2.

Figure 4.2. The Game

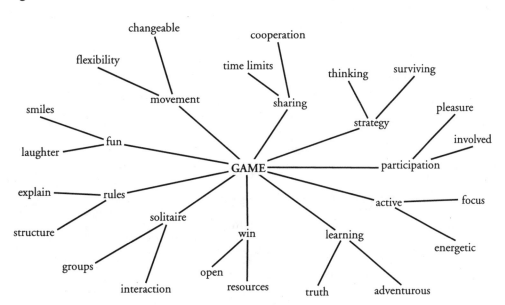

Others' Word Clusters. As you can see from the clusters below, identified by those playing the game, the game metaphor straightforwardly taps into the process of life.

- *Challenges:* Risk, adventure, cooperation, participation, taking turns, giving, receiving, choices.

- *Drivers:* Excitement, anticipation, wonder, new, imagination, creativity, eager, willing, energy, innovation, explore.

- *The People Processes:* Teamwork, friendship building, group enjoyment, together, people, with others, connect, sharing, interaction.

- *Strengths:* Abilities, mastery of skills, play your position, determination, intention.

- *Logistics:* Rules, directions, boundaries, form, principles, structure, goals, strategy, win, lose, explanation, time, compete, planned, standards, referee.

- *Emotional:* Fun, personal enjoyment, play, laughter, humor, smiles, challenging.

- *Physical:* movement, physical, coordination, athletic, exercise.

- *Mental:* Thought-provoking, concentration, stimulation, brain/mental, problem solving, learn, reflection, self-sharpening, stretch, feedback.

- *Outcomes:* Oneness, freedom, spontaneous, full of spirit.

The Really Potent Questions. If you really want to serve your clients in the grandest way possible, ask them these types of game questions:

- Who determines the rules of your Game of Life?

- Who can change the rules?

- Under what circumstances do rules need to change?

- How do you feel when rules change?

- How often do the rules change?

- What strategy do you use with the game?

- Does your strategy change during the game

- What skills do you need to play the game?

- What beliefs do you need to play the game?

- What are the purposes of the game?

- When does the game change?
- What do you need to know to play a good game?
- Can you win this game?
- How do you know when you win?
- What structure works best for this game?
- Are there times to deliberately abandon the game?
- What happens if you forget the game?
- How can you play the best game possible?
- Who else needs to know about your game?
- What happens if you play the wrong game?
- What qualities does a good game player possess?
- What is the context for your game?
- What part of the game do you like to play?
- To what extent is your game mental? Emotional? Physical? Spiritual?
- How do you relate to others' games?

✒ REFLECTION

1. What game do you and your clients play together?
2. How can you help your clients to create their own game?
3. How can coaching help clients improve their game?

Coach Angie Roote shares her story illustrating how we can use metaphors in coaching clients.

Finish the Floor
By Angie Roote

In the past few months, I have had several things going on in my life. External changes included buying my first house in a new area and starting my own coaching business. Internally I began redefining my relationships and balancing the old and new.

To remodel a room to become my coaching office, I ripped out the old flooring to prepare for new carpeting. Although I scheduled specific times to work on this project, each time I chose to do other things. When I told my coach I had made virtually no progress on my office, I began choking up and started to cry. "What do those tears mean to you?" she asked, and I blurted out, "I don't know what I'm so damn afraid of." I explained I really, *really* wanted the flooring out and the new carpet in, but couldn't figure out why I was avoiding doing the work.

In a moment of unconscious insight, I said, "The floor is like a dam ('so damn afraid'). As soon as the carpet is in place, I can begin my new career. My dam might burst. I could be flooded, swamped, deluged. I would have so much to do. No more time for myself."

The floor seemed to be a metaphor for keeping the status quo in my life. My floor was holding the process of change in check. It represented my stability, safety, the known, the familiar, the past, my "old" friendships. Tearing it out represented changing my foundation, my roots (note my last name). I feared once I did this, I could never go back.

My coach suggested the dam might look less frightening if I created a new metaphor for transformation. Perhaps I could reflect on the past and honor it. Perhaps I could be in the present. I might even dare look to the future with wonderment.

A new metaphor emerged. In my imagination I envisioned myself at the top of a bright mountain with trees overhead. Every once in a while, the moistness of dew or a raindrop dripped onto the same place on the ground. The repeated slow drip began to burrow a bit into the ground, the drip becoming a trickle. A little puddle formed and the trickle turned into a light constant flow. Overflowing, the water ever so slightly began to flow down the mountain. When I finished the visualization I felt different.

I now trust as the flow burrows deeper, the path becomes wider. The water rushes more quickly and I handle the speed as the flow gains momentum. My old floor out, the carpet in, my office complete, my coaching business begins, and I adeptly manage the success.

Example

When training coaches, I use the metaphor of the new shoe to help them learn an unfamiliar process. Designers of most shoes target a standardized foot and design a prefabricated shoe that will fit most people comfortably. I buy the shoe in my size, nine. Of course tens of thousands of other people also wear "my size." I wear it for the first time. Not terribly comfortable, although it does the job and takes me where I want to go. The longer I wear the shoe, the more it conforms to my foot, and eventually it really is "my" size. The more experience a coach accumulates, the more the coaching process and techniques custom fit the coach's personality, style, and spirit.

✿ REFLECTION

1. What was the last challenging situation you had to deal with in your physical environment? How might this situation be a metaphor for your learning?

2. What metaphor might it represent relative to your coaching business?

3. What metaphor might you choose as your bridge to transformation?

4. What metaphor might be appropriate to represent your desired outcome?

5. How long did it take for you to transition from acting as a carbon copy of your coach trainer to being in your own skin?

Stories thus far point out when coaches internally know and sense Spirit's presence. Let us move our attention to another aspect of connection to the whole—the physical environment.

Spirit in the Environment

Spirit, as an aspect of energy, shows up ubiquitously. We cannot pay attention to Spirit and ignore our environment, beginning with our appearance, moving outward into our office space, and further out into our office setting and beyond. Because the physical environment is merely an extension of self, the coaching environment needs to mirror the standards of appearance and values of the coach. Spirit lives in your choice of clothing, your surroundings, even your neighborhood and beyond. This holds true for face-to-face coaching, telecoaching, and email coaching. How would you react to knowing your coach was on the other end of the telephone wearing pajamas, sitting in bed, and clipping his or her nails with the TV on in the background, while you struggled to find your life's direction?

Your Coaching Space

What would you want to have your environment look like, sound like, and feel like for you to be supported in your pursuit of purposeful living? I pay close attention to how clients feel and the comments clients make regarding my coaching space.

Peaceful. As I look around my office I feel peaceful. Comfortable and conducive to learning are predominant themes I imagined when creating this office. No piles of paper or hidden messes in corners. One has the feeling everything is in its proper place, a mirror paralleling one of our deep desires—to be in our proper place in the universe. A water fountain offers smooth burbling sounds, an occasional duck or goose spontaneously emotes an authentic voice in appreciation of the natural beauty. Glancing outside one sees a sparkling lake, just steps away, with a melodious wind chime lazily swaying in the breezes.

Natural. Inside I see healthy plants carefully placed with attention to design and flow, wool oriental rugs, a negative ion generator, and full spectrum lighting—all chosen to create an ambiance of relaxation for learning. In sharp contrast to hotels or offices with hermetically sealed windows, my office has much fresh air and natural sunlight streaming in through large sliding glass doors. No wonder executives loosen their ties and take off their jackets. Checked at the entrance are pretenses, requirements, and artificiality—to be picked up upon departure if they wish.

Homey. In comfortable chairs, we share the same side of the credenza facing each other (not on opposite sides of the desk like opponents). A large, almost empty library table abuts the credenza, purposefully placed to create lots of workspace. This office has ample room for the notebook, the briefcase, the tissues, a cup of tea or glass of water—a cornucopia of space for Spirit and creativity. After all, Spirit sources out of space so the surroundings need space for Spirit to emerge.

Lighthearted. Tucked away, although not totally out of sight, rest some of my toys, ready to be plucked at the perfect moment: (1) a colorful paper inflatable globe weighing one-fourth ounce and only eight inches in diameter, to be called on when a client expresses or feels the heaviness of an impending decision or action. Feel the weight of the world on your shoulders? What would have to happen for your world to weigh just this little? (2) a plastic gadget with two hands that clap furiously, ready to be picked up when a client's new awareness warrants a crescendo of applause beyond my own; (3) a flashing magic wand handy when I desire to dub a client, as I did when I wanted to cement Olivia's new self-image into her foundation (Refer to Chapter 5, The Present Moment, for more about the meeting with Olivia); (4) a treasure chest of stickers and markers to bring playful creativity for whole brain activities; (5) my favorite books to remind me of the abundance of wisdom easily accessible.

Leisurely. Frequently people physically slow down when they enter my space. Plenty of time to rush elsewhere, the two-hour coaching experience allows *all* the time we need to do what we choose to do, *all* the time we need to be who we want to be. Our coaching experience does not squeeze into a busy day; it is that special part of the day when the client can relax, reinvent, and recharge.

The clothing you choose also affects the learning environment. When you dress in accord so your inner world and outer world reflect each other, you project uniformity, harmony.

I remember one morning when I really felt like wearing my Native American jewelry, casual sweater, and long skirt. But my first meeting was with a business executive. Twice I changed outfits to try to force myself to feel comfortable in more business-like attire. Ultimately I let my feelings (amplified into strong intuition) win. As he walked up to my door, one of the first phrases out of *his* mouth was, "I hope it's all right I dressed down to come today." It turned out he was part Native American!

ℒ REFLECTION

1. What does your environment reveal about you as a coach, your abilities, your attitudes, your beliefs, your values, and your presence?

2. Close your eyes and imagine the perfect coaching environment. What do you see? Hear? Feel? Smell? Touch? What step can you take this week to begin to create that space? What would make it perfect for you?

3. Which coaching outfits do you love best? Why? Texture? Color? Fit?

4. What clothes do you typically choose to wear when you coach? Did you feel comfortable in the clothes you wore the last time you coached?

One coach trainer acknowledges the omnipotence of Spirit, sharing that Spirit is in her awareness most of the time and has become, as she says, pervasive and inseparable, like fish in water.

A Fish in Water
By Vicki Escudé

My sense of Spirit has expanded through the vehicle of coaching. One reason for this expansion is that coaching is a hand-in-glove fit with my life purpose. My life purpose is to inspire personal and spiritual growth, share my ideas, and connect meaningfully with others. Every aspect of coaching as a business reflects my purpose and mission, whether it is connecting with others in a coaching partnership, or even connecting while marketing.

The amazing part of my connection to Spirit is that it no longer is what I experience during "special" times—when I meditate or read inspirational works. It has become such an integral part of my life that I do not even notice "spiritual." It is like a fish that does not notice or question water. In fact, I am mindful now when I am out of sync with my spirit, like a fish out of water.

The "coincidences" and miracles that used to jolt me with surprise now are a seamless part of my daily experiences. I have learned to know and trust that every experience is the perfect unfolding of my good and my goals and I bless whatever happens. The miracles seem subtler; it takes less drama to get my attention.

When coaching, I bring this trust to the partnership, knowing the client-partner's life is unfolding perfectly. This allows me to observe, mirror, and reflect, while honoring the dignity of his or her journey. Trust also allows me to be fully present with my client-partner and sharpens my ability to observe.

One other shift for me is that I have learned to "stalk" change, rather than resist it. "OK, what's next? How do I choose to grow?" I ask myself, as I watchfully wait for the next level of my development. I also know that the barriers I am willing to break and the depth of awareness I am willing to claim will open doors for my clients.

Spirit is not separate from me. It is everything I do and am. Even the shadow, unknown, submerged, and hidden parts of myself offer precious gifts that keep me whole. This is Spirit, too. Embracing the shadow self enables me to accept and mirror the dark unconscious of my clients.

I do not "feel" spiritual, as I did earlier in my life when I was a seeker. I *am* Spirit now more consistently.

Summary

In this chapter, you read and reflected on how to expand perspective. We have come full circle from having considered doing and being as distinct at the beginning of this section to holding them as inseparable, as in the fish-like-water example.

Noticing synchronistic patterns, coming from a place of service and gratitude, inviting cycles, honoring the dip, and using metaphors to parallel reality represent examples of coaching with Spirit. Expansion to the largest arena imaginable includes a point of view so large that any separation between coach and Spirit no longer exists. What if no difference exists between connection with self and connection with the whole? What would that look like? Feel like?

According to numerous spiritual philosophies, the whole of life experience exists solely in this moment. The future and the past have been fabricated to justify a temporal existence not present in the Spirit world. I do not intend to debate the validity of this premise, but rather to use it as a springboard for further discussion about Spirit in coaching. Chapter 5, The Present Moment, focuses both microscopic and macroscopic attention on the here and now and how this approach enhances the coach's and client's effectiveness.

CHAPTER 5 The Present Moment

ASSESSMENT

Please rate yourself on the extent to which you coach with Spirit.

0 = never; 1 = rarely; 2 = sometimes; 3 = often; 4 = most of the time;
5 = almost always

To what extent do I . . .

0   1   2   3   4   5   feel present during a coaching meeting?

0   1   2   3   4   5   assess clients' well-being during a meeting?

0   1   2   3   4   5   pay attention to my feelings while coaching?

0   1   2   3   4   5   use my feelings to determine coaching strategy?

0   1   2   3   4   5   create states of expectancy to maximize learning?

0   1   2   3   4   5   honor how much I learn from my clients?

0   1   2   3   4   5   feel comfortable allowing clients to express emotions?

0   1   2   3   4   5   feel lighthearted when coaching?

0   1   2   3   4   5   use humor appropriately?

0   1   2   3   4   5   laugh with clients?

0   1   2   3   4   5   speak my intuitive insights?

0   1   2   3   4   5   regain my spiritual connection quickly when I feel I have lost it?

0   1   2   3   4   5   rely on my body to guide me in coaching?

0   1   2   3   4   5   maintain awareness of all my sensory data while coaching?

0   1   2   3   4   5   process thoughts through my heart?

> *"As for the future, your task is not to foresee but to enable it. All true creation is not a prejudgment of the Future, . . . but the apprehending of a new aspect of the present."*
>
> Antoine de Saint-Exupéry

Inspired by this quote, I wrote the following:

Waiting

Part I
Watching the music,
Listening to the smiles,
Feeling the sounds,
I wait
and wait. . .
Part II
And begin to wonder why I'm waiting.
Now is here already.
So
I watch the music.
I listen to the smiles.
I feel the sounds
and I am happy.

This chapter, replete with delightful contradictions, is grist for the seeker of truth. Having just claimed that life exists only in the present, how can we justify the very premise of coaching? We leave the present moment every time we guide clients to create a future. Or do we ever leave the present? I do not propose to resolve this age-old philosophical paradox; however, I do hope you can use this chapter to dive deep into soul searching about your coaching relationship with the present moment and surface with increased coaching awareness and skill in expressing Spirit.

Begin by exploring why we move away from the present.

Making a Different Difference

> *"We were not put on this earth merely to make a difference in the world. We were put on this earth to make the world different."*
>
> Luke 6:17–26

The phrase "making a difference" suggests something different is needed, exposing an inherent dissatisfaction with the present. From a spiritual perspective, everything is perfect as it is. When we find the perfection in every moment, we feel peaceful and content. Why do we feel compelled to create life differently from the way it is?

Example

 Gregor entered coaching to change his work situation. An overly demanding boss and an incompetent secretary were his chief complaints. He sought a position within the same government agency but within another department. "I can't make a difference" [make it different], Gregor complained. The more he tried, the greater his frustration. While at work, Gregor spent most of his time designing and redesigning his bright future. No surprise that he had similar problems in his last two jobs.

Coaching raised awareness of his inability to find peace with the present. I played the "What if?" game by posing the challenge: "What if you had to find peace in your current situation? What would it look like? Sound like? Be like?" Playing "What if?" does wonders to open a connection to a box outside our own.

Gregor peeked out of his grumbling box and saw that his boss and secretary felt equally frustrated. In a moment of compassion, Gregor brought in a flower for his secretary. He began to understand why his boss was so overly demanding: He too just wanted to make a difference.

Slowly, with sensitivity, Gregor became more peaceful and reported that his boss and secretary appeared transformed. When he detailed their behavior and attitude, nothing external had actually changed. Only he had changed!

His lesson: No difference is necessary. The shift to an externally different world comes from within.

✿ REFLECTION

1. Do you tend to use the phrase "make a difference"?

2. Name two things different now from just one year ago. How different are they really?

3. Think of two situations in which you want to make a difference. What if you could change your relationship to these situations? What would it look like? Feel like? Sound like?

In the next client story, the coach aimed to expose a reality hidden from the client's view, changing nothing but bringing awareness to what already exists. With no vested interest in the outcome, coach, client, and the client's wife were all delightfully surprised at the result.

Example

 Dylan, an emotionally monotone executive, came to coaching to assess the possibility of retiring early from a management position in a *Fortune* 100 company to become an entrepreneur. At one point, when we discussed a particular option, I tuned in to my body and sensed heaviness. I asked Dylan what lay beneath this option and how he felt when he considered it. He responded, "I am not in touch with my feelings; my wife has a big problem with that." Because feelings contain information for us and I knew Dylan to be an explorer and adventurer at heart, I pursued this path and asked whether he would want to know more about his feelings. No resounding yes, but a weak, "OK, if you think it would help me make this decision."

Spirit work began. For me, I needed to trust I would choose a value-added direction to produce the desired result—that is, for Dylan to use the information from his feelings to make a decision. As a coach I believe it imperative to stick to a client's chosen results and outcomes. Yet Spirit clearly nagged me to add a conversation about feelings as an information source for

Dylan. I honored my intuition, let go of expectations of how it should be, and trusted . . . trusted . . . trusted.

To achieve in sports, one must recognize and interpret physical information. Excelling in sports had been important for Dylan as a child, young adult, and still now as a middle-aged man. So I surmised that he was more in touch with his feelings through his body than he realized.

I asked him to close his eyes and pay attention to where he felt something physically. He pointed to his stomach. Playfully, I suggested he name what was going on in his stomach, using any word. I avoided reference to the names of actual feelings, knowing them to be as individualistic as thumbprints. (Remember to let clients choose their own words.) He selected "wishbone." With his permission, I randomly interrupted our conversation several times during the next ninety minutes and asked him again to check inside and identify where he felt something, assigning words to the sensations. Over the next few coaching meetings Dylan's interest peaked. I intentionally did not share the list of names he selected so he would initiate the request for review. (I used the "Expectancy Principle," which you will read about later in this chapter.) When we did the review, we correlated his words with locations in his body. Curiously, themes emerged. A few meetings later I shared a "feelings list" with Dylan and challenged him to match his words with the list. He enjoyed the process and discovered he could easily sense and name feelings.

At the end of coaching, his final comment was, "I expected to become clear about my future career and I did. I did not also expect to get in touch with my feelings. My wife and I are so happy with this added bonus."

By naming something, we validate the experience. By naming feelings we also validate the body-mind connection. This works especially well with people who have had experiences in sports because they have learned the importance of paying attention to physical sensations. Spirit guided both Dylan and me to greater awareness—Dylan about his feelings and I to trust Spirit's nudges.

REFLECTION

1. Do you have any clients who cannot name their feelings or who appear emotionally monotone?

2. Do you often hear "good" as the sole declaration of a client's feeling state?

3. Might you enhance clients' success by introducing awareness of feelings?

4. What physical sensations become evident during your client meetings? For you? For your clients? Do you use this data? How?

Spirit's Physiological Presence

Spirit's physiological presence leads us into uncharted territory. Coaches staying alert in the present moment can amass more information about what goes on to better serve the client. Several years after I began coaching, I became aware of a pattern involving physical information during life purpose meetings. The pattern emerged through my physical body at first. While clients shared their purposeful anecdotes, I felt sensations building within my body—sensations most frequently located in selected places, such as my throat, my gut, my heart, and my "third eye" (centered about an inch above the beginning of my eyebrows).

Physical Place of Purpose

At the time I was studying with an amazing sports and performance coach and master NLP practitioner, Charles Parry, so I mentioned my observation to him. Parry's explanation brought me a new and exciting addition to my coaching—the concept of "physical place of purpose." Because the physical body does not *know* the difference between what is real and what is imaginary, it configures neural pathways to physiologically simulate whatever the mind offers it as fodder for thought. By reliving experiences of purposefulness, the client's body begins to feel as it did when the experiences were actually lived. When I am tuned in to the present and connected with myself, I too, feel these vibrations as if they magically transfer from client to me. For me, this provides evidence that we are all connected. These sensations align themselves with one of the body's seven key energy centers (chakras) depending on the client's context for purpose and key life lesson. For example, clients whose purpose stories tell of times when speaking and listening were instrumental in bringing satisfaction will likely experience purposefulness in the throat (throat chakra). Others who relate moments of feeling empowered when making significant choices might experience amplified energy in their navel (power chakra). Those who share experiences of self-appreciation, love, and deep caring for others could be expected to sense their hearts sending pulsating warm tingles in their chest (heart chakra).

Armed with a new gift for physical observation, I invite you to ask your clients where they experience purposefulness in their body so they can use it to make choices.

Using Physical Place of Purpose to Make a Choice

"To use the physical sensations of purposefulness to make life choices, significant and mundane, the client needs to imagine one of the choice options with as much detail and specificity as is available, then check inside for the purpose feeling. Next, imagine the other choice with the same degree of specificity and again note the internal sensations. Whichever feels closer to the feeling of purposefulness is the one that will bring greater fulfillment and satisfaction. This is information for the client. As stated earlier, the choice is still up to the client" (Belf, 2001, p. 4).

Once feelings and corresponding physicality have been identified, the challenge shifts to determining how to measure these intangibles to adeptly judge progress and success.

Example

 My client Manuel wished to feel calmer. To establish a baseline, I inquired how calm he felt nowadays, on a scale of one to ten. It would have been inaccurate to leave off the "nowadays" because he might have responded to his immediate state influenced by our coaching connection and setting. By my asking him to reply to a more general statement, he brought into the calculation the rest of his life as well. This simple question enables measurement of qualitative things in quantitative ways and surfaces an inner knowing response. No time is given for the client to detail all experiences in this time period; the wise self must answer.

As coaches we must be clear about the outcome a client wants, so I asked Manuel, "On a scale of one to ten, how calm do you want to feel in five months when coaching finishes?" Manuel answered, "Nine." Now we have a way to assess and ascertain progress. As we explored Manuel's calmness further, I asked:

- "How quickly do you recognize when you feel calm?"

- "Do you know what to do to regain your experience of calm? What activities bring feelings of calm to you?"

- "How quickly do you act to regain calmness?"

- "How will you know when you feel calmer?"

✺ REFLECTION

1. Use the above questions and discover what happens.

2. Ask yourself randomly three times a day, "How calm am I feeling now?"

3. Select a feeling and focus on it for two weeks. Every evening rate yourself on the extent to which on average you experienced that feeling over the course of a day.

4. Ask your spouse, friend, or a family member on a scale of one to ten how happy overall he or she is.

Marilyn Dabady relates her experience of how Spirit flows in her and through her, enabling both her and her clients to experience the power of sharing a present moment.

Moving Spirit
By Marilyn Dabady

Spirit is present within each person, but is it God, a supernatural being, an emotional attitude, or life energy? I acknowledge Spirit can mean many things to different people, so I offer a definition of Spirit both as it presents itself in my life generally and also when I coach.

Spirit is energy. Spirit gives me energy to pursue things that make me happy or to do something I am passionate about—it moves me to experience life fully. Imagine a time, place, or event that makes you or once made you feel euphoric. Perhaps it is the intense feeling you get when viewing a piece of beautiful artwork, winning a big championship game, or realizing you are falling in love. I might describe this feeling as a manifestation of energy emanating from the vivid colors dancing on a canvas, the intoxicating sound of a cheering crowd, or the intense emotion of joy. In any case, the experience *moves* you. That is how I experience Spirit in coaching—it moves me.

Spirit moves me to listen, trust my instincts, find my passion, and be myself. When I coach, Spirit moves me to create a space for a client's dreams, truths, and passions to emerge. In addition to sensing Spirit within myself, I believe coaching gives me the opportunity to sense Spirit in others. In that space when Spirit emerges, the client and I make a powerful connection through Spirit.

Coaching with the Flow

Coaching is one of the best models of surrendering to flow. Spirit enhances my coaching effectiveness, allowing me to surrender to flow and connect with the client. Each time I coach, I put all my attention on the client and concentrate on being in the present moment. I listen intently to what the client says and I also listen to what Spirit tells me in the message. By focusing my energy and listening to the client, I simply go with the flow. Where is the client going in this session? What is the client feeling? Where are the energy drains? What does the client need from me in the present moment in order to move forward?

When the flow of energy is abundant, I am motivated to connect with others and share my Spirit. I witness how clients become aware of behaviors or attitudes that keep them stuck and how that awareness sparks the energy needed to move forward. I enjoy the connection we share in that moment—understanding and truth ring clear as a bell. When a client and I celebrate movement toward fulfillment, Spirit moves me. Through a connection between my client and myself, Spirit creates an environment that lets each of us go with the flow.

Coaches are in a special position as participant observers. Listening intently, we learn about a client's needs, desires, and frustrations. Over time, a coach may witness discovery and transformation as Spirit moves the client toward goals.

❦

Awareness, discovery, transformation, and learning take place in the present. Being able to remain in the present can challenge even a master coach. The next section explains from a learning point of view why it is imperative for the client to be in the present to gain awareness. Several exercises illustrate how to increase the probability of being present.

Expectancy

Learning theory tells us that when a learner is in a state of expectancy, the learner becomes more involved and interested in learning. Unexpected movements stretch the body into neurological newness. Expectant means eager, hopeful, and waiting—all considered positive emotional states. Coaches aim to keep clients in an open learning mode, in a state of attention with natural rawness and receptivity to the new.

Our minds tend to take disparate pieces of information and create a whole or a "gestalt." Incompletes are mentally and emotionally unsettling. The mind resourcefully and naturally resolves the tension created by the missing piece or the unknown by supplying facts augmented with imagination. Pairing the internal experience of expectancy with an external reality containing incompletes raises a learner's antennae. When you do this you create a heightened learning environment desirable for coaching.

Learning theory also informs us that when emotions are involved, long-term memory activates, thereby increasing the chance for retention and sustainability of the learning. Coaches can use humor, surprise, exaggeration, outrageousness, physical activities, and confusion to increase the probability of long-term retention. The following four exercises illustrate how to use expectancy in coaching meetings.

Exercise

Create a handout for your client that has five numbers on a page. Explain four points while writing key words next to the first four numbers. Then engage in a different topic, leaving the fifth number blank. Guaranteed, your client's attention floats back to the empty fifth number without a teaching point next to it, curious as to what it might be. This exemplifies pairing expectancy with incompletes.

By using this principle effectively, we keep clients in a posture poised for learning. The wondering open mind is ripe for new input, guessing, questing, and playing with creative resolutions. At the same time, one aspect of our brain is delegated to this assignment; another is present and aware of the matter at hand. Because coaches create a safe, trusting relationship, what might appear to be a distraction reroutes to becoming peaked curiosity. Certainly be aware of any evidence of discomfort or tension that may arise and, if necessary, be prepared to alter course.

Exercise

Mention to your client that you have three possible angles for today's discussion. Briefly allude to each of the three, select one, and explain your plan to expose the others later in the meeting. I'll bet your client wonders about the other two with a heightened sense of curiosity.

Exercise

Show your client the forms for the technique you plan to use. Place the forms in a visible spot, although not within clear range for reading. Again you have sparked interest, this time in how the forms will be used.

Exercise

Create forms or worksheets that have missing sections, blanks, and boxes that you or your client will fill in at the appropriate time. The curious mind speculates about what will be written in.

✿ R E F L E C T I O N

1. What can you intentionally leave incomplete to trigger expectancy with your next client?

2. What can you create during a coaching meeting to keep yourself fully alert and receptive?

The Expectancy Paradox

Having claimed that expectancy heightens learning because of the element of surprise, I will now superimpose the opposite, claiming that coaches who carry expectations invalidate their ability to be fully present.

People do not operate on a predictable trajectory of well-being. A client who leaves feeling buoyant may experience intervening life circumstances and return feeling sad. We cannot be truly present unless we deliberately *forget* the last well-being state of the client.

---

1. Do you expect clients to continue where they left off from the last meeting?

2. For your next three clients, create a blank slate, a purely curious presence, devoid of any expectation, and be fully present with the client from the point of his or her arrival.

Using Humor

"Hu," the exhaling sound of the breath, is thought by one spiritual discipline to be man's first verbal expression of God (John-Roger, 1984, p. 51). Thus the word humor (hu-more) can mean expressing more of your human (God-like man) self. Humor can be an extremely useful tool in the coach's toolkit. It can heighten the experience of being in the present moment because humor involves the emotions, the body, and the intellect, all at the same time. I hope if I am wise enough to heed this truism I will develop more smile wrinkles because of the many times I lighten up my clients and myself.

In the following story, I intentionally introduced emotion into my meeting with my client Olivia to ensure she retained a new awareness. This coaching meeting segment illustrates the role Spirit plays with mobilizing emotion.

Example

 Each one of us strives to feel special and unique, yet Olivia felt she was just an ordinary person. She bemoaned her state. Nothing exciting or unusual ever happened in her life. After hearing this self-proclamation several times, I walked over to my bookcase where I keep a "magic" wand that flashes every few seconds when I turn it on. (All coaches need a magic wand for emergency use.) Putting it behind my back and turning it on, I slowly approached Olivia. Not knowing what to expect (using the Expectancy Principle), she appeared quite attentive.

With no specific idea in mind, I felt Spirit taking over as I asked her to kneel down in front of me. Raising the wand I proceeded to dub her (like a knight) and spoke these words, "I dub thee ordinary, an ordinary person, a really ordinary person, so much so that I am commissioned to give you an *extra* ordinary." We both realized what I had said and began to laugh. The instant shift with the extra ordinary helped her reframe her identity. With the pairing of positive emotion and deep laughter, this became a referent point for much of our future work. To this day, Olivia reminds me of the moment she elevated to becoming extraordinary.

The deliberate use of humor can be a powerful tool. We can be selective about choosing experiences to position into our long-term memory banks. In Olivia's case, laughter catalyzed a permanent transformation. In the moment I had walked to my wand, my mind was blank. I had no idea what was to follow, yet I sensed it was going to be perfect. Coaching with Spirit means jumping into the unknown and trusting something of value will happen.

Example

 Franci's situation was all a muddle, and she remained stuck in her complicated and tangled story. "I want to make a mean-ingful contribution, but I need my current salary to preserve my lifestyle. I want to take time for hobbies, but I have to spend so much time on work because everyone depends on me. I travel 80 percent of the time; it is very draining, so I am tired when I come home. I want to feel en-ergetic. My rent is going up and I would love to use that as the opportunity to move to a warmer climate, but I don't want to leave my friends. I would love to be in a relationship, but I don't have the energy or time to date." Each time she began to envision one life area changing, the others popped up as major obstacles. Chasing her tail, she remained stuck on all fronts.

My diagnosis after listening to the circuitous details of her woes: "You have one huge clump." Together in a moment of playfulness, we coined the word "declump" to identify a process for becoming unstuck in her recycling story. At the first sign of the pattern, she now declumps and sticks to one is-sue at a time. She even developed a personalized declump process for each issue on a separate index card, and in our meetings she structures her con-versation using her declump cards. She created a "Declump Plan" and "De-clump Action Steps." Her prognosis looked great by the time coaching was completed, at which time, of course, I presented Franci with a "Master De-clumper Certificate of Completion."

Another way to sprinkle humor in coaching is with the expression "What if?" This phrase, taken to an absurd extreme and combined with humor, can effectively disengage clients from stuck molds, as in the following example.

Example

Yugin came to coaching having made no progress on his assignment to create visions and goals because he could not remember how to do it.

Coach: *What if* a federal law required you to make progress with your homework? What might you have done to complete the assignment?

Yugin: I would have called you, but I didn't want to bother you for this.

Coach: (Teasing, with a dramatic sigh of relief) Thank you for making that decision for me. Perhaps some day I will learn how to make that choice for myself. Seriously, please at least give me a *chance* to say yes or no. Allow me and trust me to honestly answer whether it would be a bother or not.

Other approaches could have been used in lieu of a lighthearted one. The coach could have been serious and reminded Yugin to resourcefully draw on his support network. Whereas many roads might have produced the same result, why not choose to engage the fun one?

✑ R E F L E C T I O N

1. What emotions have you triggered in your clients?

2. What happened the last time you let go of any preconceived notion of what was going to happen next with a client?

3. How have you successfully used humor to facilitate awareness?

4. How can you be more lighthearted (as appropriate) in coaching?

Neutrality

Sometimes emotion blocks success. As we learned from Dylan, our physical and emotional selves intertwine inextricably. We can help clients become more fully present by tuning into our emotions through our physical sensations. Emotions attached to a past or future event become expressed in the present moment. Although clients often tell stories from a past or future timeframe, the mind is expert at distorting the past and creating a fearful future. Finding a way to separate the emotion from the story frees the client to gain perspective and move into a place of choice.

When you sense a client would benefit by distancing from an emotional incident, have the client pretend he or she is a reporter and must tell only the facts. Instruct the client to select an emotionally packed experience and retell it until there are virtually no negative physical sensations. Although this may be extremely difficult in the first few attempts, a story repeated often enough evolves into a neutral one. Devoid of emotions, the client freely generates choices and possibilities.

Example

Nancy reports becoming withdrawn and quiet during yet another exhausting meeting with her scattered and elaborate storytelling supervisor. Afraid to interrupt for fear of retribution, Nancy becomes silent. After Nancy tells the story several times and names her emotions, she moves into neutrality. Now Nancy, no longer afraid of retribution, can establish a preferred scenario, authentically expressing herself with her supervisor.

☙ REFLECTION

1. Try this exercise yourself before using it with a client. Recall a challenging client meeting. Guide yourself through repetition of the specific event to neutrality.

2. The only place you have options when driving a stick shift car is in the neutral position. You can drive forward or backward from neutral, but from every other position you have only one possibility. Similarly in the game of tennis, when standing in center court, you have more possibilities of hitting the next shot. Can you think of other metaphors illustrating increased choice in the neutral zone?

3. How neutral are you as a coach?

4. How authentic do you dare to be?

Engage all cylinders as you read a spiritual coaching moment offered by life potentials coach Ann McGill. Note the fallout from abandoning the neutral space of Spirit.

Sometimes Spirit Withdraws . . . for Good Reason
By Ann McGill

Spirit speaks to me in a silent whisper I do not hear, but perceive intuitively. When I do deep emotional work with clients, I find myself listening with my whole body, viscerally tuning in, noticing every nuance of change in emotion, every shift in energy toward fear and shutdown or relaxing into love and opening. By sharing this insight, I focus the other person's awareness on what is happening now, this moment. Often this is all that is needed to trigger valuable insights about negative response patterns.

Example

 For the first time in her life, Janey feels recognized, understood, and loved. Never before has anyone tuned in so deeply, so clearly heard her pain, and understood the fear that drives her unwanted behavior. As her emotions veer up and down, from joy to sadness to anguish and terror, it feels as if Spirit, through me, is holding her hand, cradling her in a nurturing embrace.

When I work with people like Janey who experience the world as an unsafe place, I find something very interesting happens after a strong bond of trust has been well-established and reinforced. I do not choose the moment, Spirit does.

When Spirit Withdraws

Suddenly Spirit withdraws. My ego takes over. I observe myself saying something upsetting to the client. Client reacts. Pulls back. His or her worst fear has suddenly materialized. I have proven his or her forever-held belief that "no one can be trusted."

Spirit does not return to take charge of the process until the individual has had a sufficient taste of the scary reality repeatedly created by lacking the ability to trust. Then, all of a sudden, I become aware I am once again experiencing my client on the subtler planes of existence. Once again I automatically know what to say, what the feelings are, and the kind of support called for.

When Spirit Takes Over

As I begin to speak to Janey from the heart instead of the head, Spirit takes over and communicates on deeper levels than ego can reach. Janey starts to calm down, listen, and reconsider. Instead of focusing on her fear-driven desire to flee, she opens to the possibility that this incident is not a repetition of historical events. She becomes available to learn about personal power and learn how to take better care of herself in similar situations.

I feel a rush of relief as Spirit takes over once more. Again I am reminded that ego can never accomplish the healing miracles Spirit can. I feel privileged to be a part of the process moving Janey forward, toward an increasing sense of wholeness, love, and inner strength.

✒ R E F L E C T I O N

1. In observing the entrance of your ego, how long does it take to return to Spirit?

2. Ask three colleagues or spiritual allies what they do to bring themselves back to their spiritual essence when engaged with someone else.

3. What qualities of being do you possess (such as patience, grace, and so on) that support you to move in and out of your awareness of your spiritual self?

4. Name different kinds of power that make up your personality. Which belong to your ego?

5. Ask yourself: "When should I stop being proactive?"

Embodied Spirit

The physical body can serve as one porthole through which Spirit reveals its presence. When I encounter sensations that do not seem to originate within me, I ask my clients to check inside and report their physical state and where sensations reside. Repeatedly, the location matches my own. The consistency of matches led me to hypothesize I had stumbled on information that might improve my coaching flexibility. The following story illustrates this idea.

Example

 The second time Timothy and I met, he reported a general malaise and anxiety he had been experiencing for several years. It sounded to me like therapy might be more useful because I do not have the knowledge or skill to examine historical emotional difficulties.

My awareness shifted from my thoughts to my body and I felt tightness in my solar plexus or gut—referred to as my power center. I knew this symptom had surfaced in me for a reason. Taking a risk, I asked Timothy where in his body he felt the anxiety most intensely. He pointed to the general area around his gut. "What would that part of your body say if it could talk to you?" I inquired, assuming my Columbo persona (Chapter 3). Deep within me a moment of self-connection followed as I heard myself continue, "What sound would your gut make if it could speak?" This question did not appear to source from my mind; my intuition spoke. I knew I was operating in unknown territory, yet somehow I felt certain, guided, and safe to proceed. I felt Spirit inside me physically, giving me clues as to what to do next. I knew I needed to keep my connection to my body fully open in order to preserve the connection with Timothy. Then I felt my throat constrict.

I asked Timothy what was happening. With surprise, he pointed to his throat, and in a crackling, hoarse voice he said the tightness was very focused, no longer general.

Abruptly stopping, Timothy began to cough, a lot. All of a sudden, my throat cleared. I asked, "Where is the anxiety now?" Wide-eyed, Timothy said, "I feel terrific. No more anxiety. I haven't felt this good in months, maybe years."

We concluded this part of our meeting by discussing the symbolism of the location of the anxieties. For Timothy, tension in his gut (powerlessness) paired with constriction in his throat (inability to express his truth) provided useful information as to the reasons for his anxiety.

This "technique," untrained and unlearned, sprung out of the mysterious space created when I coach with Spirit. Spirit had deliberately moved in and through my body to awaken me to new possible connections within myself, enabling me to be of greater service to my clients.

🌿 R E F L E C T I O N

1. Stay super alert to your physical sensations during your next client meeting. Jot down what you feel. After the meeting, analyze what you wrote with regard to your client's results and obstacles.

2. When you feel tired, take a chance and ask your client if the feeling is mutual.

3. What percentage of your physical sensations do you think are shared by your clients?

4. Do you think you can proactively create physical sensations as a way to invite the same from your clients?

5. How does your body "know" when truth is present?

Although in the example with Timothy I chose to address physical sensation directly, coaches can also embed physical clues in metaphors to prompt emotions to surface. The key is to view somatic information as a gift and use it. Stepping back and using *every* piece of information available in the present moment honors Spirit.

Example

 Samantha was a well-renowned water instructor and enthusiast. An essential part of her life and livelihood, water appeared in most of her coaching results. After the holidays she experienced difficulty with her children and finances and came to our coaching call mildly depressed. Her voice silently called to me to express her sadness, but she remained silent. In this case I did not feel her sadness; a metaphor appeared as a mental flash.

Spirit spoke through me when I commented, "You allow water to be everywhere around and outside of you but not inside yourself." As Samantha acknowledged this incongruence, her tears flooded out: "I have never given myself permission to cry before." Tears turned to a smile; the healthy rain shower was over, and we continued exploring ways to deal with her challenges.

The physical senses serve as one excellent gateway to enhance our ability to be in the present. Upon which sense do you rely most? Which do you forget until you feel agitated to the point where you can no longer ignore them? Have you ever driven through a city and suddenly smelled something burning? Can you recall meandering on a peaceful country road, being interrupted by the sound of a fire engine? These sensory jolts bring us to the present. Accept the challenge of having a sensory awareness day if you wish to practice returning to the present.

> **Exercise: Sensory Awareness Day**
> Select one of your senses. Commit to a "Sensory Awareness Day" and several hundred times during the day bring your attention back to that sense. For example, if you select touch, really experience what it feels like to pick up the telephone, from your inner skin to your epidermis. When you pick up your pen, feel it with every tactile cell. Several days later, pick another sense and repeat the exercise. I guarantee you will find yourself much more present in all you do, including being with your clients.

✤ REFLECTION

1. What was the last challenging situation you had to deal with in your physical environment?

2. What metaphor might it represent related to your coaching business? (For example, dirty or streaked windows might represent lack of vision; a fractured thermometer might mean temper out of control; a broken light might mean dampened vitality).

3. Using the Principle of Synchronicity (Chapter 4), note which emotions tend to be dominant in your current clients.

Sharon Wilson, master spirit coach, founder and chief spiritual officer in the Coaching From Spirit organization, shares her perspective on our topic, the present moment. You will read how Spirit Coaching requires complete intention and commitment to being in the present moment. How many times can you find Wilson using the present moment to allow the flow of her coaching to serve her client, Debbie?

Coaching From Spirit—An Emerging Form of Coaching
By Sharon Wilson

I am in awe every day of the transformative power of Spirit in coaching.

As Spirit coaches, our work is to hold energy as clients begin to connect to their "inner coach" (Spirit) and to *trust* that connection for practical guidance. Holding energy means expecting Spirit to be present in each meeting and actively looking for moments when Spirit is not present because we push it away.

Spirit coaches actively engage a two-way communication with their Spirit and believe the client is also engaged in this process, whether consciously acknowledging it or not. For example, before I meet with a client, in order to be fully in the present, I clear my energy field and state my intention to partner with Spirit during the meeting. When the meeting begins, the client and I do a verbal centering exercise to align our energies in partnership and state our intentions for the meeting. When I work with a corporate client, I may never use the word Spirit, but I encourage the client to use a concept that works for him or her, such as inner guidance, intuition, higher self, or mentor. Or, as in the case of Debbie, we may talk more about feelings and how feelings are the vibrational point of attraction for what is currently showing up.

Example

 Debbie had been invited to speak and knew this opportunity would be good for her career. Thinking about getting up in front of an audience, however, made her physically ill. As she talked about her conflicting emotions—her desire to accept the engagement and her fears— I consciously opened my heart and poured loving energy around her, creating a safe place for her to further explore those fears.

Debbie said she "saw" herself at age three, immediately dismissing the image by saying, "It makes no sense." I asked her if she had a sense of anyone else involved. She answered, "My father just popped into my mind. This makes no sense at all." We continued exploring times in her life when she had to perform in front of an audience, looking for her inner critic story. Each time, she reported that once she went in front of people, she would freeze.

When I coach, I remain in constant contact with my inner coach. For me, this contact is like having an ear piece in my ear continuously feeding me information about what to do next. Because Debbie had no conscious memory about anything happening at age three, I had asked my inner coach, "Is it appropriate to work with her around the three-year-old image?" With a "yes" answer, I beckoned Debbie to go deeper into the light, deepening her connection to inner guidance. I suggested that Debbie imagine a movie screen in front of her with a freeze-frame shot of herself at age three with her father. Even if she did not actually "see" anything, she could still get in touch with her feelings.

Suddenly Debbie began remembering a day with her father. She had been singing a famous nursery rhyme all morning. In the afternoon, her dad took her to his family's house and put her on the kitchen table and told her to sing. No sound came out of Debbie's mouth. Her father became very angry. Debbie's energy block caused her to "freeze," and she has repeated this behavior in front of audiences. We proceeded to rewrite the energy of that day. She could eliminate the incident entirely or change her father's reaction to her inability to sing or perform successfully. Debbie chose to create a new scene with her belting out the song and the entire family wildly applauding their talented little girl. As Debbie described more and more details, she began feeling the approval more deeply in her body. Together we asked Spirit to anchor this energy and feeling in her cellular structure so she would have a new physical reaction to the idea of public speaking.

Feeling the new memory as reality, she had created an inner cellular energy shift. This happened through the mystery and power of Spirit Coaching! Today, Debbie does a lot of public speaking without fear. She never performs alone; Spirit is always by her side.

❧

With Sharon's perspectives on Spirit coaching, this chapter concludes and the present moment has received the adequate attention it deserves.

The next chapter addresses our role in the creation of our lives. You have read evidence of how we coach with Spirit by designing a crescendo of connection with ourselves, our clients, and to the whole. By being in the present moment, we increase the probability of opening to and trusting this connection. If we feel connected and present, we have increased options and possibilities for responding, we have a perspective of appropriateness, and we project authenticity. In order for these to be available, we must also assume and accept responsibility for our beliefs and actions. Without acknowledging personal responsibility, we cannot hope to consistently reproduce precious moments with Spirit.

CHAPTER 6 Responsibility

ASSESSMENT

Please rate yourself on the extent to which you coach with Spirit.

0 = never; 1 = rarely; 2 = sometimes; 3 = often; 4 = most of the time;
5 = almost always

To what extent do I . . .

0 1 2 3 4 5   allow clients to be responsible for their own outcomes?

0 1 2 3 4 5   allow client attachments to dissolve quickly?

0 1 2 3 4 5   set boundaries and adhere to them?

0 1 2 3 4 5   avoid getting drawn into a client's plea for advice
or suggestions?

0 1 2 3 4 5   use forward momentum language?

0 1 2 3 4 5   allow clients to make "mistakes"?

0 1 2 3 4 5   learn from my coaching "mistakes"?

0 1 2 3 4 5   avoid absolute language such as "always" and "never"?

0 1 2 3 4 5   keep expectations from influencing my actions?

0	1	2	3	4	5	check out my assumptions?
0	1	2	3	4	5	acknowledge the influence of my beliefs on my actions?
0	1	2	3	4	5	guide clients to uncover their spiritual beliefs?
0	1	2	3	4	5	believe motivating clients to be a disservice?
0	1	2	3	4	5	pay attention to the ecology of coaching?
0	1	2	3	4	5	accept glitches as a useful part of the journey?
0	1	2	3	4	5	experience gratitude during coaching?
0	1	2	3	4	5	remember that clients already have the knowledge and skill to succeed?

SOME COACHES SAY ONE OF THE KEY FUNCTIONS of coaching is to help clients assume personal responsibility (the ability to respond), whether cognitive, emotional, or physical. When we coach with Spirit, we know self-acceptance precedes the commitment to be responsible. When one feels unconditionally accepted, personal responsibility becomes an easy choice. However, the role of the coach is not necessarily to teach personal responsibility; the role of the coach is to unconditionally accept the client, as much as the coach is able to do so, given human frailties and foibles. In this loving environment, the client usually chooses the response for the highest good of all concerned.

Delving deeper into this topic raises questions about why we fall short of full self-acceptance. Our initial inquiry brings us to the topic of thoughts and beliefs.

Thoughts and Beliefs

Starting with thoughts, we enter the chain to create our world and ourselves. Imagine each of us as a lump of clay. Our thoughts mold the clay. In line with our interest in coaching with Spirit, this chapter highlights the need for our clients and us to recognize responsibility for sculpting the clay, for choosing our thoughts and beliefs. A belief is defined as *acceptance by the mind of truth or reality.*

The Field of Possibilities. Thoughts and beliefs live in a vast expansive home known as the morphogenetic field—a field of possibilities. This powerful, abundant, high-frequency, vibrational field is available to everyone and represents the entire wellspring of thoughts. If you have any doubt, visit quantum physics and read about thoughts as energy vibrations entering airwaves. At this stage of our scientific discoveries, thoughts possess no form in the physical world of measurement unless they convert into the spoken or written word or physical action. The process of verbally sharing and writing down thoughts further increases the chance a particular thought will become magnetic because we have reinforced the thought by giving it substance in the concrete world of the senses. Thoughts and beliefs lead to words that lead to actions that lead to habits that lead to character that determines our destiny. So monitoring thoughts becomes critical for purposeful living. When we assume responsibility for our thoughts and beliefs, we take a giant step toward influencing the world—*all* thoughts and beliefs. Pay attention to any new thoughts arising in you as you read about coaching and beliefs, and consider how reframing them might assist your ability to respond.

The coach's keystone belief is to preserve sole responsibility for success within the client's power. Four coaches, Sharon Wilson, Peter Reding, Marcia Collins, and Charlotte Ward, share reflections about the thoughts and beliefs percolating within the coach's mind to help us better understand the philosophies shared by those who do coach with Spirit. Sharon Wilson starts us off on our mental journey with eight key beliefs.

Effective Spirit Coaches' Beliefs and Intentions
By Sharon Wilson

1. When you coach from Spirit, you actively engage Spirit as the primary coach in the meeting and open a two-way communication. You trust Spirit completely to guide you and your client in each meeting, even if it seems illogical. You believe in the power of connecting with your non-physical teachers and have an active conscious relationship with them in the Spirit Coaching process.

2. You easily discern true guidance from false guidance for yourself and help clients discern it for themselves.

3. You see your life and every coaching meeting as a mirror of your own inner beliefs and constantly work to let go of old beliefs and negative energy and refocus the way you see a situation with Spirit's help. You recognize every situation is about you—your beliefs, patterns, and experiences. No one else is responsible for your continued pain, disappointment, or suffering. You create your reality with thoughts and

feelings, and you can create a new reality by changing those thoughts and feelings. You commit to clearing any energy and experiences that may block you from allowing the energy of Spirit into each meeting.

4. You actively partner with Spirit in all aspects of your life and have the intention in all your dealings to actively allow Spirit in for resolutions to create a harmonious solution for all concerned.

5. You are committed to nonjudgment and to the highest good of all concerned in your relationships, and you actively release the outcome of each meeting to Spirit.

6. You believe you are connecting with Spirit, and each meeting is a sacred experience with possibilities of miracles happening. You believe and trust in the perfection of each meeting.

7. You see and feel your clients in the condition they want to be in now. You believe by connecting with Spirit that clients can accelerate physical manifestations. You respect a client's religion and belief system and simply offer a process and a framework for the client to deepen connection, learn how to flow energy, and navigate thoughts and feelings. You help clients see how thoughts impact what they attract.

8. You know you and the client come as spiritual equals. As the coach, you believe Spirit is doing the work in a meeting, and your highest self partners with the client's highest self to activate the client's inner guidance. Because our highest self is already perfect, whole, and complete, there is no hierarchical one-upmanship going on during a Spirit meeting. You and the client have come together as equals to manifest on a physical plane the client's authenticity.

❧

Peter Reding and Marcia Collins contribute to our understanding of responsibility by reminding us that responsibility involves the "whole" person. Their presentation of the philosophical beliefs of those who coach with Spirit begins with the mental foundation needed to effectively respond. A different twist in examining the ability to respond moves us into questioning the client's approach to Spirit. At the end, Reding and Collins present questions to help the coach uncover what the client perceives Spirit to be so that a coach may be able to effectively respond to any particular client's interpretation of Spirit.

Coaching the Human Spirit™
By Peter Reding and Marcia Collins

The Coaching the Human Spirit™ model honors the spiritual oneness of us all and the human uniqueness we each represent. A coach who works with Spirit honors this philosophy.

- The coach knows Spirit and is connected with Spirit to facilitate clients' innate and direct connection with clients' perception of Spirit.

- The coach continues to facilitate the clients' self-discovery of values and life purpose through all levels: body, mind, heart, and soul.

- The coach supports clients in being aware of which beliefs, commitments, and actions align with their current understanding of values and life purpose.

- The coach acknowledges clients' expanding sense of fulfillment by linking clients' values and purpose with actions and way of being.

What Contributes to Life Coaches Ability to Respond?

1. Being 100 percent accepting of client's
   - Current position
   - Willingness to move forward—or not!
   - Ongoing process
   - Decisions
   - Results and rate of progress

2. Being 100 percent present with them and for them
   - *Physically:* focusing only on the client
   - *Mentally:* knowing the client knows his or her own best answers
   - *Emotionally:* knowing the client is always at choice and all moods serve the client

   Spiritually: knowing the client is always "at one"

3. Being 100 percent supportive
   - Wants the best for the client
   - Maintains focus on the client's role in every situation

- Holds clients accountable for their self-commitments

- Acknowledges and celebrates all successes and awareness

- Focuses clients on where they want to go, not what they want to leave

- Focuses clients primarily on what they can do, not what is stopping them

- Focuses clients on building decisions and actions on the foundation of clients' values and purpose

4. Being 100 percent self-honoring

- Preparing as the coach for each session

- Being a clear channel for questions to facilitate the client's self-discovery at the deepest level of capability in the moment

- Honoring time and money commitments

- Being a model for fully giving and fully receiving

- Honoring intuition

- Being light

Uncovering the Client's Understanding of Spirit

The coach or the client may not have acknowledged it, but Spirit has and is always present. The question is not whether Spirit is present but, rather, "What can I do as a coach to acknowledge Spirit?" It is about the clients' self-discovery of relationship, existing or newly created, with their human interpretation of their spirit. Whatever our clients call divine presence, we write it down for future reference because Spirit is "infinite resourcefulness" and we want clients to reconnect with their own answers.

Questions to Uncover a Client's Relationship with Spirit

- Do you have a relationship with a divine presence?

- What do you call it? God? Spirit? Higher Power?

- What does your relationship consist of?

- What do you do to connect consciously with (using the client's name for Spirit)?

We hear over and over again the coaches' bedrock belief that clients have their own answers and the role of the coach is to bring those answers forth. *Why* is this so important for the coach to believe? How is this belief tied into the very essence of being human? In exploring this belief, Charlotte Ward makes a compelling case for the absolute necessity for both the coach and the client to be empowered with responsibility.

Entitlement
By Charlotte Ward

Coaches choose to support clients in the best way possible; however, there is a decision each of us has to make that is not so easy. It concerns the business of giving advice.

I favor supporting clients to generate *their own* advice. I believe each of us comes life-equipped with an exquisite personal guidance system, a state-of-the-art gyroscope that self-corrects for life purpose, if we coaches *allow* it.

One of the fundamental coaching precepts revolves around who owns the change. A divining rod for those coaches tempted to give their clients advice instead of supporting their coming to their own answers is this great question: "Who controls the power to make the change?"

I say *change* because presumably people who seek coaching do so to stop something or start something that they believe will be more beneficial than the way they have been being and behaving. The very desire to make a change comes with the human territory. We lifetime learners bore easily. Restless for new challenges and successes once we have conquered the old, we are born nomads of the mind.

People Desire Change

The fact that people desire change is good news for coaches. Herd animals that we are, most of us want company as we "travel." Determined to grow up, we learn to decide more and more for ourselves, but we frequently seek advice in how to change *safely.* From parents and caretakers, we widen our circle to peer groups, friends, spouses, and partners, then teachers and mentors in a broad range of professions.

We arrive at an oasis of wisdom, albeit always temporary, by some fabulous combination of measuring the facts, logic, big picture, and feelings connected with each scenario. Our inner guide is the triumvirate at our core—beliefs, hierarchy of values, and purpose of life. With so many considerations and so much at stake as life itself, no wonder we want help. No matter how large or small our question seems to be on the surface, we ardently desire that each decision accurately express our core. We seem to have a basic and urgent need to match what we do with what we are. In a constantly changing world, our rigorous consistency of actions with life purpose is the glue that lets us keep ourselves together. By every decision we prove over and over again, "I am still *I.*"

By supporting clients in the first meeting to determine their life purpose, SUN coaches go immediately to the core of human work. By supporting them in subsequent meetings to shape their lives consistent with their recognition of their core selves, we provide a useful proven template for the possibility that they can choose to align themselves, as pleases them, in all areas of their lives. Many coaches say that the supreme joy of coaching is seeing clients increase their awareness and take personal responsibility for becoming resourceful to achieve consistently the outcomes they want. In fact, those client outcomes are our purpose for coaching.

Out of my years of studying neuro-linguistic programming (NLP), I have come to appreciate and respect each individual's "knowingness." A tenet of NLP philosophy holds that clients have their own answers. The advice I give is likely to be on *my* life purpose. It may or may not match my client's need. It could be off in myriad ways, by a fraction or by a mile.

Clients hire coaches not to tell them what to do but to manage the process of their discovering what to do. We can relax. We don't have to take on the burden of other people's decisions; we just have the delightful creative job of guiding the process.

Just Guide the Process

Coaches may well be aware of resources that their clients are not. Many of us think it appropriate to ask whether the client wants information. Oftentimes coaches can ask strategic questions that lead to client discoveries and realizations. But whenever clients think of their own answers, they are much more likely to succeed in the change.

Dr. James Brew, the obstetrician who coached the home births of my children, told me of the early years in his profession. He said he would arrive soon after the family called and stay through the labor. Not only would he encourage the woman for the sometimes long hours it took, but also he would breathe with her and finally push with her until the baby was born. Inevitably he found he was going home exhausted. Many times he had considered quitting his obstetrical practice because of the personal toll it was taking. "At last," he smiled, "I understood the difference between birthing and coaching. I realized I did not have to *bear* the baby myself, I only had to *catch* it."

Gathering these ideas into a potent tool, I believe we show ultimate respect for the client by clearly separating tasks. It is the coach's mandate to inform the prospective clients in the introductory meeting and remind them as they proceed through the program that they have given us the assignment to guide them to provide a plan and strategies to stick to the process. The clients' self-appointed task is to solve their problems and to choose better ways of doing and being their lives. They own their own problems and they own their own solutions.

I'll bet not one of us wants more problems, questions, and challenges or whatever other term we apply to the category of "What shall I do?" If we do not want the problem, how then do we have a right to the solution?

At the heart of the matter waits the well-known existential question "Who am I?" We set clients to answering with *their* purpose statement, which we readily acknowledge can only come from them. They would probably laugh at us if we tried to shape their life purpose for them. How could a coach possibly offer one syllable to that private essential statement of self?

I propose that "What shall I do?" is the existential twin, the action part of the personal equation. Both these questions are rhetorical. As such, I think generating answers just as rightfully belongs to the client because they are the only ones who can own the action.

If we want to coach for personal responsibility and autonomy as outcomes, we need to employ respect for client entitlement all along the way. Then we have the supreme reward of catching precious human beings as they emerge in the world.

❧

We move from the birthing chamber to the coaching office to review my own experience, where life was delivered in a different way. With my client Glen, I experienced moments of terror regarding my ability to coach with Spirit, until I was *able* to return to a space of trust and find the necessary *responses* that entitled him to be responsible. It would have been so much easier and familiar—in my outdated pattern of believing I am the wise one with answers—to have given Glen an answer, but instead my strong coaching beliefs gave birth to a different outcome.

Example

 Glen was an unassuming young man in his late twenties, feeling stymied trying to find the right career. Hand-to-mouth finances, uprooted from assorted living arrangements, generally feeling aimless, he grasped at coaching.

Time with Glen challenged me. I even questioned my basic coaching beliefs because I rarely felt as if what we were doing was of value, other than at a superficial level. He always seemed down, pessimistic, and mixed up like a pan of scrambled eggs. He vehemently rejected going back into therapy. As a coach I just wanted him to become aware of the link between his state of mind and his life picture. When our coaching arrangement came to an end, he wrote that coaching had been useful and he was sorry it was ending. I disagreed with the first comment and agreed with the second.

I lost touch with Glen until three years later, when he *happened* to catch me by phone in between client meetings. Sounding congested with despair, he lamented how his revolving door choices had not differed since we worked together. Having no idea what to do, I asked the seven magic words: "How can I be of service now?" When he proceeded to tell me how he had been walking the streets for two days and sleeping outside on a park bench, I simply asked, "What one step could you take to clean up your act and move you in the direction where you truly want to go?" He replied, "Take a bath. I haven't had one in a week." I asked him to call me right after the bath and to remember to bless the dirt going down the drain because it had served a purpose. He agreed.

After we hung up I realized I was shaking. I felt totally incompetent. Nervously I awaited the phone's ring. All the "shoulds" danced around in my beginner's brain. I should have connected him with a social worker. I should have told him where to go for help. I should. . . . Glen did call back and we engaged in a brief conversation about what step he could take next.

A year later, Glen called again to thank me for "saving his life." He confessed he had not mentioned the loaded gun that he held to his head during our conversation. He decided not to pull the trigger because I did not try to convince him to do or be somebody else. All I did was *ask* him what *he* could do, not tell him. Claiming this to be a pivotal point in his life, he realized he had choice. In the space of two months, he proceeded to seek out and land the job he wanted.

This experience humbled me to the magnificence of our profession, where coaches believe questions supersede answers, where we believe in people's responsibility for their thoughts and choices, and where *all* we have to do is unconditionally accept our clients.

🌿 R E F L E C T I O N

1. Note your coaching beliefs. Which would you not compromise, no matter what?

2. Catch yourself giving advice. Immediately ask your client what he or she would have done if the advice had not been given.

3. Increase awareness of when you ask for advice and keep a log. Check whether you are skirting responsibility for self-generating possibilities.

4. Bite your tongue when you feel the need to give advice. Ask a neutral question instead and listen to the response.

The progression from thought to action begins with thoughts and moves into words. When the same words repeat often enough, patterns form. Limiting beliefs, such as "shoulds," spread like poison ivy, coloring perceptions, eroding self-esteem, and altering context. Because these patterns are more difficult to detect by the one who develops them, a coach can and must bring these patterns to the client's attention so new language can be introduced and perhaps substituted. This next section addresses the concept of the spoken word, honing in on a few particularly limiting words that give clues to limiting beliefs: absolute words, the meaning of "free from" versus "free to," and how to sidestep the feeling of relief that is always attached to the past.

The Absolute Continuum

Verbalized thoughts are words. We learn how clients perceive the world by listening carefully to their choice of words. By guiding clients to accept responsibility for thoughts and language, coaches help clients increase the probability of obtaining the results and well-being they seek.

The probability for an absolutist thinker to achieve *everything* is nil. Those who live in the pressure-filled absolute world would do well to reconfigure their mental settings to the "relative" channel. Drawing on some fundamental spiritual principles, we can explain why. Life is process, not outcome, we read in most spiritual teachings. Socrates wrote, "Nothing ever is, but all things are becoming." Spiritual antennae up, we can nudge clients to understand that absolute language offers no flexibility. Deleting words like "never," "always," and "every" can make the difference between success and failure. The "absolute continuum" can assist clients to be more perceptive to their own language as well as to the language of others. This is illustrated in the following story.

Example

 Alma committed to reviewing her coaching materials *every* day. One day missed, the commitment broken, and Alma's already low self-esteem plummeted yet another notch. Which word destroyed the possibility of success? "Every," of course.

The following simple and fun exercise can be used to open the door to the continuum and subsequent learning.

Exercise

Invite clients who speak in absolutes to create a line representing the continuum with "always" at one end and "never" at the other (see Figure 6.1). Have fun placing other words on the continuum, such as frequently, periodically, rarely, sometimes, occasionally, and so on. Challenge clients to see how many other words can be added. Suggest they invite friends, family, neighbors, and others in their support networks to participate. In future meetings, keep the continuum visible and use it to reconstruct language, thereby increasing flexibility of thoughts and chances of success.

Figure 6.1. The Absolute Continuum

Always ——————————————————————— Never

✤ REFLECTION

1. Name three beliefs that seem closely linked with your destiny.

2. Name three disparate beliefs. Find their correlation anyway.

3. Consider the phrase, "It doesn't matter," which suggests an "I could care less" or a blasé attitude. When choosing to say, "It doesn't matter," do you *really* mean you do not want something to matter? To materialize?

4. Create your own absolute continuum. How many in-between words can you find?

A different twist on absolutist thinking takes us to the firewall of judgment, tainting our perceptions of people because rigid thinking entombs. Coach Kathy Kelly created an internal game to assist her and her clients to flip the box open and regain a perspective of encompassment.

The Other Side of Judgment
By Kathy Kelly

To support my efforts to become a better coach and maybe even a better person, I have been paying attention to my tendencies to come to quick judgment of people, to size them up in a simple and crisp way. Sometimes, these tendencies lead me to focus unduly on the part of the person that needs "fixing," the negatives. So I have been trying to get a bigger look at things—to see the gray present in most any truth—and to see the positive flip side of these unfavorable judgments. To enable me to better see these bipolar opposites, I play a little game with myself. It's simple. Each time I catch myself sizing someone up in this discerning way, I ask myself, "What about them *is not* such and such?" I challenge myself to turn over the coin. And if I find I cannot readily answer the question, then I seek out the answer in our conversations and in my observations.

For instance, I recently met a "southern belle." Soon, I caught my inner voice, "She is so typically southern . . . so conservative . . . so 'stand by your man.'. . ." While this person did have these qualities (usually my judgments are not totally off base—they are just one part of the whole truth), I forced myself to look for the other part. I found, layered just under the surface of her seemingly down-south simplicity, a highly educated leader, business-woman, and breadwinner. She held onto her southern persona but had become a modern woman too.

I have concluded it is much easier to label people in black and white terms than to acknowledge the complexities of the human spirit and to seek out the sublime. As a coach, there is a temptation to latch onto a client's obvious "issue." This way we (smugly) have them all figured out, and all that remains is to help the person see the light. Of course, this is not the coaching way. Coaches are inquisitive, looking for more. Amazingly, when we strive to check out our intuition—to look for the opposites and delight in the many unopened doors in front of us—we can truly find the sublime, the divine, the radiance in all of us.

☙

✺ REFLECTION

1. Think about a few clients and write down something bothering you about each. Now ask the question: "What is the opposite of what bothers me?" Do you see the whole picture differently?

2. Think about yourself and a few things that bother you about who you are. Ask yourself: "What is the opposite about what bothers me about me?"

Free From or Free To

Spirit moves us forward so we can have new experiences, growth, and learning. Coaching with Spirit means maintaining forward momentum. Motivation theory tells us we can choose to move away from something or toward something. Coaches can decipher motivation by listening carefully to a client's language. The field of neuro-linguistic programming deals a lot with this concept, so here I will only address my pet peeves, the phrases "free from" or "free to" and "relief."

When I ask a client to identify desired results, I often hear the words to be "free from stress," "smoke-free," "free from pain," or "debt-free." "Free from" language describes an anchor to the past. I choose to encourage clients' movement toward the future, so I ask, "If you were free from stress, what would be there instead? If you were free from smoking, what would be different? If you were free from debt, describe your new relationship with money."

Often clients have been so attached to their past, they do not have the words to describe an alternative, nor have they ever thought what would transpire if different from the familiar past. Emily's story serves as an example of this.

Example

 Emily came to coaching to find her life's work, experiencing frustration at not knowing where to begin. A plethora of possibilities flooded her imagination; however, her reality had no relevant opportunities. Deep in her soul she sensed her purpose was to end suffering on the planet. When I asked Emily to describe the planet when suffering would end, her mind blanked. Never having considered that picture, she lacked words. *My* head was spinning with words like "peace," "upliftment," and "harmony," but I stifled the urge to fill in the blanks for her. For homework I suggested she open to synchronicities that may provide the answer.

Three weeks later she bounced into my office affirming, "If suffering ends, people will *ascend*. I realized it while I was waiting for an elevator staring at the word 'ascend.' All of a sudden it came into focus—ascension!" Now she had something to pull her forward. Within two weeks a real job possibility arose—one enabling her to contribute to ascension. Leaving coaching, she marched her ascension banner high into action.

✤ REFLECTION

1. Listen carefully for the word *free*. Remember you have just been given a clue into the mental operation of your client. Note the context (free from or free to).

2. Keep the conversation open when a client uses the word free to describe what she or he does not want. Keep asking questions until desires are positively expressed.

3. Pay attention to *your* use of the word free.

One feeling often erroneously thought to be acceptable as a positive feeling is "relief." Feelings of relief still latch onto the past. To help the client uncover the appropriate feeling to catapult into the future, simply ask, "After relief subsides, what replaces it?" Some positive quality of well-being will likely substitute for relief. I often sense a seawall of blocked energy release when clients shift from past to future.

We sometimes mentally fabricate stories to interpret others' behaviors. To be fully responsible for our interpretations, we need to check their validity. Ida thought she figured out her coach's thoughts. Was she surprised! In this example, read why it became important to have her verbalize her thoughts, thereby freeing her up to be responsible to do the same with others.

Example

 Ida projects as a confident, intelligent, and successful woman. For one of our coaching exercises, I invited her to select a color from the marker dish so I could record some data. I observed her touch, lift, and set back down two or three colors before she selected one and set it down with emphasis and a deep sigh. I allowed space with my silent speech (Chapter 3). Approximately fifteen seconds elapsed. Under her breath she muttered almost inaudibly, "You must think me so dumb." I asked her to elaborate. "It took me so long to choose a color. I'm wasting your time on something so unimportant," she said with a deep sigh.

Coach: What was that sigh about?

   Ida: Frustration! It always takes me so long to make up my mind—about anything.

Coach: What were you thinking while you were choosing?

   Ida: What color should I pick? You must think I'm dumb because I can't make up my mind. I'm wasting your time. I try to look intelligent, but you can see right through me.

Coach: Are you interested in hearing what I was actually thinking?

Ida appeared surprised to consider she might not have guessed correctly.

Coach: I had a lot of thoughts while you selected a highlighter. First, I wondered whether you would select the color I am wearing. Second, I tried to guess whether the color would be the same as that chosen by the last person. Third, I pondered which color I would choose given the colors already on your chart. It never occurred to me to judge or criticize you.

Ida's jaw dropped as I spoke. A coachable moment!

Coach: Is it possible you might be second-guessing others too? Might you find it useful to check out your assumptions about what others think? Would you like to ask a few people whose opinions you respect and trust?

Ida: Absolutely! I can't believe I made that all up. What an insight. That's so liberating.

⁂ R E F L E C T I O N

1. To what extent do you ask clients to elaborate on their thoughts?

2. What assumptions do you make about what clients think about you? Do you verify validity?

3. Which of your current clients is the most transparent? The least? Contrast the two and see what you learn from the comparison.

4. What evidence do you have about your own transparency?

To this point we have reviewed how the beliefs that reside in the thought realm can manifest into action. The coach is a sleuth, capturing beliefs, proceeding to the end result as evidenced by the action, and retreating backward to the source of action, the mind. To delve inside the mind, we need to listen carefully for what clients do not say and encourage clients to verbalize their beliefs.

Diametrically Opposed Beliefs

Sometimes the word *responsibility* carries the negative connotation of burden and heaviness. Some people rebel from responsibility because it appears to rob them of freedom. This does not have to be a choice, because both freedom and responsibility can exist simultaneously. On the spiritual plane, everything exists at the same time.

When coaches encounter diametrically opposed client wishes and behavior we can handle this in the following ways:

1. By helping the client become aware of the contradiction;

2. By examining the client's context, ecology, or values to learn what is beneath;

3. By considering each side of the equation to see how each might evolve in the future if left untouched; and/or

4. By inviting the client to explore how the two might become synergistic.

In the following example, read how Kyle's coach helped him to recognize his diametrically opposed beliefs and to see that he had a choice.

Example

Desperately craving direction and career clarity, Kyle resisted doing homework to ferret out his options. I used my hands to dramatize the contradiction: "On the one hand, you came to coaching to become clear about your life direction, specifically your next career. On the other hand, you continue to return unprepared to move forward. Please tell me what is happening with each hand."

As Kyle stared at his left hand, he began speaking about his love of Montessori school as a child and how traumatized he felt when pulled out and put into a traditional school system. The former was full of options, exploration, possibilities, a smorgasbord of choices, and excitement of the unknown. The latter (his gaze switched to his right hand) reeked of goals, requirements, and mandates set by others. So if he set goals and closed his options, he would be eradicating excitement and could no longer be in a state of curiosity. Life might become predetermined and uninteresting—a very dull prospect for Kyle.

How could Kyle have both, that is, set goals and preserve his curiosity? I fanned his curiosity by asking him to explore how setting goals and keeping options open could thrive together. We labeled this homework his "Hand-I-Work Project." With each piece of progress he would clap his hands together, symbolic of success.

As a result of coaching, Kyle shifted his focus to keeping possibilities open within his job instead of leaving.

Misguided beliefs create reality distortions, not just for clients, but for coaches too! During the coach training process, coaches often face their limiting beliefs, as in this example with Margaret and Bettina.

Example

 Coach Margaret and her new client Bettina had their first meeting, for which Bettina paid her monthly agreed-on fee of $250. The second meeting time was arranged—and passed—without Bettina's appearance. Margaret phoned; no one answered. Margaret called again—three times in the next couple of days—and did not hear from Bettina. Annoyed and lacking confidence, Margaret called me, asking, "What should I do now? How should I handle the agreement that states clearly Bettina is liable for payment if no cancellation notice is given?"

Margaret shared her fear that Bettina had *not* found the meeting valuable as an explanation for why she did not show up. Further, Margaret was sure Bettina would not want to continue and was avoiding her by not returning phone calls.

Which avenue for guiding the discussion for learning could I take? I remembered the wise words of coach and author Vicki Escudé: "Congratulate your mind when fear stalks you because it is doing its job well! Then gently begin introducing new thoughts" (2000, p. 62). I followed this reflection with the possibility of reframing because "It is by reframing thinking that you can see the positive possibilities for seemingly impossible problems [opportunities]" (Miller, 1994, p. 80).

I began coaching Margaret with this question, "What beliefs are present for you *now* given the current state of the situation?" Margaret was taken aback, expecting to receive the advice she asked for, not a challenge for internal reflection. In response, she confessed she believed she was not giving value and could not be a good coach. An avalanche of negativity continued—Bettina would stop coaching, would not pay, and a very uncomfortable showdown would ensue after several more phone calls and letters threatening suit. After hearing herself spout such pessimism, she paused and self-judged with a huge, "Wow!" (Her fears had done their job well.)

Next I asked her to identify beliefs that might support the outcome she desired. Bettina would resume coaching and pay on time. From that vantage point, Margaret exposed some new options for behavior and calmed down, reestablished her confidence, and phoned Bettina again. This time Bettina answered, sounding relieved to hear her coach on the phone. "I wondered what happened to you," Bettina started, "I went to your house for our meeting last night and you weren't there." Putting puzzle pieces together, they realized they had put different dates in their calendars. Bettina had a family emergency during the time Margaret thought she scheduled the meeting and had to leave town for two days. She felt very disappointed when her coach was unavailable on her return. Furthermore, her teenage son had erased all the messages during her absence.

Margaret learned a valuable lesson. Assumptions and negative expectations serve no purpose other than to erode well-being and create undesirable possibilities in the morphogenetic field. We must guard against getting stuck in expectations. "Expectations is the place you must always go to before you get to where you're going. Of course, some people never go beyond expectations" (Juster, 1989, pp. 19, 20).

Having just stated that expectations can diminish coaching effectiveness, let us cross to the other side of the street and see how Coach Trainer John Collings used expectations to aid his client in clarifying a desired outcome.

Spirit at Work
By John Collings

Henrietta works in an office of seventeen people, representing a variety of personalities. Her boss, a control addict, changes rules hourly. It was really difficult to know which side of the fence she was on at any given time. Her negative feelings about her boss even resulted in shouting matches between them in front of the entire staff. In these moments Henrietta felt full of turmoil. Additionally, if someone started gossiping or complaining, others usually joined in, creating even more disharmony. Negativity traveled quickly and her co-workers invited her to participate in the downward office spiral.

As her coach I asked what supportive thoughts would increase harmony during these moments of turmoil. Henrietta replied she wished she could remember everyone is an extension of the Creator—even her boss. If she could choose internal harmony as her reaction, then her experience of work would be positive.

She set her goal as harmony in the workplace, choosing to be an outsider to the gossip and complaint society. To reinforce her belief that everyone is an extension of the Creator, I probed further: "If you had this belief consistently, what would be different?"

Henrietta replied, "Whenever I am having thoughts or feelings of ill will, I will keep them to myself. I will train myself to focus on God and myself as an extension of God. Shifting my focus to the other person who triggered my first negative thought, I will say his name to myself and affirm he is an extension of God, too. I will continue to link the name with these positive statements. By affirming this over and over again, my mind will stop the train of negativity and will shift from whatever is at stake (which I will remember is not important) to our connection with God (which is important). In this way I can experience harmony in myself and in my work environment."

In my work as a success coach, my first course of action is to work with clients on increasing their ability to respond with purposeful thought and action. Henrietta chose harmony as her way to live purposefully. It is the presence of Spirit that enables us to take the language of life purpose and put thoughts into words and words into action.

↝ R E F L E C T I O N

1. What other questions might a coach ask to facilitate transformation to a harmonious inner experience?

2. How do clients know whether they succeed in altering their internal experience?

Personal Integrity

The final topic in our discussion of beliefs and responsibility is about the personal integrity of the coach. Ethical coaches do not impose their beliefs on clients, even a seemingly benign belief such as "It is good to finish what you begin." Many clients engage in coaching to become motivated to complete things they start and have not finished. Because the spiritual spectrum does not have a beginning or an ending, every part of the process is necessary. Being responsible does not necessarily equate with having to finish everything we start.

Imagine dozens of partially completed projects in your client's environment, yet he persists in beginning new projects. You might begin by asking him why it is so important to complete projects. "I should," he might meekly answer. "Who says so?" you persist. He has no answer.

I do not want to suggest that all clients' projects remain incomplete. Completion is neither good nor bad. I question whether clients seeking assistance in completing actually *do* want to learn to complete because often the motivation becomes acquired through external pressures, societal or parental. When one feels truly accepted as someone who prefers incompletes, then, interestingly, one can move from "should" to "choice" and may decide to complete some of those incompletes. The amazing power of love and acceptance can bring us to empowered choice.

ℰ R E F L E C T I O N

1. Look at your personal beliefs as a coach. Have you bought into any societal or parental beliefs that you now inadvertently pass on to your clients?

2. What if being responsible meant leaving things incomplete? How would this impact your actions today? Your choices? Your well-being?

3. What if you felt a greater responsibility to yourself for finishing a project rather than to a societal norm?

Beliefs are the seeds of unexpressed action. When beliefs bloom, they become words. Ultimately actions speak louder than words. This next garden of discovery brings us into the realm of action.

Action

Observe the Obvious

Coaches can assist clients by observing the obvious to help clients realize what beliefs underlie behavior. The following stories give glimpses into the power of accepting responsibility for choices made. Note in each example how the client is able to respond (respons-able).

Example

 Luigi appeared down and energetically flat when we first met. I had offered him a free coaching experience to explore whether or not coaching would suit his situation. Toward the end of the experience he had perked up a little, yet still seemed heavy with some unspoken burden. It seemed as if someone had punctured his life tire and air was seeping out.

He chose to continue coaching and two weeks later returned, expressing how drained he felt after our first meeting. "I feel I have no more hope," he muttered, slumping down further in his chair. "Years ago I imagined what I wanted my life to be and now, having had it all come true, I feel empty and hopeless instead of satisfied."

I observed gently, "If you were completely hopeless, you would not have pursued coaching. Some part of you must feel your hope. Give yourself credit for being here. That part of you is the part I intend to coach."

Luigi straightened up with fuller presence, "I am here; that's right. I must have some hope inside me. Let's get going."

By observing the obvious, I brought Luigi into the present, where we could connect. Luigi claimed ownership for his choice to show up and be coached. When we assume responsibility for our choices, we feel empowered; when we feel empowered, we can co-create our lives.

☙ REFLECTION

1. Think about three actions you took this past month. What values underlie those actions?

2. What choice did you make prior to engaging in those behaviors?

3. When was the last time you showed up in a situation you knew would be challenging? Did you give yourself adequate credit for showing up?

From Tension to Attention

We have all the knowledge and skill to handle the life situations handed us. Even Meredith.

Example

 "I feel overwhelmed. I experience ongoing tension. I have *so* much to do and not enough time." Meredith said this with a deep sigh and a nervous laugh that masked her real concern.

For the first few meetings I let Meredith fill up her "results basket" to the hilt. Her charge was to identify the *most* important things she wanted in her life. Every two weeks the list revealed twenty-five-plus "most important" items. Each time Meredith returned having achieved 60 to 70 percent, burdened with feelings of being overwhelmed, tense, and guilty for not having done it all. The third time she observed, "I just have too much to do."

Waiting patiently for six weeks for this comment, I inquired, "Who chose those twenty-eight items and decided they represented the *most* important? How many items would be on the list of someone who experienced something other than overwhelm and guilt?"

Meredith's eyes lit up almost defiantly childlike. "Ten!" Ten items comprised Meredith's next results list.

Two weeks passed.

"I did it! I achieved what I wanted!" she squealed with delight. "*And* my boss came in with a new project and I told him I had a full plate of priorities. Can you imagine he accepted that with no questions asked? I felt terrific!" Meredith continued with commanding insight, "I created all the busy-ness to make me seem and feel important. I didn't really feel important, though, because I couldn't get it all done. Now I feel important because I focus on what is *most* important."

Meredith moved from tension to attention. When she felt empowered to select what to put her attention on, tension disappeared. When Meredith realized she was responsible for her choice to overwork, she considered a different choice. Guilt gone, Meredith's mirth restored, we laughed as I wrote down this hypothetical license plate as a summary of her learning: "Gee•you•ill" (guilt)—implying guilt makes one ill.

✒ R E F L E C T I O N

1. Name three times you believed someone else to be responsible for your feelings or behaviors. Reflect further. What if you were actually the responsible party? Does your perception of the other person change?

2. What does feeling guilty mean to you?

3. How do you know when you feel guilty?

4. Do *you* feel responsible for helping clients obtain results?

5. Why do you think you feel guilty?

Resistance to Commitment

SUN coach Lana Acola reflects on why it is sometimes difficult to commit. Her musings bring insight into why we resist making progress toward the very goals *we* set for ourselves and how we can transform this resistance into responsible movement.

Sometimes I resist commitment to pursuing visions and goals because I do not want the responsibility; however, by not acting, I eliminate choice and opportunity.

Pursuit of goals is a doorway to learning new lessons, discovering and gaining new insights. Taking responsibility for my visions and goals requires me to trust the wisdom of my heart, to honor its requests, and to commit to act. When I have faith in the process, I am enriched by the journey, no matter what the destination. When I remember this, I gain courage to move forward in realizing my goals and visions.

Dealing with resistance to making commitments led me to develop a "Guideline for Winning" (Belf & Ward, 1997, p. 71), a very powerful one for me: I choose to identify with my light while learning from my shadow.

This guideline reminds me that my visions are the best and brightest part of me searching for expression and that the obstacles I face, such as discouragement or indecision, are merely temporary states of mind—not me.

Keeping this guideline in mind helps me hold an image of the possible for myself as well as for my clients.

By identifying with the highest nature of my clients and myself, it is easier to see the things that get in the way of our visions and goals as passing illusions, certainly to be dealt with and learned from, but not permanent or fixed. We can learn from these shadows while focusing on our light and, as a result, gain the power and courage to take action.

❧ R E F L E C T I O N

1. What do you understand about the relationship between commitment, responsibility, and choice?

2. Name two times you chose not to respond. What was the outcome?

Putting all the pieces together—*connection, the present moment,* and *responsibility*—we discover the full power of coaching with Spirit. Read the following delightful story submitted by a coach in the coaching process herself. Marvel at this trilogy of perfection: the right question (demonstrating the connection between coach and client), the high level of client astuteness to tune into and trust the language of the physical body (revealing the client to be in the present moment), and assuming responsibility for receiving this information. Armed with all three and paying attention to the clues Spirit leaves along the way, the client charges right into action to experience success. "The quiet words of the wise are more to be heeded than the shouts of the ruler of fools" (Ecclesiastes 9:17). This verse in the Bible illustrates the benefit of being receptive to wisdom, no matter where it comes from—even fleas.

Spirit Is in Fleas
By Jeri Costa

One of the indecisions I faced while being coached involved taking action in a key relationship. My own coach, very much attuned to my commitment to Spirit, also recognized my offbeat and somewhat irreverent sense of humor. She posed the following insightful consideration: "What would it be like for you to ask Spirit to give you direction or an answer in an entertaining or irreverent way?" I was delighted with the prospect.

Perhaps I subconsciously set the stage by deciding to connect to Spirit in my "Angel Wash" bubble bath. I began meditation in the usual manner, going within and stating my intent. Almost immediately I felt a persistent itching on my leg and arm. This unwelcome distraction caused me to take a closer look. I found at both sites a cluster of small well-defined red bumps. From what authority I do not know, I determined they were flea bites. So much for this meditation I thought, until it hit me: "Hello, remember what you asked for! What could be more outlandish than the presence of fleas in this divine connection?"

So amid the steamy water and fragrant mist I awaited enlightenment. Drifting back to childhood, I found myself sitting on my mother's lap listening to her read from one of my favorite books, *Beyond the Clapping Mountains*. I had spent hours listening to these tales of the personified struggle of the wildlife in the snow-covered tundra and the icy glaciers of Alaska. I could hear her voice: "Once upon a time before the white man came to Alaska, there lived a mouse and a flea. They were the best of friends."

My divine guidance was taking me back to the musing of a flea in a book written well over a half century ago. I would find that even the title had significance. There was a legend telling of two mountains that would clap together; and when birds migrated they had to fly between these mountains in order to continue on their journey. Those fearful or not strong enough to make the trip would be crushed between them.

For me the message was clear. In the story of the mouse and the flea, they were forced to separate in order to survive and move on to a better life. As for the birds, they could not go around the mountain, but only through it. So, too, it was for me. I thanked Spirit for the clarity and immediately resurrected a copy of this childhood storybook, as I suspected there would be more insight, amusement, and guidance where I had least expected to go.

✢

Ecology and Coaching. The story you have just read is ecological. By that I mean the coach paid attention to the client's environment—in this case, the focus on Spirit and an irreverent sense of humor. I believe coaches have a responsibility to be ecologically aware while coaching. Our responsibility mandates using questions and methods to bring the most effective result for the client by taking into account the environment, in the very broadest sense of the word, in which the client moves. If we ignore ecology, we will find our clients cannot sustain learning.

❧ R E F L E C T I O N

1. Have you noticed any clues in most unusual places that show up in a timely fashion and seem to advance you toward achieving goals?

2. Do you remember to thank Spirit for these clues?

3. Consider how you might more ecologically approach your coaching.

4. Are you ready to do CPR (connection, present, and responsibility) with your coaching?

For Managers Only

To this point, I've used the term "coach" to refer to my readers, although I describe a wider audience in the Preface. In particular, managers, who are often burdened with a myriad of day-to-day tasks and responsibilities, may find it hard to connect with some of the principles of coaching with Spirit. Yet most managers are already familiar with and in fact are practicing many of the elements of coaching. They just don't call it coaching. Any of the management responsibilities could be a starting point for considering a manager's opportunities to coach with Spirit: interpersonal communications, motivation, supervision, delegation, employee monitoring and evaluation, planning, solving and identifying problems, making decisions, budgeting, training, and public relations. Each offers daily opportunities. Zoom into your typical work environment, experiment with these, and notice what happens.

Scenarios

To help you get started in recognizing opportunities to coach with Spirit, consider how you'd respond to the following scenarios.

1. Your team meets to solve a systemic problem. *What if* you began the meeting with five minutes of silence? *What if* you collectively created a metaphor for the problem and the solution?

2. In the middle of a staff meeting it becomes clear you have reached an impasse. *What if* you stopped all talking, asked everyone to tune inside, listen to inner chatter until it quiets, and then proceed by asking internally, "Why is our project important?" and "Why is that important?"

3. Your employee's performance slacks. You realize you could do a much better job if you did it yourself. *What if* you truly believed and trusted your employee to be capable of solving the problem (when in doubt, let the client figure it out), and *what if* your definition of delegation changed from meeting to assign and monitor tasks to allowing more silent space within which to create new possibilities?

4. Your employee, a new father, has become increasingly late for work. *What if* you tuned into your somatic sensations before speaking with him? *What if* you approached this discussion with the attitude, "How can I be of service now?"

5. You disagree with your boss on a strategic direction, such as how to reduce expenses by another 12 percent. *What if* you stopped action, and you and your boss allowed extra moments of connective silence before jumping in to solve the problem? *What if* you played the *What if?* game?

6. The approaching deadline on your big project seems impossible to meet and your computer system breaks down. *What if* you took ten minutes to center within yourself, allowing for an entirely new and different approach to surface? *What if* you allowed your intuition to guide your next steps?

7. You experience great frustration at continually coming to loggerheads with a very competitive colleague, and you have an urgent meeting with her today. *What if* you took a few minutes in your office before you met to consider what might be "bigger than the issue of the moment"? *What if* you let go of attachment to whatever outcome you desire and entered the meeting feeling neutral?

8. You dread having to deliver a poor performance evaluation to your employee. *What if* you took a few minutes of quiet time before you meet with him?

9. Two new employees join your department. *What if,* as part of their orientation process, you help them learn their personal mission statements and how those relate to your company's mission statement?

10. Your company is undergoing yet another reorganization, and the rumor mill reeks with speculation and fear. *What if* you convened a meeting with your staff for the purpose of creating a ritual for those who might be asked to leave *and* for those who might stay?

Summary

This chapter took us into the third key principle of coaching with Spirit—responsibility. Branching into the two domains of being responsible, we began with thoughts and beliefs and finished with action. We reviewed two philosophies containing beliefs of those who coach with Spirit; delved into the core coach belief of entitlement; looked at how to listen for and expose unfounded, distorted, limiting, or diametrically opposed beliefs; and examined particular words coaches need to be alert for that often trigger unsuccessful responses. We progressed from thoughts and beliefs to words to action, where we concluded with the importance of clients and coaches being responsible for their choices and actions in an ethical, ecological fashion. At the end of this chapter, in a section called For Managers Only, I provided ten specific, challenging managerial situations that might benefit from a coaching with Spirit perspective.

When we coach with purposefulness, downgrading what is not on purpose to the background, letting go of attachment to results, trusting that what happens is for the highest good of ourselves, our clients, and all others concerned; when we are in the present moment, available, connected to ourselves, each other, and the whole, able to choose our responses in a state of wonder and curiosity, and being of service; and when we are grateful for all of this, then we coach with Spirit.

We have now firmly established the relationship between coaching and spirituality and identified the three key principles needed to coach with Spirit. It is time to check out the validity of these principles in different arenas within the world of coaching. In Chapter 7, we will study the marketing process to see whether and how these principles appear. Next, we will examine the executive realm of business, noting whether and how these principles show up, highlighting issues unique to coaching executives (Chapter 8). Broadening our scope of exploration in Chapter 9, we examine instances of international coaching to learn whether these principles hold true in different countries. To conclude our analysis in different realms, we will reveal what clients say about their coaches who claim to coach with Spirit (Chapter 10).

To coach with Spirit, we need clients! Read the next chapter to learn what Spirit has to do with marketing.

CHAPTER 7

Marketing Coaching with Spiritual Fluidity

MOST OF THIS BOOK focuses on preparing for, conducting, and reflecting on client meetings. In order to have clients, we must first attract them. If we wish clients to be receptive to coaching with Spirit, we must acknowledge that marketing our profession also involves tapping into the reservoir of Spirit. Without integrating Spirit into marketing, one appears shallow, missing a vital piece of the whole. Henry Ward Beecher said, "Education is the knowledge of how to use the whole of oneself."

Fluid Like a River, Not a Faucet

I chose the metaphor of water for this chapter because water flows. Unless we artificially manipulate it through the kitchen faucet, for example, water in its natural setting does not turn itself on and shut itself off. It continually and perennially flows. In the same way, how counterproductive to think marketing is something to turn on and then shut off. Only artificially and with negative consequence do we abort our natural state of being, cutting off our pool of energy or overflowing until we drown. When I behave, think, feel, and flow like a coach wherever I go, wherever I am, I attract a tidal wave of clients.

Persons who have not been in sales prior to entering the coaching field frequently think of marketing as a discrete, dreaded activity instead of an extension of coaching. They miss the boat when they express undercurrent wishes to just coach and not market.

Spirituality and Sales Splash Together

Although spirituality and sales are not often mentioned in the same sentence, four spiritual principles and a six-step marketing process can converge to facilitate swimmingly successful client attraction. A number of these principles have already been sprinkled in earlier chapters in the context of client meetings. Revisiting them with the topic of marketing reinforces their presence in every droplet of our coaching ocean—our daily events, overall business, profession, and the power of coaching in everyday life.

Four Ways Spirituality Enhances Marketing Effectiveness

Principle 1. The Principle of Attraction

Who I am greatly influences the type of person I attract. If I claim to be a person of integrity, I likely attract prospects and clients with integrity. On the other hand, if I question my own competence, ability to market, and ability to close sales, I can expect to find prospects who have trouble making commitments. Myron's story illustrates a common occurrence among beginning coaches.

Example

During the marketing segment of a coach training program, Myron lamented that none of his three potential clients had the finances to afford coaching. Later in our coaching meeting, he voiced concern about the large number of coaches competing for the few possible clients in his area. Drawing on the proximity of timing of these two comments, I set out to help him splash out his belief.

After using the Synchronicity Worksheet (see Chapter 4), Myron acknowledged it might be more than a coincidence that he had been attracting financially unstable prospects. Drained from his torrential effort, he admitted great distaste for the competitive market in which he found himself. To expose his beliefs, I asked him to guess what beliefs people afraid to pay for services might hold. He replied, "Lack of abundance and scarcity of resources." Proceeding further, I asked him to reflect on underpinning beliefs of people with the mindset of a competitive world. Myron said, "Competition frightens *me* because there might not be enough for everybody; hence, I must believe in lack of abundance and scarcity of resources."

A light bulb went on in Myron's brain, bringing about his watershed. For the first time he saw how his beliefs created his experience. Regrouping quickly, he developed a new belief: "There is plenty for everybody, including me." I reinforced this new way of thinking by reminding Myron that there is no other just like him in the entire world, so how could *he* possibly have any competition? Later that week he phoned to tell me one of the three prospects found a way to afford coaching and signed up.

Furthermore, seeing through his different lens, Myron began to seek out collaborative arrangements with other coaches; he found a way to connect and share the human and financial rewards of coaching.

Principle 2. The Principle of Learning Mirrors

We have opportunities to learn how we operate, think, feel, and act from every interaction with another person. If we experience waves of discomfort marketing or selling, the potential client also probably experiences discomfort. We can use our inner world as a barometer of the external. Some coaches appear reluctant to charge or adequately charge for their services out of fear the client may not find coaching valuable. This belief functions as a breakwater, keeping them from success; I ask these coaches to consider a new assumption.

If we believe we deserve to be paid to learn, we drop through a new porthole to expose a drastically different point of view. Instead of tacking on what value the client may attain, the sails come about to look at the value a coach may receive. Because personal discovery is one of the primary values of those who coach, it would be hypocritical for us to help others learn and not be committed to learning ourselves. Committed to our personal growth and discovery, we know every client brings us ongoing waves of learning opportunities. If we are eager to pay for learning, we must accept that those clients attracted to us (Principle 1) will also be willing to pay. This reframing validates why we must charge for our work.

Example

 In one moment of waterlogged weakness, I agreed to allow Duncan to coach a colleague for free. Duncan had been ambitiously marketing for several months to no avail. Each time he had to mention the fee for his services, he almost eagerly, and with relief, let the potential client go. Yet he desperately wanted a client to try out his new coaching skills. Interesting outcome!

Happy to have his first client, Duncan reported the first two meetings proceeded smoothly; glitches only began at the third. Twice his client called to reschedule, then missed the rescheduled meeting, claiming travel as the legitimate excuse. Grasping at any straw enabling him to continue, Duncan offered longer meetings, more frequent meetings, even weekly telephone check-ins. After additional client postponements, excuses, and three months elapsing, Duncan managed to snag his colleague in the hallway. Appearing sheepishly apologetic, she confessed, "If I had been paying you, I would have taken it more seriously."

Duncan attracted the perfect client to teach him (and remind me) the lesson of reciprocal worth. As Terrie Lupberger already professed in Chapter 3, I too truly believe the clients and the coaches-in-training I attract come into my life at just the right time to help me learn my lessons. I trust in the continual flow of clients to support my continual learning.

❧ REFLECTION

1. What beliefs do you hold around the match between your value and your client fees?

2. How comfortably do you voice the price of your coaching service?

3. What do you see in your coaching marketing mirror?

4. Mentally scan your current client load. Do you have even one client from whom you have not learned anything?

5. List five things you have learned from your clients this year.

6. How do you handle a client who becomes dependent on you and calls or emails all the time? Does your mirror reflect you have difficulty setting your limits?

Mirror, mirror on the wall, which one of us is the greatest learner of all? In this next section you will have the opportunity to hold up the aqueous mirror and dive into the current of connection. Be careful. You might drown because some clients become too closely connected—overly dependent. If you spray droplets of "tough love" to set the channel marker boundaries, all the while asking good coaching questions, you can rescue both yourself and your client.

Principle 3. The Principle of Connection

This principle has been a pivotal theme throughout this book. It spawns our golden coaching rule—treat others as you wish to be treated. If you treat people with respect, you can expect respect back. If you give a client a shoddy deal, watch it boomerang back in the future. Remember how you felt when you received a referral from a client you coached years ago? My favorite marketing story introduces you to Gerda. I take the risk of sounding arrogant by sharing my long journey with Gerda—a true tale of a sale springing out of the deep respect I hold for people's abilities to make their own choices.

Example

 Six years intervened between when I met Gerda and when she signed my coaching agreement—six years during which I tracked her life progress with respect, interest, and caring. After our first encounter, when I asked Gerda if she would like me to be her coach, she told me yes but she could not begin right away. Asking if she would like me to contact her at some future date prompted a "yes, please" response. Honoring her request, I called five months later and once again she reported she was not yet ready. Genuinely interested in supporting her intuitive right timing, I initiated the third contact, at her request, a year later. Honoring her decision, I trusted her to know. Another year passed. I felt it prudent to check whether Gerda *really* wanted me to persist, so I assured her she could say no to me. She said that she really did want me to keep checking in. Throughout a few more check-ins and years, Gerda and I established a special connection. I kept my word as promised (respons-able) each time she set a timeframe for a call back. Gerda experienced empowerment by knowing she had permission to comfortably reassess at each juncture.

During these six years, the coaching profession changed dramatically—coaches abounded all over, much like Salvation Army Santa Clauses on street corners at holiday time. In the interim, several coaches had approached Gerda to ask if she wanted coaching.

When Gerda called me and said, "I am ready; now is the perfect time," I smiled a Cheshire Cat grin. She elaborated, "I must tell you I am amazed and surprised to have never felt any pressure. You seem to really care about my circumstances and me. That's why I choose you as my coach, even though many others asked me."

Example

To market my coaching, I called a prestigious interior designer, Colette.

Teri-E: Hello, I'm Teri-E Belf. I'm a success coach and our connection is
        through Molly.

Colette: (sounding obviously rushed and stressed, as if ready to terminate
        our call before it began) I have all the success I need, thank you.

Teri-E: That's terrific; I only work with successful people (poignant pause).
        Perhaps you are referring to your career or finances. Do you go to
        the gym as often as you would like? Is your life in balance?

Colette: What did you say you do?

This example illustrates connection through words. Did you catch how I used encompassment? (See Chapter 3.) By using her language, I kept the connection and conversation open and gained a client.

Take a glimpse at another example of encompassment in the context of marketing.

Example

In Chapter 1 you read about beginning the coaching process by guiding a client to learn life purpose. Sometimes when I mention this to a potential client, I hear, "I already know my purpose. My purpose is to serve God."

I reply, "Many people say their purpose is to serve God. We want to find words to describe your unique way of serving."

By encompassing this response, I establish rapport instead of a barrier.

☘ R E F L E C T I O N

1. Pay attention to the next sales call you receive. Was encompassment used?

2. What is the longest time between when you met a potential client and when the coaching agreement was signed? Analyze your behavior to note what worked. As a matter of fact, log all your successful marketing experiences, with specifics as to why you succeeded.

Connection brings the word networking to mind because, without connections, your client load might not exist. We have looked at how encompassment connections bring clients. Sometimes encompassment must be avoided in the interest of ethical conduct. Keep this next story out of your networking net.

Example

Imagine attending a typical networking event in which a career management consultant begins talking to you about someone who turns out to be one of your former clients. What a coincidence! The counselor asks how the coaching went and whether the client was satisfied, hinting at an interesting untold tale underneath. The dilemma? You want to remain in the conversation and continue pursuing this golden networking opportunity, but your ethical flags signal something amiss. Let the consultant know right away that you do not discuss client activity as a matter of professional ethics. Say you would be happy to talk about other things. *Even if you just admit this person was a client, you are in violation of your agreement to honor confidentiality or at least anonymity. Caution:* These conversations can appear suddenly; tack to a different direction. You must!

Principle 4. The Principle of Greatest Good

Obsolete are sales strategies with one winner and one loser, where the focus is on dispensing a product or service for financial gain. A sale involves something far more important—connections and opportunities to bring out the best in your clients and yourself. Everyone has a chance to experience winning, whether a sale is made or not.

People often ask why I offer a one-and-one-half-hour introductory coaching experience free. I view it as a win-win. For me, there is a big difference between the actual coaching program and introducing the coaching process. When in a coaching arrangement with a client, I have a signed agreement that lays out the coaching fee, program structure, responsibilities, and expectations of the coach and the client. Additionally, we must mutually agree on the results that constitute the coaching program. Introducing the coaching process for marketing purposes is a one-shot deal. At the end, the potential client has received something of value, whether clarity, an idea, a possibility, a chance to dream, a deep belly laugh, a moment to relax in the middle of a busy day, a feeling of increased esteem, or a deep connection. I feel privileged to facilitate that added worth for free. Secondarily and very much in the background is the question, "Will this person become a client?"

Often I find myself having such an enjoyable time meeting new people courageously exploring windows of possibilities that I am surprised when they say yes, they want me to be their coach. So entranced am I in being of service and learning from them and about them, I forget one of the reasons for this free meeting—marketing.

The Toughest Coaching Choices

Even when things do not go exactly as expected, the coach must adhere to the principle of greatest good. Marketing (the process of finding the client) also raises the question whether you are the "right" coach for this client. Some of the toughest choices facing coaches are whether to persist to keep a client, whether to terminate the coaching process prematurely, and whether to refuse to coach someone altogether.

Every coach has a story or two or more about these choices. These are important stories because we grow from them and become better coaches. Because of our commitment to personal discovery, we can count on receiving our fair share. Read how Spirit plays an important partnership role in these three incidences.

Example

 Sheryl, a Marine Corps officer, appeared for her life purpose meeting looking like a condensed package of pure muscle. Moving with restriction appropriate to a petite yet powerful woman in charge, she held tight facial features and sported straightjacket clothing. Her words were thought out in advance, every one carefully calculated and strategically planned. Sheryl pensively inched through the life purpose process, having difficulty recalling times when she experienced fulfillment and satisfaction. To her great astonishment and dismay, she found that her few purposeful stories shared themes of loving serenity and surrender to her intuition, quite contrary to her modus operandi. After validating the accuracy of this realization, she went home to ponder further.

Sheryl did not arrive for her second meeting. When I called her home, her husband angrily told me never to call again, adding that her first meeting with me upset her too much. I wrote a letter directly to Sheryl, but received no response.

I was quite shaken by this event. Clearly the contrast between Sheryl's life and her purpose was enormous. At that point I had several options: I could feel lousy, worry about Sheryl, or question my ability to accurately assess the readiness of a person to do this work. Numerous other negative possibilities swam around my mind. Instead of staying stuck in this vortex of negativity, I asked Spirit to teach me what I needed to learn from this to make me a better coach.

Spirit spoke clear as a bell: Trust the process. People take what they are ready for. Each person's journey is made up of openings, peepholes, crevices, and fissures. The timing is always perfect in the big scheme of things, although it may not appear so from your limited vantage point. Sometimes you plant seeds and may not be around when they bloom.

Example

Mahalia committed to coaching with the key desired result being to learn how to manifest results. At the same time, I noted she repeatedly mentioned poor financial and career decisions as evidence of her lack of trustworthiness. Displaying a "poor me" mentality, she also expressed difficulty asking for what she wanted. She found making choices grueling for fear she would make the "wrong one" yet again.

At the second meeting, I experienced her indecision through sundry, wavering spoken "spins" as she considered moving or staying put in her job. *I* had difficulty remaining focused on our conversation. The next meeting centered around making decisions with my intended goal to have one of her six choices clarified so she could stop ruminating (her favorite word). My strategy to discuss this resulted in yet another series of ponderings, hesitations, and uncertainties, even around the question about whether to proceed with coaching or stop.

I chose to stop being Mahalia's coach. Stopping clients is not my preferred practice. To my dismay, I also realized that Mahalia could and would chalk up this experience as another one of her poor decisions.

Although I felt like a flop, I gained an invaluable personal truth. When I connect with Spirit and quiet my mind, I become aware of what should be obvious, but sometimes becomes lost in life's myriad details; that is to say, I can trust my physical reaction to provide an accurate diagnosis of my situation.

I am glad I clearly spoke my truth about *my* inability to coach Mahalia so she did not feel rejected. Whereas she was disappointed, she accepted a referral to a colleague and thanked me for my honesty. These tough choices were all about me, not about the client. Contrast the emphasis in how the following statement can be delivered: "I cannot coach *you*," versus *"I* cannot coach you." Accepting I may not be the best coach for everyone humbles me.

Example

 The third event involved Sharma, who over the phone explained she wanted to become a coach so she could pay off her bills and set aside three months of savings as a cushion while she pursued her dream—to write poetry. After she left, excited to begin her new lucrative profession, I reread her enchanting poems and knew within my soul her choice to be a published poet dramatically dwarfed her passion to become a coach. Her focus needed to be on her passion, not a roundabout detour. Spirit spoke strongly and clearly. In good faith I could not take Sharma's money; I would be without integrity. Leaving a message on her answering machine, I strongly urged her to reconsider her decision to coach as a profession. She misunderstood me, believing I thought she could not become a coach. To the contrary I explained, "I think you would be wasting your time and money to sidetrack with coaching and I completely support you to go straight for writing."

To make a short story even shorter, one month later Sharma called to thank me profusely for questioning her admittance into the coaching program. She now had a publisher who agreed to an advance, enabling her to concentrate straightaway on her calling. Sharma was on her way, direct route, no detours, and my integrity has not been tested again.

❧ REFLECTION

1. Identify the last three tough choices you had to make in coaching. How have these situations contributed to you becoming a better coach? A better person?

2. Can you think of the last "detour" you took, seduced by financial gain instead of choosing a route congruent with your purpose and values? What were the consequences? What was the "cost" of the lost opportunity?

The Six Steps to Fluidly Market Coaching with Spirit

Marketing with Spirit occurs when you are *not* proactively marketing. It feels magical because nothing visible seems to happen at the moment of success. As in all other venues, much happens behind the scenes, planted seeds of connection begin to sprout, and, as in the natural world, everything has its season to bloom. In the example of Gerda (earlier in this chapter), Quimby (Chapter 11), and the perfection of events that unfolded with Beryl (as you will soon read), we can see the timing of connections can happen as if by magic, without force, without pressure, with trust. When we allow the charisma of Spirit to weave, successful marketing transpires.

Please understand that one cannot market by sitting at home meditating, cocooned within a cozy blanket. All four spiritual principles must play a role in the marketing equation. Marketing begins with making a connection. No connection—no sales!

The following six steps* apply to marketing and also are found at the heart of coaching with spirit: stillness, creation, connection, action, completion, and acknowledgment. All are essential and in this sequence.

Step 1. Stillness

Every moment presents meandering spirals of mental stimulation and with each exhale the possibility of returning to stillness. Most spiritual practice values quiet time. We meditate, center, and learn other mind-quieting techniques to become still. We do this because we hope Spirit appears in the silence. Do you remember the last time you slowed down and took a deep breath before making an important phone call? What was the outcome? That moment of stillness probably paid off.

Stillness allows time for connection with Source, internal connection, assessing intuition, assessing physical sensations, and quelling emotional impulses. Stillness, the first step, is most frequently skipped in our eagerness to jump ahead to the next step, creation.

---

*Appreciation to Dr. Elaine Gagné, executive coach, consultant, facilitator at The Franklin Covey Leadership Center, and certified SUN coach, for permission to adapt her Creativity Cycle to marketing.

Example

SUN coach Joan C. King reflected long before she entered the coaching profession. Beginning the manifestation process with stillness enabled her to become clear about how she might be of service. As a neuroscientist, King knew the value of accessing Spirit to support manifestation of results and well-being from both the physical and spiritual points of view. In the stillness came the description of her perfect client.

The "Perfect Client"

- Acknowledges Source

- Understands life flows from Source

- Already acknowledges external circumstances emerge from internal processes

- Is willing to learn how to manifest results and well-being

- Responsibly pays the fee

- Has multifaceted resonance with me

- Is healthy enough to fulfill the coaching commitment

- Expresses joy in life

- Is eager and ready for growth

As a consequence of her stillness, King creates "perfect" clients.

Step 2. Creation

Mental creation emerges out of stillness. Creation includes planning, visualizing, and affirming. In this phase ideas emerge—ideas for approaching a sales call, marketing a product, or making a presentation. The best salespeople imagine a successful outcome prior to actually connecting. In King's example above, the clarity she gained from her quiet time allowed her to easily devise a marketing strategy. Because thoughts do create our reality, we must think and behave in alignment with the success we want.

Consider adopting two useful beliefs I hold in my imagination regarding marketing. First, I have fun attracting clients. Second, attracting clients is easy for me, as the following true story illustrates.

Example

 "Hello, what are you doing in my vacuum cleaner?" Taken aback by these words as I answered the phone, I regrouped and invited an explanation. While the caller had been vacuuming, her vacuum ground to a halt. Turning it over she found my business card. With an appreciation for synchronicity and a trust in the process, she called to say whatever I do, she wanted it. Have I attracted a story to reinforce my belief that attracting clients is easy? Because I do not typically give out business cards, we never did figure out how my card showed up in her house—much less her vacuum cleaner!

Intellectually, many agree our inner world determines our outer reality; however, how can we experience this internal-external relationship more consistently? With greater awareness of spiritual principles, we can have more control and fun in marketing interactions and more likely get what we want (clients, financial rewards, and ease in the process).

Example

At one point I decided to challenge my spiritual belief that attracting clients can be easy. I mentioned to my husband I wanted to visit Sunrise Ranch in Loveland, Colorado, and I wished I could have a client nearby. I had no contacts in that area. Nothing more happened with that topic—at least on a visible plane. Two days later the phone rang and the caller asked if I still coached. When I replied affirmatively, he told me his sister, who lived far away, had been cleaning out her office and found an article about me in *Bottom Line: Personal* written three years earlier. She faxed him the article, adding a note to be sure to call me and sign up. Can you believe he lived in Denver, Colorado, just an hour away from where I wanted to visit? Never again have I doubted how powerful the creation phase of the marketing with Spirit cycle can be.

Step 3. Connection

As we have documented, being in the present plays a vital role in coaching with Spirit; so too in marketing with Spirit. The essence of a successful connection is the salesperson's ability to be in the present, that is to say, continually calibrating and recalibrating wishes, needs, feelings, and thoughts, for oneself as well as for the prospect. From a spiritual perspective, every connection with another person is an opportunity to be of service, not merely to sell a service.

Step 4. Action

Actions, predominantly talking and writing, project us out of the intellectual into the external world. We demonstrate products, explain services, call potential customers, and draft proposals. In the same way that just thinking about being responsible produces no action, neither does thinking about a sale produce a sale. Sharing thoughts with potential clients does!

Another way to examine action routes us to the desire to coach—even before the prospect says yes. *What if*, in the process of marketing your coaching service, you had the opportunity to give someone, even a complete stranger, an experience of empowerment. The secret: You can, every time you introduce yourself.

How to Empower Prospects. Eavesdrop on a novice coach conversing about coaching. You will likely hear a lot of talking from the coach as he or she tries to say as much as possible during the open window of time while the listener's attention remains at a peak. At some point, the unempowered listener becomes overloaded with auditory stimuli and tunes out. Unfortunately, I have heard this filibuster countless times.

Let us rewrite the script, setting the stage in a Chamber of Commerce meeting. The roles reverse and the listener will assume control. You, the coach, quickly keep returning the volley at the beginning of the conversation. "What do you do?" "I am a success coach." "What is that?" "I am a vehicle to help you go from where you are now to where you want to go." "How do you do that?" "I begin by helping you discover your life purpose." Hear how I engage in marketing aikido, saying very little, *allowing* this person to take charge and ask for more information?

Good, I have tapped into the listener's curiosity. At the soonest possible moment, I lob the power back to the listener, who is empowered to flick the on-off switch at any time. Repeating this pattern brings a sense of empowerment to the listener because the listener gains control of the process and content. This becomes a successful marketing technique *only* if the coach is authentic. Let us eavesdrop further.

"I have always wondered about my life purpose. Are you some sort of therapist?"

I will now intentionally advance to the "close" when I test whether the interest is sufficient to produce action. If you begin your close prematurely, your listener will predictably back off and ask you another question.

"I sense you are interested and I would be delighted to share an experience of coaching with you. When would be a good time?"

Every time the listener asks for more specifics, the listener regains the leadership role. And every time you return the ball to your listener's court, the listener's sense of empowerment increases. Our listener is not yet ready to commit time.

"Can you tell me what we would do in that meeting?"

"I would guide you to obtain a clear picture of the results you want five months from now. You would have had a real experience of the process instead of just talking about it. Do evenings or days work better for you?"

At an unconscious or subliminal level, the listener concludes that being with you feels empowering. People choose to spend time with those who provide empowering experiences. You have just increased the chance of the listener being eager to spend more time with you.

One final note on the topic of empowering and marketing. Bartering, the process of agreeing to exchange services with no remuneration, serves to disempower potential clients because it promulgates limiting beliefs.

In coach training I often encounter situations where coaches, eager to start their coaching businesses, inquire if they can barter coaching for something else, such as massage therapy, nutritional counseling, website development, and so on. Admittedly I hold a strong bias against bartering. First, bartering in the United States is illegal unless you intend to report it on your tax return and pay the tax, even though you received no tangible compensation to deposit in your bank account. Second, by asking to barter, you proliferate your belief and your client's belief in your lack of self-worth. As a coach trainer, I will not reinforce this limiting belief because it does not support success. Think about it. Have you ever met a financially successful person who asks to barter?

ℓℓ R E F L E C T I O N

1. When you catch yourself talking too much, remember why you have two ears and one mouth.

2. Listen to someone marketing coaching. What proportion of the time is the coach listening versus speaking?

3. Tune in to your next prospective client. Do you think he or she feels empowered? What evidence do you see and hear?

Step 5. Completion

Incomplete actions, as well as lack of follow-through or follow-up, drain energy and deter us from focusing attention in the present. A distracted mind misses cues and cannot fully connect. In sales, completion translates to closing the sale, identifying appropriate next action steps, obtaining customer satisfaction, and asking for referrals. Without these activities, we remain in the process of selling, rather than closing the sale. Both spiritual teachings and sales emphasize the importance of completions.

Beryl Allport, a SUN coach, shares her own memory of the path to finding and embarking on an entirely new career in coaching. See how many completions you can find in her narrative and be aware that, if at any step along the way she had allowed an obstacle to block her progress, the outcome would have been different.

My Journey to Coaching
By Beryl Allport

My journey to be coached and become a coach was totally guided by Spirit. When the right book or person appears just when needed, Spirit is at work. Such was the case for me in February 1997. At the time, I felt totally drained in my career as a regional manager fund raising for several charities. Charity cutbacks made survival difficult, and the small, intimate, and caring company where I worked joined with a huge company focused more on paperwork and income than the charities, clients, or us.

One Saturday in February I was browsing in a health food store when a magazine headline story, "Living Your Dreams," caught my eye. This sounded too good to be true, so I took it home and buried myself in the story about a woman who had worked with a life coach to change her life in order to follow a passion and become more fulfilled. The end of the article listed pages of coaches. I had never heard of a personal life coach. Having coached baseball and other sports, I was only familiar with sports coaching. Most names were coaching individuals, four were schools, all were in the United States. I contacted all and when I communicated with one person in particular, I immediately knew I was in touch with an intuitive, spiritually inclined soul.

I made an immediate decision to be coached—the prerequirement to any hope of becoming a coach—journeyed to the United States, and began a new direction in life. These events, I believe, were totally guided by Spirit.

During the next six months I rode the waves of many emotions and tests from fear of giving up a paycheck to excitement at the possibility of becoming a coach. I had already been facilitating successful wellness retreat weekends for three years, connecting me to an entire community of holistic practitioners, many awesome participants, and my personal practice of yoga and meditation. Coaching seemed like a natural business addition in alignment with my soul.

The actual decision to make this transition was difficult because I was more than sixty years old with no other source of income or security. When Spirit strongly wants to move me in a direction and I pay attention to the tugging, I feel like I have no choice but to follow! I quit my job, finally deciding to "go for it." I took some money out of my retirement savings plan, had business cards and brochures made, visited lots of network meetings, and began coaching.

Now, several years later, many other messages from Spirit have transpired. I have been and am blessed with clients attracted to me by Spirit; I believe whoever comes to me is exactly who is meant to, for both of us. I learn from every client as we feed each other's souls.

Step 6. Acknowledgment

The last step in the marketing with coaching process is to celebrate success along the way. Find a way to acknowledge yourself after five cold calls. Better yet, delete the phrase "cold calls" from your vocabulary. The word "cold" does an injustice to one who has a sincere interest in connecting with another human being. Cold describes ice, icebergs, ice cream cones, frozen ponds, and glaciers—not a motivation to extend oneself to a warm-hearted individual.

Celebrate three times when you introduce coaching to someone you did not know. Applaud yourself aloud after spending two hours writing an article about coaching.

Cheer when you complete a business ad or new web page. Genuinely thank your prospective clients for allowing you to share your enthusiasm. Enthusiasm accounts for 80 percent of marketing, I learned in the Professional Speaker's Club of Toastmasters.

Remember to acknowledge yourself for your enthusiasm, too. Acknowledge yourself for every step you take, large or miniscule, that moves you toward your goal. Then allow a moment of stillness to express gratitude for all the ideas, connections, actions, and completions you experienced along the way. Whether you coach internal to an organization or as a self-employed entrepreneurial coach, please do not wait for your annual performance review or even weekly staff meetings to take stock of your successes.

Stop right now and acknowledge yourself, and *now* again. Your self-esteem is proportionate to your self-acknowledgment, so let yourself unabashedly know your magnificence. Internal praise and gratitude keep us healthy and enhance self-esteem.

Summary

On an intellectual level, most of us agree that our inner world does determine our outer reality; however, we may not yet experience it as regular as a metronome, without missing a beat. With a greater awareness of spiritual principles, we have more control and fun in our sales and marketing interactions *and* we are more likely to get what we want (clients, financial rewards, and ease in the process). Honor the four principles and follow the six steps listed above and watch your client base stream in.

To this point I have presented the three spiritual principles and showed how they can be applied in one area, attracting clients. In the next three chapters, I explore the application of these principles to subsets of the population, beginning with executives, followed by a look at the international scene, and finally, an examination of how coach leaders view coaching with Spirit.

One of the questions I was asked frequently while writing this book was whether coaching with Spirit works with executives. Turn to Chapter 8 to read what I found out.

Executive Coaching with Spirit

ASSESSMENT

Please rate yourself on the extent to which you coach with Spirit.

0 = never; 1 = rarely; 2 = sometimes; 3 = often; 4 = most of the time;
5 = almost always

To what extent do I . . .

0 1 2 3 4 5   allow feelings to be discussed while coaching executives?

0 1 2 3 4 5   discuss purposefulness or life purpose with executive clients?

0 1 2 3 4 5   invite Spirit into the executive suite, overtly or covertly?

0 1 2 3 4 5   recognize the presence of Spirit?

0 1 2 3 4 5   target sustainable learning instead of what is useful right now?

0 1 2 3 4 5   release expectations and beliefs from my cultural
conditioning?

0 1 2 3 4 5   connect with the Spirit of the executive?

DO EXECUTIVES REQUIRE A DIFFERENT FORM OF COACHING than others? Do executives acknowledge Spirit in their world of work? Does connecting with executives require additional skill sets? Can coaching be used to transform a management mindset into an executive one? As I listen in varied settings and coaching arenas, I hear myths about the exclusivity of executives. These myths impede effective coaching and need to be dispelled.

Myths of Coaching Executives

1. Executives do not possess the same desires, conflicts, anxieties, purposefulness, or purposelessness as other clients.

2. Executives climb the ladder of success to the pinnacle of the organizational pyramid and finally feel fulfilled.

3. Executives like being on a pedestal and viewed as superhuman.

4. Financial benefits make the executive's life easy.

5. Executives do not need to feel acknowledged and nurtured. Satisfaction programs are fine for employees, not for executives. The 360-degree assessment process provides all the positive feedback an executive needs.

6. Praising the boss is wrong.

7. Coaches must use different competencies to coach executives.

In my experience, executives do not need a distinct form of coaching (Belf, 1998). When it comes down to our basic spiritual needs—to understand purpose, feel connected, be of service, and be engaged in meaningful work—executives are no different from anyone else. Behind closed doors in the safety of the coach's office (or in a natural setting away from the office) most appear interested in and ready to discuss how business and Spirit intertwine. What follows are several executive coaches' experiences that challenge some of the above myths.

Let us begin with a look at purposefulness and its relevance in executive coaching.

Personal Purposefulness

Robert Witherspoon, a renowned executive coach, believes that deeper values and a sense of purpose tend to enhance his coaching effectiveness. Prior to each coaching meeting, he taps into an aspect of his life purpose, *to bring out the best in people,* often stating it in some way during his initial client meeting. Witherspoon explains that life purpose falls under one of the roles coaches assume with executives, that is, the role of coaching for an executive's agenda. He writes, "Sometimes the sessions border on life coaching, as the executive considers his or her life purpose and personal challenges" (Goldsmith, Lyons, & Freas, 2000).

Dr. Elaine Gagné, a respected international coach, considers life purpose as the first step in coaching her executive clients.

Executive Coaching: Antidote for the Seduction of the Times
By Elaine Gagné

So many people today are seduced into living imbalanced lives that imbalance has become the norm, the red badge of courage worn by the harried and exhausted chargers in our workforce. Many will not recognize this as a problem until they reach burnout. Burnout can take many forms: illness, dissolution of relationships, irritability, loss of energy, problems in thinking, decreased ability to perform routine jobs, utter collapse, and more.

My job is to help people at various stages along this path, hopefully sooner rather than later. I work with successful professionals. Unfortunately, they attribute their success to their crazy work style—the one leading to burnout. They fear that, if they change this work style, success will vanish. I help them see the folly in this thinking.

At the core of this syndrome is people's inability to be clear on *what* they truly value or to *know* their true value and contribution. I use the following simple formula to guide our coaching relationship.

Phase 1. Be Quiet

We get into a quiet space in which we can ask the questions, "Well, who *am* I anyway?" and "What am I doing here?" These may seem like dumb questions; however, they are questions some people never stop to think about as they go through life reacting to circumstances and people, making choices serving those circumstances and people. When they stop long enough to see where they fit into the whole scheme of things, they may realize they are strangers to themselves.

I take them through a series of exercises to put into words what has been forever present at the core of their being—each of their personal mission statements. You may ask, "What does a personal mission statement have to do with professional work?" If a person has no solid foundation in what he or she is all about as a person, his or her professional work will ultimately lack the richness possible only in a truly fulfilled person. Truly fulfilled people never experience burnout.

The outcome of this phase is to be able to say: "I know who I am."

Phase 2. Get Connected

The next step in the formula is to get the person to examine every aspect of life and see how each area affects the other—to take time to connect the dots and look at what needs attention first. Here is where a person becomes clear about how he or she wants life to look. Even for those people who want to focus on their professional lives, we nevertheless identify other areas, keeping the big picture in mind and helping to monitor the effect of these other areas. Becoming clear about goals and objectives enables us to create a plan to achieve them.

The outcome of this phase is to be able to say: "I know who I am" and "I know what I am here to be and to do."

Phase 3. Take Action

Now it is time to take action on the plan. Many people experience failure by not executing their well-made plans. I assist people in creating plans supported and set up for success. In ways that work for them, I hold them accountable for that success and the learning that goes along with taking action.

This is the area in which I do the bulk of my work. Each session takes us further toward the being and doing goals. *Doing* goals may be pretty familiar to the successful professional; however, they may take a slightly different bent. For example, how does a person learn to say "no" so he or she may say "yes" to something even more important? *Being* goals pose the greatest challenge. For instance, how does a person accustomed to moving at a rapid pace learn to *be* calm, peaceful, and even serene in situations normally creating stress, reaction, and craziness?

The outcome of this phase is to be able to say: "I know who I am," "I know what I am here to be and do," and "I know how I am going to get there and how I can ensure and experience success."

Phase 4. Celebrate

This step is often overlooked in the American culture; it seems most people are trained to move on to the next thing as soon as they accomplish what they set out to do. Celebration is a critical step when we look at changes that have occurred, who the person had to become to make those changes, the power of those changes, what was learned, and, most of all, to honor the fact that he or she *succeeded!*

Celebration comes in many forms—although primarily acknowledgment of some sort. Regardless of its form, acknowledgment honors who people have become as they move into the next cycle in the spiral of personal and professional growth.

The outcome of this phase is to say: "I know who I am," "I know what I am here to be and do," "I know how I am going to get there and how I can ensure and experience success," and "I know how I can feel the deep pleasure of that success."

This simple model—Be Quiet, Get Connected, Take Action, and Celebrate—can take people from utter chaos to confident, consistent forward movement as they become free from a killer seduction and learn to deepen self-awareness and their sense of contribution.

Purposefulness proves fair game in the executive suite, but what about Spirit?

Spirit and Executive Coaching

In my work as an executive coach, I help executives get better results in two ways. First, I help them assess their leadership and create their development plan using criteria such as strategic planning, customer and market focus, process management, and business results, to name a few. *Note:* These criteria are based on the coveted Malcolm Baldrige Quality Award Criteria that gives organizations guidelines for stellar results.

That is the easy part. Getting results is what the Western culture is all about. When one is pointed in the right direction, knowing how to focus attention and time, results follow.

More difficult is to coach for the expression of Spirit—for who a person *is* under all that goal setting and achievement—thereby tying people back to what they truly value and their unique contributions in their worlds. This type of coaching requires courage from all—both client and coach have to stay true to the vision of deep and rich fulfillment. Many entrenched mindsets and habits must be challenged, torn up, and let go—sometimes leaving an unfamiliar and often frightening emptiness in a place that feels like a world spinning out of control. A leap of trust is required. The client must be able to temporarily step off a cliff, having faith the golden bridge beneath will be there for support. The coach must stand firm in offering encouragement and at the same time preventing reversion to the comfort of the familiar.

The outcome of this courage and persistence is deeply rewarding for both client and coach. I feel it a great privilege to coach clients to deepen fulfillment and see how this fulfillment can affect their worlds.

Example

 Jean was the epitome of professional success. From all appearances, she "had it all." But Jean had a persistent and nagging feeling something was not right with her world. She sensed her relationship with her husband and children was taking on surreal qualities, going through motions, yet missing key events. Her time with friends seemed superficial; she sometimes felt as an observer in her own world. Jean felt tired and "old." All of this had been creeping up on her for a number of years until she had accepted this state as her reality. All of this masked her true yearnings, fading more each year.

When Jean got back in touch with what she really wanted, a dam broke—joy for what she rediscovered, sorrow for what she missed. She realized how entrenched she had become in her lifestyle and gained some glimmer of what it would take to extricate herself. At this point, our real work began. A number of times Jean lost heart and opted for status quo. My job was to keep her vision in front of her and to continue to ask what she wanted to do with her dreams. I challenged her to say "yes" or "no" to the dreams—just thinking of them made her come alive. We focused on who she was becoming in her process of discovery. We used each discovery as a stepping stone for greater depth and self-awareness.

Every session and in between each session yielded learning. While Jean noticed some change right from the beginning, after ten months she noticed significant changes with her family, her work, and her health; her whole life had changed. She says she is a "different" person. I remind her, "No, you are just more of who you really are and have been all along."

❧

Acknowledgment

Dr. Gagné alludes to the importance of acknowledgment. Let us poke deeper into the myth that executives must be truly fulfilled because of their status, widespread recognition, and fat wallets and pocketbooks.

"I wish I could receive some praise. It's lonely up here." I caught these words muttered under the breath of an executive vice president who just finished praising a manager for a proposed management-supervisory recognition day—a coach's Kodak™ moment, an opportunity to coach an isolated executive.

My self-appointed mission became to delve into the topic of executive fulfillment and acknowledgment. Many approaches came to mind. One angle was to discuss the importance of asking for feedback from others. Another was to question why loneliness was a problem. I could have had the executive rank values or explore what type of positive feedback would be useful. I might even have suggested working with subordinates, the board of directors, or other stakeholders to teach when and how to deliver praise. It does not matter which direction I chose; the point is I believe it is important for coaches to include this topic intentionally when coaching executives and not to wait until you might hear an almost inaudible slip of the tongue: "It's lonely up here."

As a result of coaching, the executive increased his level of awareness about the importance of asking for acknowledgment and began to experience greater fulfillment at work *and* in his personal life.

❧ REFLECTION

Use any or all of these questions to assist executives (or anyone) in broaching conversation about acknowledgment:

1. How do you like to be acknowledged?

2. Who might compliment you?

3. What feedback leaves you feeling appreciated?

4. Can you coach your executive team to offer positive acknowledgment?

5. Do you believe that praise from subordinates is appropriate for executives?

6. What would meaningful positive feedback sound like to you?

7. How can you proactively recruit praise?

Executives Talk About Feelings

Another myth prevalent in the coaching industry suggests that talking with executives about feelings and emotions is strictly taboo. Executive coach Timi Gleason regularly challenges this myth and reports extremely effective coaching resulting from communication about emotions.

Leaders as Emotional Risk Takers
By Timi Gleason

Sometimes I find it challenging to let clients explore possibilities without trying to jump in and "tell them the answers." There is great beauty in the minds of deep thinkers, although they can be *so* slow to process coaching questions. There is also great beauty in the hearts of those quick-acting leaders who believe they should be able to eliminate their pesky employees who take the fun out of managing. In one of my cases, I was able to go behind the client's thinking to be supportive.

A general manager wanted to know how he could get rid of one of his key managers, Ramon, who did not have the drive expected of him. He saw Ramon as an argumentative, insubordinate loser. As long as we focused on the facts of the situation, possibilities were nil. We needed to reframe so my client could start moving forward and away from his self-imposed stress. I suggested we try a pleasant imagery exercise.

I had my client imagine himself on one end of a continuum (a long line) and place Ramon, facing him, on the opposite end. When I asked him to pick a symbol to represent Ramon's energy, he picked a roaring lion (King of the Jungle).

It took him a few long seconds to think about how *he* wanted to be symbolized. With his eyes still closed, a gentle smiled crossed his lips as he sat up straight and happy. He chose a knight because, as he explained, "I am in service to my employee as his manager. I want to learn how to calm Ramon's attitude toward me and either be able to mentor him or support him to move on. But I want to do it as *his* Knight." Truly, Spirit was present! The rest of the exercise went smoothly, and a plan of action for resolving their issues followed in the days to come. Communication opened up like never before, and both men began to move forward in their career development.

✧

Connection

Another false myth about coaching executives is that it is difficult to connect with them because of their lofty perspective. Dottie Perlman, an executive coach, shatters this widespread view in the following story.

The Transformed Attorney
By Dottie Perlman

When Curtis, a practicing lawyer and Harvard Law School graduate, first came to me, he admitted he had no idea what he was getting into. He did recognize he was feeling confused, stuck, and directionless and that he needed help. Coaching was a foreign concept, and he was skeptical about whether I, or anyone, could make any real difference for him. What happened as we proceeded together can only be attributed to coaching with Spirit.

Most of his initial apprehension and anxiety disappeared after our first meeting because, as he revealed, I had created a safe space for him to open up to vent his feelings and frustration comfortably. He felt heard. Appreciating my empathy and understanding, he sensed he could trust me and be his real self with no barriers.

Just Be Present and Available. By just being present and making myself available for him to pour out his anger, his many walls, his voices of "should" and "have to" began to collapse. As he emerged and revealed himself on a much deeper level, we slowly peeled the onion to get to his untapped core essence.

I shared an article I had written dealing with the emotions of change and asked Curtis for his feelings and reactions. He expressed enormous relief hearing that he was not alone and learning that others share similar feelings as they go through the roller coaster ride of change.

Coaching Magic Occurs in a Safe Space. In coaching with Spirit, connecting with the client is key and can even become magical. Over the next few weeks in a series of in-depth meetings, I gave Curtis permission to experience "not knowing" and "not having all the answers immediately." Being a lawyer, this was particularly difficult for him. I remained a neutral sounding board, letting him take us in whatever direction he needed to explore. As I continued to be present and receptive, Curtis became more engaged and invested in the process. Curtis's outlook gradually transformed from being angry (outward-directed negative energy) to being more reflective (forward-looking positive energy). I probed deeper. Little by little Curtis was willing to let his guard down, be vulnerable, and thus open the doorway to inner truths for further exploration.

In the middle of a particularly lengthy meeting, I asked Curtis what motives had originally led him to pursue the legal profession. I listened intently to the spoken words and heard underlying unspoken yearnings as I distilled and extracted what really mattered to him. Together we delved deeper and identified the core values of his authentic self and what he saw as his purpose in life. He transformed by aligning his new career, organization development, with core values. Today Curtis will tell you he has never been happier.

This is the magic of coaching with Spirit—being fully available for the client. Curtis is a classic example of how allowing Spirit in coaching can make a profound difference in the client's readiness and ability to search within and rediscover authentic self.

Executives Have It All

Those looking up at the executive suite perceive that fame, fortune, and an eagle's span of control make up the entire formula for business happiness. Not so, according to those who coach executives. Something else is missing, and that something brings executives to coaches.

Exposing the Executive's Spirit by Coaching in the Wild

My arena for executive coaching appears rather traditional as compared with the stories I received from others. Whereas my clients and I do sometimes relocate onto a deck boat or stroll along a lakeside path, this appears stodgy compared with the sailboat regattas, cowboy canyons, fishing excursions, and sand dunes you will read about in the stories that follow. While pondering why so many executive coaches chose a natural setting to coach, I chanced on this plausible explanation: "Language is the very voice of the trees, the waves, and the forests" (Merleau-Ponty, 1968, p. 155).

When I read an unsolicited email from Dave de Sousa, excitement welled up. Out-of-the-box thinking characterized Dave's approach to executive coaching. Sometimes a coach needs to help the client let the lasso out and follow it to the end so life can be viewed from a different angle. I particularly applaud Dave for being tuned in to facilitating his client's transfer of this unique experience into the executive's world.

Dan's Canyon
By Dave de Sousa

Dan, president of his own twenty-six person consulting company, worked extremely hard to satisfy his clients. His tenacious spirit, driven to provide solutions to some very complex client challenges, was far above the norm. Under his leadership people did whatever it took to complete an assignment, whether long days or all-night work sessions. As you might suspect, the other areas of Dan's life were slowly shrinking—classic burnout creeping up—the signs all there.

As Dan's coach and friend, I offered to include him on my yearly horseback adventure to the remote mountains of southwestern Colorado. Then came the excuses: I can't ride. (I'll teach you.) I may get lost. (I'll guide you.) I can't afford the time. (You won't have any if you don't slow down and get away.) He finally agreed, and we set up a plan that would put us both in the wilderness on horseback in mid-September.

When new challenges arose, he met them with the same determination present in his work. He was forced to "get ready" for his getaway. Because of the high altitude and the physical demands, I encouraged him to start an exercise program. Just the thought of getting ready picked up his spirits, changing his attitude about the other areas of his life.

I set into motion my plan to rent horses and teach him my crash course on horsemanship. Leaving a week before Dan, I went into the mountains by myself and made arrangements with the cowboy, from whom I rented the horses, to drop Dan off at the trailhead. I would meet them there and our adventure would begin. Perfect timing! As I crested the last hill before the trailhead, Dan arrived. We loaded up the packhorses, climbed aboard our trusty steeds, and headed down into the canyon out of which I had just climbed.

Picture this: I lead the way with my packhorse in tow and Dan, who up until that time had never even seen a real live packhorse, let alone led one, inched his way down a steep slope.

One crystal-clear afternoon we let the horses graze in a lush alpine meadow. As we rested near a huge blue spruce tree listening to the elk bugle in the distance, I said to Dan, "Remember this valley, this meadow, this tree, these sounds and smells, and this sky and return here often." Dan named this little valley "Dan's Canyon."

Indeed, the trip and especially "his" canyon have become firmly etched into his memory, enabling him to revisit daily from any location on earth. He just closes his eyes, allowing his Spirit to whisk him from his hectic world of business and deposit him under that magnificent blue spruce.

Our relationships, experiences, and memories shape us and our Spirit responds to their urgings. Because of the need for executives to get away, the necessity for them to meet unique challenges, and my personal and spiritual experiences—in and out of the wilderness—I have taken my "next step" and created the "Extreme Cowboy Adventure."

⊱

As a way of gaining perspective in the middle of an executive's workday, Dave's client learned to visualize and recall the memory of a faraway adventure resplendent with challenges akin to those in his business.

✧ REFLECTION

1. In what ways have you cast out lassos for your clients? Coaching in unusual environments? Keeping unusual props in your office? Painting outrageous hypothetical scenarios to turbocharge the imagination?

2. How do you increase the guarantee for sustainable learning from once-in-a-lifetime experiences?

The following coaching story submitted by executive coach Beth Hand draws the parallel between the courage needed by executives to be in charge of an organization's destiny and the same courage to be in charge of one's personal destiny. "You can't run from destiny," coach Dawn Courtney reminds us. "It will always find you."

Leading Is a Courageous Act
By Beth Hand

One frame for describing my coaching comes from fishing—something I grew up doing. In my twenties and thirties I competed in marlin tournaments, spending long days about seventy miles offshore in the clear, warm blue of the Gulf Stream and the deep blue of the Atlantic. I fished onboard different makes of boats, including several Bertrams sportfishers. In heavy weather and depending on the boat's relationship to the waves, the Bertrams tended to roll from side to side—however always righting themselves.

When everything falls apart or seems to, I hold for the client that place of "righting," available even in the worst possible conditions. The place of righting is a place of spiritual trust—a place where we can acknowledge and be in the full range of motion. It offers balance even amidst imbalance.

I coached an executive whose organization was targeted for a merger with a larger one with a different mission and identity. Many meetings and conversations led the executive to believe his position might be in jeopardy or his freedom to make strategic decisions might be radically changed. We began by acknowledging the dreadful situation, the possibility of demotion, the dissolution of the organization, or the chance of a major reallocation of organizational resources. After his initial anger, he immediately wanted to take action and strategize. I invited him to consider the uncertainty of the future, questions it might raise in his different roles as a leader, a colleague, even as a family member and friend. Without insisting, I continued to invite him to be in that emotional mix of not knowing, even feeling helplessness. Our organizations often deny leaders the experience of such feelings and our Western culture insists we make the briefest acknowledgment (if even that) of changed events and move on quickly to the solution. It's the end result that matters, we insist, rarely the process. With that perspective, we lose the richness and inspiration that can arise from fully experiencing not knowing.

When my client deeply acknowledged the many different ways he was challenged, his tone, his body, and our conversations began to change. He started to accept this "whole thing," this full range of motion. Even his strategizing changed as he began to envision new possibilities, some even more exciting than before. Coaching enabled him to experience the proposed merger in a way that led him to make different choices in relating to his employees. Acknowledging uncertainty, he made no promises that "everything would be okay." He immediately established "safe" venues for employees to express concerns. I think what I offered was to hold that place of trust, helping him embrace the whole while letting the "righting" occur as naturally as the rolling in heavy seas.

꙳

Sail into the next story, where the result of coaching a group of executives transforms the entire culture of the organization. Note how these coaches used the three coaching with Spirit principles—connection, being present, and responsibility—as the foundation of their adventure-based work.

Exposing the "S" Word
By Ed Shulkin

As I was packing to go to college, a seasoned collegian who had weathered the eye dropping, sometimes brain numbing, often all-night study sessions took me in hand and with loving guidance said, "If you want to be popular and not be seen as weird, avoid all discussions about politics and, for God's sakes, religion or spirituality." Those words ring in my ear on a regular basis now—especially the "S" word.

I am an organizational culture builder. Using adventure-based learning and coaching, I work with organizations and senior people within them to build cultures based on teamwork, respect, emotional intelligence, values, and spirituality.

Our college dorm room sessions now have become work environments, and in these work settings many of us avoid acknowledging a Higher Power, a universe, a something "out there" that drives and guides us along the path we refer to as purpose.

Spirit is in our language. We do have permission to use words like coincidence, serendipity, synchronicity, connection, psychic, déjà vu, universal, and others referring to what we believe is going on out there. Why? Because deep down in our heart of hearts, deep in our soul, in our gut, throughout our bodies, in the places we live, we believe something is going on out there. But in order to get "out there" we have to get "in there," and that might be described as the "S" word. My work with one particular client illustrates what I mean.

I had been working with a client company for more than five years when the CEO finally said to me, "I don't like the way my managers work together." Pressed to tell me more, he described attitudes of mistrust, fear, suspicion, and competition existing within the organization. This was my opportunity to move the company forward.

"What are you doing culturally to produce a different environment? What if you had a culture of fulfillment, a place where every employee was encouraged to achieve personally and professionally? How would you like to lead an organization based on creativity, balance, and commitment to sustaining higher productivity because of ownership of shared values and visions?" He looked at me, smiled, and said the magic words every coach longs to hear: "Yeah, if only."

Retention. Within a month we had embarked on a six-month journey designed specifically to create the kind of culture I had described that day. In my work I try to match events with desired outcomes. The key to learning is retention. In our model for adventure-based learning, coaching assures retention.

The Regatta. We began with a weekend event I call the corporate regatta. I chose the regatta, a sailing event that takes place on twelve-meter yachts, because of the perfect fit of group size and dynamic. Participants are taught to perform a specific task on the boat; teamwork is required for success.

Starting with total lack of experience meant creating the team, its personnel, the mission, the communication techniques, the confirmations, the skills, and the attitudes necessary to win—a daunting task under the best of conditions. Complicate this task by throwing together a group of people who came from an organizational culture having a different set of values and the issues rise to the top like flotsam. Using the yacht and its required tasks to create metaphors for the real world, the teams were trained in the "how to" of yacht racing. Daring to expose their soft underbellies, they found themselves willingly laughing about weaknesses in skills as leaders, communicators, mentors, and humans. Truly an opportunity to transform!

For two days the teams learned and honed their skills. Among other things, they learned to be emotionally, mindfully, physically, spiritually, and socially connected and in that space almost effortlessly achieving needs and wants. Yes, there was a race. Yes, the team with the best preparation and execution won. But the real fish caught was the understanding of how the human condition—the "S" word—could be welcomed at work.

We embarked on a six-month journey that day. An individualized coaching program was developed to maximize the effect of lessons learned during the regatta, each senior manager matched with a coach. We focused on creating adaptability and balance into the coaching model so members had tools that applied to their entire life experience. The coaching model, individual sessions interspersed with monthly whole-team sessions, provided feedback and observed behavioral and relationship changes.

Outcomes. At the end we had a team, a culture, and, more importantly, results. Sales grew at double-digit rates for the first time in several years; time to market was cut in half; turnover was reduced by more than 20 percent. And, for me, the most exciting accomplishment of all, the company made two acquisitions and successfully integrated them into their culture. Today coaching is a major part of their human development strategy. The difference between the good performers and the great performers is the presence of coaches.

❧

Earlier we exposed the power of the metaphor in personal coaching. In the executive coaching realm, Carl Ingram and his client literally and physically jump right into the middle of a different landscape in nature to co-create a magnificent metaphor, taking both on a spiritual journey.

Coaching the Nature of Spirit and the Spirit of Nature
By Carl Ingram

A coaching colleague and I were sauntering on a restored beach and a metaphor for Spirit restoration emerged from our dialogue. How can a walk on the beach inspire the nature of Spirit through the Spirit of nature?

Introduction

My work as an executive coach creates openings for coaching colleagues to connect with the nature of their Spirit. One way I accomplish this outcome is to engage the Spirit of nature. I meet with colleagues outside our offices, preferably in parks at a picnic table, hiking on a wooded trail, or strolling along a beach. Experience has taught me that when we experience nature firsthand we create opportunities to connect with our inner nature and our spirit.

The more a leader connects with Spirit, the better the leadership because direction for leadership comes from Spirit guidance and engagement with other people in the workforce. Astonishingly painless to say and thorny to do, leading from Spirit takes open-hearted reflection and strong-hearted action with a willingness to receive from others. Our problem-solving mind seeks a soothing remedy. Reading books in search of action-step prescriptions only distracts from an appointment with Spirit. Through nature, Spirit is always calling to make contact.

Advantages for Coaching Colleagues Outdoors in Nature

1. Leadership mantles drop sooner outside the organizational setting.

2. Without the corporate persona, leaders begin to notice their true Spirits.

3. Instead of walking the walk and talking the talk of the parent company, leaders walk a mile in their own moccasins.

Advantages for the Coach

1. It is easier to fully show up in Spirit.

2. In nature, it is easier to set aside academic learning, drop the agenda, and forget the last session.

3. It is easier to be in the moment.

4. It is easier to listen and compel self for a breakthrough.

5. Openings create Spirit to come forth.

Advantages for Colleague and Coach

1. Metaphors offer alternative viewpoints to better know and understand present and future situations.

2. Nature offers metaphorical opportunities as broad as the sky.

Examples of nature-based metaphors abound: the cycles of the seasons, death and rebirth, the process of development, roots before blossoms, the necessity of fallow wintering, life as mystery, following one's path, and encountering Spirit as part of everyday life.

Coaching in nature, not a method to be relied on exclusively, is part of a variety of ways to engage the coaching colleague. In my coaching I include personal and work history, assessment with standardized measures, agreements of how we work together, and outcomes. The outdoor coaching evokes the capacities of intuition, being present in the moment, and moving with feelings. On the other hand, the world of work is based on a rational way of knowing and understanding. My well-disciplined conscious mind tracks objectives to ensure congruence with personal mission. Other times in coaching I use my rational mind for different outcomes. The coaching colleague needs a balanced way of engaging heart, mind, *and* spirit.

My coaching colleague Jim contributed why he found the outdoor coaching experience valuable: "Getting out of the office and into nature worked well for me. It lessened the influence of my past environment and corporate position. I was more comfortable, especially in the natural settings available around San Francisco, California. Being out in nature aligned me with my desire to better integrate my work with my values. One of my values is to help our society preserve and value our natural environment. So being outside worked for me on a number of levels."

Coaching Relationship. Jim and I formed a coaching relationship to assist with his transition from senior director of international recruitment for a multibillion-dollar-a-year engineering consulting firm. Deciding to leave his prestigious senior corporate position, he searched for a vocation or calling where he could live his spiritual values and contribute to the betterment of the world without forfeiting his spiritual self. He experienced an emptiness and restlessness. The focus for our coaching was discovering who Jim is beyond his successes and failures. We found Spirit emerging.

Some of the ways Jim expressed Spirit in his life included environmental advocacy, creative leadership, a witty manner, and artful singing. However, his spiritual vision had narrowed as a result of his undergraduate training in business, an MBA from Stanford University, and twenty years in the corporate arena. Spiritual horizon too limited, he sought to reclaim his fuller and complete spiritual self.

After six months of coaching, we enjoyed taking turns choosing the location for our meetings. The restoration of Crissy Field in Golden Gate National Park in San Francisco attracts many ecologically minded volunteers. Jim found solace and rejuvenation in rolling up his shirtsleeves and replanting native flora. Jim chose Crissy Field to show me his part in the large restoration project.

Internal and External Restoration. Jim says, "It was especially important for me to share a part of my 'new world' with Carl. One of the things I started to do immediately after leaving my twenty-year career was get my hands in the dirt with the beach restoration project. Once we were at Crissy Field, Carl was interested in understanding what had been done to this land and sharing my excitement about my involvement."

The Spirit and beach restoration metaphor emerged from our conversation. For the mile trek back to the parking lot, we decided to walk on the wet sand next to the water instead of on the paved path. Our conversation meandered across many topics, and we were enjoying a quiet walk together when we found ourselves attracted to a sand dune where replanted native flora had taken root. Jim reached over the low fence and pulled out a non-native plant, Sea Rocket. He began talking about how much effort is needed to restore the salt marsh and to weed out the exotic plants floating in on air and sea. The wind swirled the sand around my feet. I felt a spark of insight and I began to talk about the similarities between beach and Spirit restoration. Jim sparkled and encouraged me, joining with ideas to grow the metaphor.

The Metaphor Emerges. My words flowed as my rate of speech accelerated. It seemed the Spirit of the land entered every pore of my body, nurturing the metaphor. Time disappeared. My feeling of oneness expanded as my focus narrowed to hold only Jim and life on the beach. I felt goose bumps. When I feel tingles over my back, I know I'm engaging something greater than myself.

We volleyed ideas back and forth. Jim became animated, pointing at plants, the sea, and the sand. As I took the psychic and spiritual perspective, he would bring up another idea about life on the dune. Soon we were synergistically with each other's ideas, creating a metaphor together. We don't know who said what, when, or why—we only knew we were touched by the Spirit of nature and connected by the nature of Spirit.

Walking back to the parking lot, we reflected on the experience of being moved by Spirit. We felt closer to each other, having shared deeply from our hearts and minds. Our usual good-bye hug lingered—the untrusting part of ourselves trying to hold onto the moment. The wise part of ourselves knew that we were to cherish the learning but kiss this moment as it flew by.

We have used this metaphor as a reference for Jim's development. As he becomes more himself, he speaks more clearly from his heart. As a result of his spiritual restoration, Jim does not work as hard; his rewards are greater; his leadership is less commanding but more magnetic; he attracts people to follow. The more he humbles himself, the more others elevate him and his actions.

Jim had the following to say about his coaching experience: "Overall, what made my coaching experience powerful was Carl's commitment to bring a Spirit and energy to enhance my life. I'm now able to act more congruently with my values. The result is that I'm calmer and more trusting that things will turn out fine."

The arch of our coaching shifted from the perspective of succeeding on the corporate ladder to discovering personal path. When dwelling with his true spirit, Jim now has the courage to explore career options to apply his leadership skills as an environmental advocate.

In summary, the more we flow with our natural psychic environment, the more our personal evolution is in harmony with the natural cosmic universe.

❧

❧ REFLECTION

1. Where did you feel Spirit breathe into you?
2. Where do you find the Spirit of nature and the nature of Spirit?
3. Look around in your backyard or across the street. What aspects of nature touch you most?
4. Formulate a question about something going on in your life. Take a short walk in nature. Be open to nature giving you the answer.
5. What psychic weeds could you pull up to be a better coach?
6. What does restoration mean to you in the context of coaching?

In this next story we relocate to a typical office environment. You will recognize familiar content and process used in coaching nonexecutives, further dispelling the myth that coaching executives is different. With courageous openness, Rebecca Chan Allen offers a look inside her executive coaching world, sharing feelings and fears about coaching executive development with Spirit. What makes this contribution so intriguing is that we go behind the mental, emotional, and spiritual scenes of the client *and* of the coach.

Working with Spirit: Coaching Executive Leadership
By Rebecca Chan Allen

Coaching with Spirit is an emerging transformation process in which both coach and client have to let go of cultural conditioning and yield to the call of the Spirit. This narrative is about the transformational journey of my work with executive leader Tywyn Jones [TJ is a composite character and case]. During the journey, it was difficult to know whether success was achieved. In retrospect, the transformation was quite remarkable. By connecting with Spirit, TJ transformed herself from a functional expert into a confident executive leader. Although the journey was unpredictable, it follows some classic patterns of change. I call these patterns the "Three Turns of Transformation" (Allen, 2001). First, I will tell you about TJ; then I will discuss the turns of transformation.

Connecting with Spirit

TJ was a brilliant engineer who had a successful track record bringing new products to market. When offered the "ZCom" presidency, she was thrilled and saw it as an opportunity to realize her vision. Cherishing a dream of creating a company where talented people from all backgrounds could fulfill their creative potential, she and her family moved from Canada to the United States, anticipating adventures and challenges. To her dismay, she soon felt overwhelmed and immobilized.

When a former client first referred ZCom to me, I did not realize it was an answer to my own prayer for transformative engagements. It turned out that TJ was not looking for cross-cultural workshops. Her request was more personal. She felt stuck and was looking for ways to regain her creativity. We decided to meet every four to five weeks.

Looking back at the four-year period, we could both see the emergence of Spirit in our work and in our lives. The success came through three cycles. I call these cycles the "Three Turns of Transformation."

The first turn is about connecting with authentic power by moving from the ego to the self. I use self to mean the individual. The second turn is about connecting with others through Spirit. The third turn is about following our bliss by shifting from fears of scarcity to embracing abundance. Each of these turns shifts us from the illusory fears and desires of our restricted egos to the serenity of Spirit or Self. When Self is capitalized, I use it to mean the universal Spirit, the intelligence resident within the individual.

The Ego and the Self

Spirit is the universal creative energy and intelligence within and around us. By tuning into Spirit, we can achieve our purposes and goals naturally and effortlessly. However, due to social and cultural conditioning, we can become distracted by fears and desires and become trapped in the turmoil and confusion of economic insecurity, social approval, and egocentric power. When we recognize the natural creativity of the Self and follow its gentle guidance, we can be freed of confusion and weariness. Our goals will realize themselves. Our performance targets will be met.

The Three Turns of Transformation

Now we look at the "Three Turns of Transformation" in my coaching journey with TJ. The turn of transformation refers to a cycle of change in coaching in which a major barrier to Spirit is overcome, (re)turning to Spirit, our natural center. A change cycle is a process of unfolding to reveal a truth or reality—usually not straightforward. In fact, during the unfolding, you may not be aware anything is changed. The effect of transformation can catch you off guard. You go through a seemingly long period in which nothing appears to happen. Then, suddenly, you are able to see, feel, or do things in a totally different way, recognizing a reality there all along. That reality is Spirit or the Self within and around you.

Turn 1. Accepting the Power of Spirit. The first phase of coaching was focused on TJ finding her center of power and fulfilling her mission to establish a thriving enterprise. TJ knew that she had the vision, talents, and tenacity to achieve her goal but was at a loss as to why she was stuck.

TJ's strengths were her intelligence and warmth, her passion for work fueled by her love of challenge. Although she drew inspiration from mystical wisdom and prayers, she was not comfortable about her own spirituality and tried to de-emphasize that aspect of herself.

To mask her discomfort, she would sometimes join in dismissive jokes, although inwardly she called on Spirit for help. This outward denial of Spirit cut her off from a source of energy she needed to transform herself from a functional professional to an executive leader. Without the support of Spirit, it was difficult for TJ to leave her comfort zone.

In her comfort zone, she was confident and effective. But when she dealt in matters outside of her discipline, she acted in ways she thought an executive would act. Coming under the influence of unexplored social-cultural conditioning, she adopted an executive wardrobe and tried to use business lingo. Her effort to conform to cultural expectations landed her in no-win situations.

To help TJ shift out of her comfort zone, we explored her unspoken fears. By making the fears concrete, TJ could begin to deal with them and make them manageable. It turned out that, despite her reservations about following corporate norms, she was unwilling to abandon the rewards that came from adopting the conventional aggressive no-nonsense approach to business. She was concerned that embracing Spirit would mean a deviation from accepted norms. That in turn would lead her organization to view her as "New Age," goofy, or unskilled as a business executive. She thought accepting the power of Spirit would stigmatize her and make her the butt of jokes.

I asked TJ to catch herself when she was stressed and ineffective and when she was spontaneous and creative and to keep a simple log of these moments. From this exercise, she learned that when she was in touch with her Self, she experienced no negative chatter in her head. Once she abandoned the executive script in her head, she stopped feeling the need to act like an executive. She discovered she was perfectly at ease in the corporate workplace—at home there as much as anywhere else. Accepting the power of Spirit was easy, for it was an authentic power within.

Her acceptance of Spirit in her work opened TJ to new horizons. TJ had prided herself on being a self-taught manager, never needing management training. She finally went to an executive program. There she discovered the path to executive leadership was not about acting out restrictive scripts or having certain outward appearances but, rather, it was a journey to openness, a journey to the Self.

Turn 2. Connecting with Spirit in Others. Another barrier to Spirit was her fear of differences. In her job, TJ had to work with diverse teams of functional experts in finance, accounting, information technology, human resources, and others—fields she felt she needed to stay on top of. She found some of the people and their subject matters passionless and uninspiring; her inability to connect with people outside her discipline diminished the enjoyment of her job.

To help TJ connect with Spirit in others, I asked her to discover the bliss centers in others. I asked her how she could tell when people were passionate and inspiring. "When I can see sparkles in their eyes," she said. As an exercise, TJ was to observe when she could detect sparkles in others' eyes as well as when she was able to bring sparkles to others' eyes. From this activity, TJ became more mindful of how she related to others. Instead of viewing others' expertise as a source of personal humiliation and inadequacy, she became comfortable in learning from others. Instead of viewing others as separate beings competing for recognition and approval, TJ began to see them as collaborative colleagues for innovation and synergy. This new vision brought ease and enjoyment to her relationships.

Turn 3. Manifesting Spirit. Despite TJ's success, she was plagued by fears of scarcity and job insecurity. These fears hampered her ability to pursue her visions with confidence. She wanted to make sure she had enough money in the bank before risking the pursuit of bliss—implementing her vision of a creative organization. To explore this barrier, we worked on articulating the conditions for fully following Spirit.

TJ learned the amount of money and the conditions required were both moving targets. She realized that as long as she was influenced by the demands of ego and social conditioning, she was constrained. However, when she asked the Self for guidance, she learned the Self had no requirement or conditions. The Self in her had abundant energies, creativity, time, and freedom. This discovery helped TJ let go of fears and manifest her potential.

In the above, we looked at a client's transformation through Spirit. Next, we look at the coach's turns to Spirit.

The Coach's Three Turns

Intertwining TJ's journey was my own transformation as coach. In this journey, I learned to let go of preconceived ideas of how to work with Spirit in corporate settings. Here are my three turns.

Turn 1. Freedom from "Shoulds." Just as TJ struggled against social scripts for executive leaders, I learned to recognize the "shoulds" about corporate coaching and consulting in my head. Although I was keen to integrate Spirit in my work, I was reluctant to go whole hog on authenticity. I feared being myself would cause me to lose control and expose my weaknesses. So sometimes I pulled back from being completely candid. For example, I saw early on that TJ was hesitant about moving out of her comfort zone, but I did not address the issue until it became a problem.

I also learned that whenever I conformed to what I imagined a successful coach would do, it took my mind away from the emerging situation. For example, when I was fearful that I would be seen as not doing anything and therefore not earning my fee, I overcompensated by promoting an unimportant initiative.

Turn 2. Partnership. Coaching with Spirit is a co-creative process in which coach and client contribute to one another's learning and support mutual transformation. The work is a partnership. In our case, the idea of partnership was implicit rather than a built-in objective. When we started the coaching, we related as coach and client. The explicit goal was TJ's development and success. But as we worked together, we realized that increasing mutuality could produce better results. I had to make the conscious effort to ask for feedback and share my own aspirations and struggles. Just as TJ benefited from connecting with others through Spirit, I gained new capacities and partnerships.

Turn 3. The Gift of Spirit. Another barrier was my own economic insecurity. I became attached to working with ZCom and fearful of losing my connection with the company. Sometimes I allowed my attachment, although mostly unconsciously, to influence my decisions. Instead of reaching solutions effortlessly, we were mired in conflicting ego polarities.

To be freed from ego-generated work, I had to confront my own fear of scarcity. I worked through the same process as TJ in figuring the amount of money I needed to purchase my freedom. Like TJ, I discovered the ransom was a moving target. I now know that creative freedom is a natural gift. It cannot be bought. Moreover, this gift is free for the asking from the Self.

᠄ᠥᡃ

Competencies Used to Coach Executives

One of the myths listed at the beginning of the chapter suggests coaches need unusual competencies to coach executives. As you read executive coach Alan Shusterman's three examples, note the familiar spiritual themes—connection with self, connection with another, being in the moment, the power of silence—and see whether anything novel arises.

The Power of Spirit
By Alan Shusterman

Coaching with Spirit? I can't imagine coaching without it.

For me, Spirit is at the heart of coaching, that is, connecting with the client on a gut level, accessing and trusting intuition, being in the moment, and letting the moment and intuition take you in the direction that best serves your client. Spirit is the foundation of masterful coaching, the foundation of any coaching relationship producing extraordinary results.

Coaching is not a mechanical process; it's not about knowing all the answers or always knowing what to do. Spirit is the essence from which the art of coaching emerges. The challenge of a truly masterful coach is to successfully nurture spirit, honor it, trust it, call on it, and build on it. When selling coaching, focus on results. When coaching, focus on Spirit and let the results speak for themselves.

Keys to Connecting. Spirit is about connecting with clients and connecting with ourselves. Self-awareness, empathy, and authenticity are keys to connecting with others and to coaching with Spirit.

Coaching with Spirit frees clients to be honest with the coach and thus honest with themselves, enabling clients to be vulnerable, take chances, and open doors to positive change.

Spirit guides the coach to abandon preconceived notions, let go of self-ego, and make the right move at the right time in service of the client. Out of Spirit arises the perfect question at the perfect moment, leading to powerful insight or learning.

Recognizing the Presence of Spirit. How do I recognize the presence of Spirit in my executive coaching relationships? What difference does it make? I knew I had successfully coached with Spirit when, at the end of our first meeting, my new client, a top executive on the fast track with a perennial *Fortune* 50 company—and a stranger just two hours earlier—marveled, "Wow. I've told you things today that I've never told anyone else before."

In the same way, I felt the presence of Spirit when, at the beginning of a coaching meeting originally intended to focus on strategic planning, my executive client had the courage, trust, and comfort to reveal he was experiencing great difficulty in his marriage, a monumental situation overwhelming everything else in his life. We proceeded to have an open and painful discussion about deeply personal issues he had never shared with anyone else. As we parted that day, he expressed his heartfelt gratefulness for our discussion. Two weeks later we proceeded back down the road of leadership development, his primary coaching focus. Two months later he learned he was to receive the promotion he had been seeking for so long.

I also recognized the magic of Spirit when, as a novice coach, I listened to my executive client describe a difficult situation encountered the day before, not resolved to his satisfaction. The answer popped into my head—that is, *I* knew how he *should* have handled it. As a well-trained coach, I also knew *not* to tell him what to do (or what he should have done), instead asking coaching questions to facilitate his discovering his own answer. Whereas I knew the questions I could ask—the correct textbook approach to take—I instead heeded my intuition and remained silent. After moving on to discuss another issue at length, lo and behold, the client returned to our previous discussion and said, "You know what? What I should have done was. . . ." Indeed, he found the answer and learned a valuable lesson that would serve him well thereafter.

Can I tell you how or why I chose to remain silent when I did? Can I give you a guideline for the right move to make in other similar situations? No. All I can say is this: Nurture the Spirit in your coaching relationships and have the courage to trust it will guide you to make the right move, for that particular client, at that particular moment.

In the corporate world, results are what matter most. Talk about Spirit, intuition, and the like does not necessarily sell well. While coaching with Spirit certainly has a profound and higher meaning to me, while it represents an ideal of how to connect with our fellow human beings, and while it is my passion, the bottom line is that it works. I am convinced and my anecdotal evidence shows no process is more effective for developing top-notch managers, executives, and leaders than coaching.

❧

Summary

From the sampling of executive coaching stories I received, it appears from a spiritual point of view that the process of coaching executives and nonexecutives is the same. Other elements may and probably do differ, thereby requiring executive coaches to learn or prepare for executive coaching with a different knowledge base, assessment tools, leadership skills, and so on. However, spiritually, coaches still need to be vigilant about personal purposefulness, connection, being in the present, and responsibility.

We have one more hypothesis to check out—whether or not coaching with Spirit varies in other countries. So pack your coaching bags to travel to the next chapter to read what coaches around the world have to say about coaching.

CHAPTER 9

International Coaching with Spirit

DO PERSONAL AND PROFESSIONAL COACHES who work abroad with various cultures experience the same themes as those who coach in the United States? Does the coach who professes to coach with Spirit take on a unique persona in different countries? Are any aspects of a coach's customized blueprint transferable to other cultural settings? Are spiritual issues the same?

I invited a number of coaches who coach with Spirit to contribute their perspectives. Although it is important to be sensitive to, recognize, understand, appreciate, and value the diversity of different cultures, the question remains: "What are the essential elements for coaching with Spirit anywhere?" To go beyond my borders, I emailed fifty-five International Coach Federation (ICF) chapter heads inviting them or anyone they knew to share stories about how they coached with Spirit and included here every reply I received. So we learn about coaching with Spirit from coaches in The Netherlands, Canada, France, the United Kingdom, and Indonesia.

Stories from Five Countries

From The Netherlands
By Julia Ferguson Andriessen

One example of coaching with Spirit is a session with my client "William." I received an email from him earlier in the day that had been sent to a variety of family and friends. It was a beautiful and magical story about the death and transition of his father that had happened since we last spoke.

My first reaction was one of shock, as William had not cancelled our coaching session for that evening. I was concerned for him and his family, as the death was unexpected and his father lived in another country.

Also, I noted in his emailed story that his African culture has a beautiful and powerful way of relating to one's "transition," as William put it. I was, however, feeling a bit raw myself that week, as it was the second year since the death of my own father. I was concerned I might not be able to handle the call, that my emotions might get in the way of my coaching abilities.

Sitting quietly for a while, I decided that because I had made a promise to my clients to be with them through everything, I would listen and support William that night during our phone session.

About five minutes before William's call, I sat in my office and prayed. I prayed to my Higher Power for guidance, for the words that would be appropriate and helpful to William, for strength, and the gift of truth. I asked to be a vehicle to share what William could use. I asked to listen with my heart and to stay present.

It was a wonderful session. I listened to William share about his father and what an inspiring man he was. While sharing about my father's transition and the issues surrounding immigrants in a different country separated from most of one's family (William and I both live in Holland), I felt a warm presence. A healing light and energy enveloped and nurtured us throughout the hour-long session. I found the beauty in his culture's approach to death very healing; he enjoyed and found strength in quotes from a book I selected that talked about death ending a life and not a relationship.

A few days later on April 12, the date my father died, I received an email from William thanking me for my support and sending greetings to my father—he knew I would be "talking" to him that day. He asked if I would also ask my father to send a celestial email to welcome his father to his new life. I felt Spirit walking into my office again as I read this email and felt the warmth.

Coaching offers many opportunities to help people, guide them to their life purpose, and give them support to reach their destiny. This session will remain a guiding light for me to remember that my ego has no place in my coaching sessions, and when I live my path guided by Spirit, I am the best coach I can be.

∾⅌

From Canada
By Beryl Allport

Coaching with Spirit for me is always asking Spirit to be present and that results be guided from the Spirit of our higher selves. I feel blessed to know Spirit is everywhere as energy—in and around us all. Spirit creates lightness, light, and heartfelt experiences. All feelings are energy and these energy messages alert awareness or consciousness. If I listen and heed, I become mindful moment-to-moment, being present and totally alive to experiencing self, others, and life. Living consciously also creates the awareness of synchronicities—those things, people, and incidents mysteriously appearing at the most unexpected, appropriate, and meaningful times.

My visual metaphor for Spirit in action is a horse in the wild, running freely with mane flying in the breeze, whinnying sounds of sheer joy, and kicking heels high to exercise abundant energy. Spirited is feeling free—a goal that coaching helps me and most of my clients attain.

During my own experience of being coached, living my own experiences, and now witnessing the varied experiences of my clients during their coaching process, I felt and continue to feel the presence of Spirit. Intuition is Spirit in action, listening to the inner nudges creating awareness of living in the moment. Being present in every moment with clients and myself is what I call coaching with Spirit.

Life Purpose—A Spiritual Tool

A most incredible awareness tool in the coaching process is establishing life purpose. It is our divining rod to stay aligned with Spirit. Once we know our purpose, we can more easily understand how Spirit guides us. During coaching experiences, Spirit constantly prods and pokes, saying, "Listen, feel it, do it." When a client embraces Spirit, an awareness of the next step or risk emerges; when action is taken, it feels right.

Here in Canada, and for me personally as well, there is a strong Native American-influenced connection to nature. I believe in the powers, energies, and influences of nature on our being and am guided to live and inspire accordingly. The stillness rhythms of the breeze and streams, the cycles of the sun and moon, seasons, the messages from the animals and birds, the practice of yoga and meditation, all allow the guided messages to surface as intuition and make coaching possible from this place of awareness of Spirit.

As an elder wise woman, I am now in the role of being an inspiration. May I continue to be aware of Spirit and follow my path. My totem is the great blue heron, and as I connect to that energy, I experience the balance of stillness and focus with its powerful wingspan and direction in flight. As I live my purpose, "To relate from my unified spiritual self creating worthy and adventurous memories" and share coaching with Spirit experiences, I am grateful for the mindfulness of the moments and messages reminding us that when Spirit guides us, we create. If we don't heed the messages, we fall off track and experience stresses, challenges, and accidents.

I believe all of the above is Spirit at work, and each client story reveals life maneuvering through personal rivers, streams, and falls. Spirit is present when we feel "in the flow"; Spirit is present when we are given necessary lessons.

When I coach with clients, I ask for help, I ask for a sign, I ask for guidance. When I open a book to just the perfect page for a client, Spirit is present. When I phone clients for no particular reason just when they are in crisis, Spirit is present.

While I was riding the waves of turmoil being coached, my coach intuitively trusted I would be exactly where I needed to be to make the decisions Spirit was guiding me to make. I now do likewise with my clients; I am guided as they are. I trust it will be as it is meant to be.

I believe when one is open and trusting of a process and just lets it happen, even if not as originally planned, the outcome is totally guided by Spirit.

From France
By Margery Miller

I love to think people are the same all over the world, and in many ways they are. We all have certain emotions, moods, and types of characteristics. Until I spent time coaching clients in France, I did not really understand how cultural differences would surface.

I found spiritual differences in France in that people there have not been acculturated to see the range of choices they have—this perception coming from class and religious structures that have existed in Europe for centuries. It is not endemic to my American clients to see potential as limited; they perceive restrictions having more to do with finances or relationship issues.

Why is the presence of choice part of spiritual makeup? Because only through acknowledging choice can we truly begin to self-actualize. For me, self-actualization is the ultimate spiritual work—and a life-long process. Those people who see themselves on a spiritual path tend to understand the ongoing nature of commitment to a life of growth and change.

Example

One client, Genève, is the head of a graphic design firm and definitely an entrepreneur and leader. Caught in the mire of a loveless marriage, she found it extremely difficult to break away. Genève was not the same woman when she married many years ago. Although she no longer practiced the Catholic religion, she felt bound to the system because it had been a church marriage. She was afraid to step out of the box and declare her freedom. It did not help that according to French law, if one party abandons a spouse, the other can take all accumulated assets. So my client, emotionally separated from her husband, remained at home carefully plotting her course of action to gain freedom.

Obviously she experienced a great deal of pain associated with her situation. Genève's family did not condone divorce and her husband could not understand why she could not just stay home and bear children instead of having a demanding career. The level of awareness of people around her was very different; she felt isolated and alone in working through her problems.

Coaching helped Genève move forward enough to move into a spare bedroom, see herself as an independent woman, and begin to make choices that worked. Had a woman who believed in her unlimited potential not coached her, would she have come this far? Difficult to say, but obviously the support of a coach who had a cultural background espousing unlimited potential helped her tremendously.

Example

Another client from Great Britain owned a technical training business in Paris teaching French companies. Having a difficult time setting boundaries with employees, Edward wanted them to like him and remain with the company. In the French culture, I found there is a strong sense of entitlement about jobs—hence it is difficult to fire people. Because France is a socialist country with a strong clamp on free enterprise, Edward had a difficult time finding the balance between compliance with the laws and setting down basic ground rules enabling his business to succeed. His challenge was to learn to like himself more, to find his own value. Gradually, as he placed more importance on himself, Edward began to be clearer with those around him.

Both of these clients suffered from lack of self-value. Slowly, as they developed a healthy self-respect, learned to listen to their hearts, and cleared away brain noise obfuscating their thinking, they began to see their potential as independent adults. As a result of coaching, their culture had less influence than before. Certainly, my American clients have the same problems, yet in my experience, they seem to break old patterns more quickly than my European clients.

Realizing I experience freedom of thought, I have become more grateful for the cultural choices I have taken for granted!

From The United Kingdom
By Aboodi Shaby

A common theme in Eastern philosophy is we can have happiness without struggle and without needing the external world to change. My client, Sean, learned this spiritual wisdom through our coaching. When I suggested to him that sometimes the worst thing that can happen is to achieve what you want, he agreed it sounded weird. I asked him to think about it, and I proposed a few imaginations for his consideration.

Guiding him to envision himself really keen to have something, say a new job or car, I pointed out he would likely spend a lot of time thinking about what it will be like when he owns it. I fueled his imagination further: How spiffy a new car would look parked in his driveway and how good he would feel driving down the highway with cool sounds on the stereo, receiving envious looks from people as he drove by. Or how he might feel when landing the job of his dreams, the pride he would experience going to work on his first day, new feelings of importance, and, later that night, telling friends how lucky he is. I could see by Sean's face he was imagining how happy he might be when he finally acquired these wishes.

I then invited him to pretend after weeks of wanting the new car it finally arrived. Continuing with act two of this visualization, he drives up to the garage in his old car, excitedly takes the keys to his new dream from the salesman, gently slides into the car, turns on the ignition, and zooms away. Thrilled to bits with it, he feels like he has really achieved something and he proudly drives home to show his partner and friends. They all admire it, making appropriately envious sounds. How happy he is with his life and his new car.

Act three begins by projecting a week or a month into the future. Eager to go to work, Sean climbs in his still-new-looking, shiny car, but he is running late and just had a row with his kids before leaving. Instead of feeling happy, he dreads the day ahead. What happened to the happy feelings? Sean and I explored this familiar-sounding paradox so he could increase his awareness of the relationship between internal feelings of happiness and external changes.

How often had he wanted something, looked forward to the happiness he hoped it would bring, only to succeed, and then experience disappointment soon after.

What would happen if he didn't get it? Sure, he would be disappointed, but he realized that disappointment, like the happiness, would soon fade. He admitted his kids would still love him if he did not obtain that "perfect" job. He would still smile at people who smile at him. His ongoing happiness would be largely unaffected by the things he most thought would make him happy! This realization was the beginning of Sean's greater happiness. Now he knows those external things will not increase long-term happiness, and he can take smaller steps to increase his ongoing happiness.

Those little habits—smiling more, resolving to spend some time each day doing something you really enjoy, taking time to meditate daily—whatever your circumstances, will do more to increase your happiness than that new car, job, or girlfriend. Try it and become happier, like Sean did!

. ∾୬ℐ

From Indonesia
By Carol Fleischman

Several years ago I lived in a fishing village in Indonesia for nine months working with an organization whose purpose was human development. We provided training and processes to develop the potential in the village people beyond their own vision. We were invited by the country and then by the village of Bubun, in North Sumatra. Our two-year task was to help them plan for their future, train them in leadership skills, and coach them to take responsibility for carrying out their plans.

We were a team of five—three Westerners and an Indonesian couple, Laiya and Sutiah, who translated for us as well as became trained. We were also provided with a team of four young Indonesian men who had various levels of education and spoke some English. Although I did not speak the language, I know coaching is about working with people to discover their purpose in life, articulate vision and goals, live out values, get results, contribute to their world, celebrate life, dare to risk and change, and build community. We used this vital dynamic process, whether with a group or an individual:

- Acknowledging the past (history, successes),

- Keeping focused on the vision and goals,

- Naming what presently blocks vision from happening,

- Determining necessary new strategies, and

- Launching a new action plan.

Results were celebrated regularly, and the dynamic process continued to reinforce ongoing movement to the desired state. Certainly we needed translators, but most of all we needed to stand steady with our coaching methods and processes and model the possibility we anticipated from them.

Important Considerations

Honor the Culture, Build Rapport, and Establish a Caring Partnership. We were not there to Westernize them or impose our beliefs or other aspects of our culture. This experience required us to be completely flexible. Workdays began in the wee hours of morning for both men and women. They arrived back from the river or the Straits of Malacca mid-afternoon. Life in Bubun was quite simple and predictable, yet we got to know the people—all the human dynamics of a community were evident. People had lived out of the same roles for generations with not much chance to imagine anything differently.

Friday was gotung royung, the community workday. Along with the village people, we swept the narrow village paths, chopped down the fast growing lalang, and trimmed the cemetery.

Our Coaching Philosophy and Beliefs

Every Human Being Has a Purpose in Life. Every one has a unique contribution to make to the world, unique qualities, and a solid set of values. We knew that if those purposes were discovered, new passion and new meaning would catalyze the spirit of every individual. Our intention was to create an environment that offered opportunities for this to happen.

Every Human Being Has a Vision. Somewhere in everyone's subconscious lie hopes for the future; these may be latent (unarticulated), but they exist. Our task was to facilitate a shared vision that included the hopes and dreams of every human being.

People's Behavior Is Based on Their Image

- People operate out of images they have; women in Indonesia consider themselves to be of a lower status than men.

- Images control their behavior; women continue to play the role of wife, mother, and servant.

- Messages inform images and shape behavior; women did not expect to be educated, included in decision making, or invited into the mosque.

- New messages change images; when women receive messages that they are significant human beings and have a contribution to make, their images shift.

- New images change behavior and people's lives transform; women begin to take responsibility and take on leadership roles.

Our task was to shift the images of the people so they operated out of the possibilities of their human potential, therefore catalyzing the Spirit and forward movement of the entire village.

Transformational Events

Our Arrival. The village, composed of 174 families, greeted us when we arrived, graciously providing meals for several days while we settled into quarters specially built for us. A village celebration welcomed us with music, food, and a long meeting in the community center—an open-air building. The room was filled with village men; women and children crowded by the windows outside. The next morning as we strolled around to see what the village looked like, we saw a band of thirty to forty women coming to meet us. They asked us what our roles were in this project, wondering how they could be involved in every aspect of the process. We invited them to the planning event, scheduled for a week later, and asked them to be involved in creating a community garden that would benefit all families. The ground was tilled that same afternoon. We also engaged them in creating a preschool to provide care for more than eighty children as soon as possible. Resources were needed, space needed to be established, and word of the event needed to reach the entire village as soon as possible.

The Planning Event. We immediately worked with the villagers to organize a weeklong planning event inviting government and university representatives and people connected with resources for village development. A village logo was created, shelters for the workshops built, mandis (bath areas) constructed by wells, and food and lodging organized. The women showed up and situated themselves in the front rows as the event began. Everyone had a chance to speak their hopes and dreams, challenges, and actions to overcome the challenges. Programs were developed and responsibilities assigned.

Clues of Spiritual Revitalization

- New energy is triggered, displayed in sparkling eyes, smiles, and faster gaits.

- Passion is ignited and more "doing" happens as the "being" is accelerated.

- People's lives become balanced as they add a variety of meaningful activities.

- People experience their engagement as significant.

Example

Ibu (meaning mother) Rukiah played the role of village hostess. She was a lady of spirit, probably in her late fifties. She lived with her daughter, who was married to the village leader. Her role was to arrange all social and other events in the village: weddings, guest arrangements, funerals, holidays, and Islamic celebrations. Everyone respected her and acknowledged her role.

Something new happened to Ibu Rukiah a few months after I arrived. We posted an announcement and open invitation of leadership training. Our goal, in one week, was to train twenty-four people (three teams of eight) to facilitate community forums in other villages. We were delighted when many of the illiterate women, Ibu Rukiah included, arrived eager to be a part of the first day of training. It worked well because with our translator's help we taught them how to ask questions, and one who could write recorded the answers. When we configured the three teams we were surprised that everyone was reluctant to have Ibu Rukiah on their team.

Holding to our philosophy that everyone has a contribution to make, we selected and taught Ibu Rukiah specifically to set the context for the community forum. We had images drawn that she could point to as she spoke. Her role was to welcome people and give the "New World/New Human" talk—basically conveying the world in a time of great change in which new technology connected us all and challenges and opportunities were affecting countries and people across the globe. She was to tell people in her village that a new movement was happening where people, working together, focused on addressing challenges and building opportunities. She was to point out that Bubun was a demonstration of how that could happen and invite them to be a part of the movement.

As we traveled across choppy waters to our village assignment, I wondered if it would work. When Ibu Rukiah finished, the entire crowd of people packed in the schoolhouse and gave her a long-standing ovation. A new Ibu Rukiah emerged from that moment forward. She became a visible force in the village, encouraging other women to be health caretakers and to be involved in all the new programs defined in the planning event. When the village "sent me out" nine months later, she had someone write down a poem she created saying we would always be connected and the way to remember was to look up at the moon and think of each other.

Example

Aida was a single young woman, probably in her early twenties. Most young women in this village marry as teenagers. She limped quite dramatically with a leg handicap hidden under her sarong, the common article of clothing all women wore. Aida, as all able women in the village, left at 3 a.m. every morning to go out in the shallow parts of the river to gather karong (shellfish). They arrived back in Bubun mid-afternoon. The karong were loaded on the Desa Pontei boat that went into the market every night to be sold to buy rice and other necessities for family sustenance.

Aida was a front-row participant at the planning event and attended every planning from that time forward. She became the lead person in developing the initial women's industries—sewing and padong (basket and rug) weaving—as well as helping to create a cooperative so rice and other commodities could be bought in bulk, thereby reducing costs for each family. Aida was a busy lady. Her trips into Tanjung Pura, the market city, and Medan, the capital city of North Sumatra, were aimed at making connections with cottage industries, finding instructors, and being the liaison to grow the industries. One day we crossed paths, both on our separate missions. She was radiant, walking at an unbelievable pace, calling out to me, "Bubun bergerak maju!" which translates, "Bubun is on the move."

Example

Fatimah, the wife of the village leader, was one of two to three women in the village who had some education. She was a quiet, unassuming woman, playing the role of housewife and mother, expecting her fourth child when we arrived. During the first week after our arrival, a preschool was created and immediately more than eighty children were enrolled, freeing up women to play other roles. Fatimah, beaming, took responsibility for coordinating the sewing of uniforms, developing curriculum, and training other teachers. Soon she was making contacts in Medan for resources and began training women in other villages to create their own preschools.

Example

Sutiah was dutifully a wife, mother, and cook, the wife of Layah and mother of Merci. Her second child was on the way and it was obvious it was not her desire or choice to be on the leadership team in a fishing village. She sulked a lot, especially when she discovered her translation abilities were needed in so many capacities. It was important for us to be a role model for her, teaching her how to be a coach as she worked with the various programs. It was wonderful to see the new Sutiah emerge, catalyzing so many women to take responsibility for their futures, moving as a team, and replicating the work of Bubun in another village.

These are just a few of the many lives transformed in a few short months. Bubun became a demonstration village for North Sumatra because the people evolved and made the difference. My Bubun experience reinforced my coaching belief that every human being, in any remote part of the world, has the potential for growth and fulfillment, which is what coaching is all about. After many years, Bubun continues to be the most profound coaching experience I have had.

Summary

Coaching with Spirit appears to be an international phenomenon. I concede the sample is small and offer no statistical evidence as to the accuracy of my data. I do find it telling that those international coaches who chose to respond offered stories demonstrating the three key principles of spirituality as bedrock for their work. Self-selection may be the reason and, as it is outside of the scope of this book, I leave it to others to explore further.

We have broadened horizons by peeking into the world of executives and traveling abroad to other lands. Next we open the windows wide to see what coaching with Spirit looks like from those with the greatest visibility in the profession, our coaching leaders. The next chapter brings us into the minds, hearts, and spirits of prominent coaching leaders, selected because of their prominence and influence in this field. Diane Hetherington, the interviewer and a senior coach and coach trainer herself, begins by sharing her passion for coaching with Spirit, suitably setting the stage for the interviews. After reporting the results of the interviews, she provides an added bonus, a list of thirty-five practical and philosophical tips offered to anyone who wishes to increase the ability to coach with Spirit. To conclude, Hetherington weaves the patterns together to exhibit the coaching with Spirit fabric. It is amazing how many commonalities abound among our coach leaders.

CHAPTER
10

Coach Leader Perspectives on Coaching with Spirit

Diane Hetherington

I BELIEVE EVERY ONE OF US is on a spiritual journey, whether we are aware of it or not. When I coach with Spirit, I hold sacred space for my client's exploration in any of the following three intelligence areas: cognitive, emotional, and spiritual. A lot of work has been done in the area of cognitive intelligence and more recently in the area of emotional intelligence. The notion of spiritual intelligence is at once newly defined and as old as Socrates and Plato.

Spiritual intelligence is

- How we address and solve issues of meaning, purpose, and value;

- Our desire to connect to something larger than ourselves;

- What generates our capacity for transformation;

- What allows us to change the rules and to create new possibilities;

- The source of our vision, looking at what can be in the light of what is;

- Our conscience, supporting us in taking a stand to do the right thing; and

- What leads us to generate bottom-line results that support and sustain us.

How do we use our intelligences in an integrated fashion for maximum outcomes? These are learned capabilities, innate potential that can grow and develop over time.

Coaching with Spirit supports that development, helping clients to find meaning in life and to realize full potential—facilitating the discovery of what fosters and what hampers the flow of Spirit. This chapter also offers tips for coaches to nurture their exploration into what supports and hinders them from consistently coaching with Spirit.

Fourteen Coach Leaders' Viewpoints

What do senior, seasoned coaches believe about coaching with Spirit? Fourteen prominent coaching leaders were interviewed for their perspectives and experiences on coaching with Spirit, some by email, most by phone. Many coached before there was a profession called coaching; many are coach mentors and trainers. They coach for leadership development and they educate executives to use and teach coaching in their organizations; they coach for organization change and to create coaching cultures; and they support clients in career development and creating success.

I asked the following questions:

1. What does coaching with Spirit mean to you?

2. What is your experience of coaching with Spirit?

3. What thoughts do you have regarding coaches/coaching and Spirit?

4. If you were to give one specific suggestion to coaches who want to coach with Spirit, what would it be?

First, read the responses from questions 1 through 3, attending to any similarities and differences beyond the individual's style of expression. At the end of this chapter is a list of suggestions—ABCs to increase your coaching with Spirit—that I culled from the interviews that will support coaches to develop their spiritual intelligence to coach with Spirit.

Julio Olalla, President, The Newfield Network

I have been coaching for about eighteen years, since before it was called coaching. I began in 1983 in Canada and to this day I say that I love my chosen path and am very grateful I have taken it. Coaching with Spirit evokes a lot of things to me.

The Intuitive Response. Coaching offers an intuitive response in the world today. There is a lack in this area. We have focused so much in the arena of the conceptual and left out the human dimension. We are called to a full expression of life. I see a desire for that learning connection. Capital technology comes cheap. We need to learn ways to work and be together. People need to generate meaning and purpose and to connect with their work. This calls for inclusion of the fullness of the human experience— emotional, biological, and conceptual. Leave out any of these and something is missing. We need to embrace the wholeness of human experience in the act of learning.

Profound Trust. Profound trust is required as coachees are listened to with all their concerns and know they are able to include every piece of themselves and their issues as part of the learning process.

Mystery. A good part of coaching is in the realm of mystery, no matter how brilliant the coach. We never see the full person in front of us. We need to accept that. The moment we think we know fully, we become so righteous we cannot coach.

Listen for the Passion. Coaching with Spirit means the ability to listen for the passion, for what moves the coachee. The coach engages in a close, deeply felt connection, not in a detached approach. In our society we miss the ability to have intimacy. Coaching is somehow a very intimate conversation dealing with profound issues. It requires a lot of trust to build tremendous empathy.

I feel privileged daily and blessed to connect to so many different human beings. I experience a permanent connection with gratitude.

Observe Yourself Observing. Human beings often confuse assumptions with reality. When people cross the threshold of being able to actually observe themselves observing, that is a beautiful moment. People express deep gratitude for that moment, that opening. My whole life in coaching has included an incredible number of people who have expressed that gratitude.

Enlarge the Frame. A coach generates a lot of humility in the best sense by supporting the coachee in transcending the smallness of the self. A person faces huge issues placed in a small frame. As we enlarge the frame, the issue becomes small in the large frame and allows the coachee to transcend. That moment of transcending the self is a very spiritual experience, opening one to the mystery and magic of life.

By enlarging the frame, clients break the small jacket of rationalism. Very often I receive letters thanking me for that experience. It is not religious. Many had thought this only belonged to the religious, and it is not so.

With a Spirit of Service. I cannot think of coaching without a spirit of service. Without a sense of service, gratitude, and love, coaching becomes mechanical. Look at your transformation and then coach from service. Do not be afraid of your wounds. Your wounds are assets; when *you* have been there, you are more able to honor and respect where your client is.

Coach more in the spirit of serving the coachee than in the perfection (or great wisdom) of the coach. I am continually amazed at how little we know, at how much pain is there. This is a more serious issue than professional ability.

Frederic M. Hudson, Ph.D., President, The Hudson Institute of Santa Barbara, California

Coaching with Spirit, the centerpiece of all coaching, means working from the deepest place within the client. It might be called "the center," "the soul," or "Spirit." What it is called does not matter. What does matter is that the place that seeks coaching transcends the ego needs and wants of the client. Such a place is characterized by some of these qualities: urgency, ultimate concern, quest, yearning, feeling empty or full, seeking deep, being sick of usual and banal, and a sense of ego transcendence. The coach meets soul with soul, Spirit with Spirit. Spiritual coaching is not so much about words or conversations, but about a spiritual relationship between two people on a shared journey. That relationship is the potent center of transformation.

All of my coaching is coaching with Spirit. I begin with the topics and concerns the client brings and then search through questioning for the deeper yearnings implicit in those topics and concerns.

A Third Ear. The coach must have "a third ear" for spiritual discourse, or else the relationship with the client is not spiritual coaching. The coaching relationship becomes more of a peer coaching quest, as the client and coach share words about the journeys they are on. The coach maintains a clear distinction between false spirituality (the "fluff" of the nonmaterial world) and true spirituality (those words and images that bring life, mission, and human connections into perspective).

Fran Fisher, M.C.C., President, Academy for Coach Training; Founder, Living Your Vision®

Coaching is the sacred space of unconditional love where learning, growth, and transformation occur naturally. Coaching is a spiritual process incorporating all aspects of us. It is here today as a modality whose time has come, emerging naturally out of the human consciousness as a new level of our human development. Coaching supports us in our spiritual quest, and every single client and student validates this. Underneath whatever a client wants to accomplish is a desire to increase satisfaction—that is, a spiritual quest.

Coaching is transformational. The presence of Spirit is the essence of the human being, the individual. As coaches our job is to support clients in accessing their essence and learning how to manifest that essence in every aspect of their lives.

Coaching is a spiritual process—a process of empowerment—and something that rubs off. When I ask coaches what they love most about being a coach, the response is usually about their own personal transformation. Hanging around coaching calls them to do their own personal work. It is a "walk your talk" profession.

D.J. Mitsch, President, The Pyramid Resource Group; Past President, ICF

Coaching with Spirit means coaching through the voice of Spirit—a power both within and yet bigger than the coach and client. It means energetic connections transcending the direction of our minds as we listen and respond to the most compelling voice within.

I view the pyramid, our company logo, as a symbol of going beyond what is known into a state of discovery. In my life I have learned we are truly spiritual beings having a human experience, living in a human body, reacting to situations, learning to love others. It is from that perspective, going beyond what is known, that I coach people and am surprised and delighted by what they are capable of being and doing when they listen to the wisdom of their spirits. Most create the experience of attracting, as if by magic, what they most want. They have all become purposeful in how they live and work. The key formula to accessing the hero within is to surrender, tell the truth, clarify intention, and accept that all is well. I follow this formula to help access the voice of Spirit in coaching conversations.

A Spiritual Conversation Beyond. Coaching in any language on the planet gives people access to their truths and inner wisdom. Coaches are here to work beyond the barriers of language, culture, and religion to help people answer the quintessential question: "Why are we here?" And perhaps the answer is that we are here to learn who we really are as spiritual beings. It may even be bigger than that—it may be we are here to learn to really love others.

Coaching is a spiritual conversation designed to access wisdom, and wisdom is the soul's consistent message or truth. Coaching is a context for a conversation waiting to happen—it is about the exploration and not something to know from the mind. Trust and be present to the process of discovery and synchronicity!

Linne Bourget, M.B.A., Ph.D., Executive/Change Leadership Coach

Coaching with Spirit means three things to me, from the most mundane to the most exalted: (1) to have a high positive view for the client and be an advocate for the very best, highest level of client success and happiness; (2) to use my highly developed intuitive guidance, to listen to that little voice guiding me in what to do and say and what the client needs; (3) to say a prayer or invoke spiritual connection before I start a meeting. I may ask for special help for a client who is going through difficult times or I may share directly with my client a spiritual perspective.

I am a fifth-generation spiritual intuitive and have always included intuition as part of my work. I have a spirit-based practice. Most of my clients do not know and would not be comfortable knowing that fact. In talking with colleagues over the years, I realize my clients have been able to move through their issues more quickly, to develop a much more positive sense of themselves, and to achieve positive results. There is less suffering and difficulty in the process I take my clients through.

Coach Only Where Clear. Be clear on your spiritual purpose and your own spiritual path and be able to honor those of your clients, even when dramatically different from your own. Where your spiritual path is not clear, you cannot be effective in coaching people; coach where you are clear, not where you struggle. It may be tempting to work through your problems with your clients, but it is not professionally responsible. Healed wounds need to come to a critical mass of clarity on an issue before you can hold yourself out as an expert.

Seek Deeply Trained Coaches. Coaching with Spirit is valuable and vibrantly helpful for clients, if applied by "deeply trained" and highly responsible coaches. Deeply trained means two things: (1) having expertise in the content of your client and (2) having skill in your own personal and professional process. It means you have done your homework, can get out of your own way, and can be available for the client.

The downside is that right now coaching is fashionable and some coaches and clients are overly eager to jump into Spirit without adequate preparation. While coaching looks easy, in fact, it is not something everyone can do. It is important to be able to put your own needs aside and come from an unselfish place.

Rich Fettke, Speaker, Coach, and Author

Coaching with Spirit means connecting with those parts that have people feeling fully alive—in other words, finding what is truly inspiring to the client while still honoring what is inspiring to me. In my coaching, clients often do something they did not believe they could do. When people overcome fears or push what they call a personal limit in their past, they feel this aliveness. They see more clearly what is around them.

Sometimes I take clients out on a 100-foot rappel, or a rock climb, or a bungee jump. They say, "No way am I going to do that!" Then an hour later they do it! For the rest of the day, the week, the month, and often the rest of the coaching time they say, "Thank you so much for inspiring me to do that. I have applied the same lessons I learned out there to my business life and it is amazing. I feel very fulfilled."

Coaching is absolutely vital. People want to feel alive. They want to live with spirit and enthusiasm. As humans we are compelled to grow and learn, beginning with that first crawl or step. Coaching with Spirit allows people to keep honoring this need to learn.

Agnes Mura, M.A., M.C.C.; Master Executive Coach; President, Agnes Mura, Inc.

What coaching means to me is something very practical. My background in learning to live a spiritual life is practical and eclectic; I learned as much from Christianity and Judaism as I learned from Buddhism and other Eastern philosophies and Zen.

I consider myself a secret agent for the forces of Spirit from inside the mainstream. I think that the power of transformation cannot come from just sitting on a mountaintop and meditating. Transformation has to come from the practice of everyday values, like integrity and respect, honoring the unity of all things and all people, searching for the common ground, and skewing bigotry of any sort.

Practicality.   These are practical principles of living and the foundation or the common thread of most religions. I do not ask people what they believe. I watch how they live and then I tell them what beliefs their lives prove out. This is, in fact, a major part of my coaching. I look at the discrepancies between what people say and what they do—the espoused vision and the lived vision. No matter what they think they believe, I tell them that what they live is a belief that looks different. I consider what people do and how they act toward and speak of others to be the real proof of their spirituality, no matter what theory they have learned or what they do on Sunday morning.

Taking a Stand on Values.   I find enormous common ground with people from a multitude of different backgrounds and I am hired often for multicultural situations. These are cultures I am not directly familiar with, and yet I find easy common ground based on those fundamental values that have guided my life. I literally require my associates and my clients and my friends to take a stand on these values. They do not have to agree and they do not have to follow them, and I will provoke a conversation that makes them take a stance in that regard.

Breakthroughs and Shifts Come from Attitude Changes and Changes in Perspective, not from Efficiency Tricks.   It is hard to think of any coaching relationship where coaching with Spirit is not at the core. If we are not careful as coaches, we can become an organizer of people's lives. We can get lost in the goal setting and implementation tricks, and just get people to be more efficient. That is a big trap for coaches! We learn techniques and can feel quite fulfilled as a coach because we achieve some results.

Practical spirituality for me is something transforming the way someone sees people, not just the way somebody thinks about immortality.

Great Coaches Have a Few Grey Hairs.   Regarding qualifications and competencies of a great coach, I think there are a lot of good coaches, yet what makes a great coach? Great coaches have a quality of presence from having lived and understood the principles of how life works over the years. They tend to have a few gray hairs, sometimes premature gray hairs, because of what they have overcome.

It is important for senior high-achieving, successful, authoritative executives and business people to feel they have a peer sitting across from them. This calls for a good spiritual foundation, the sense of having overcome a few things and having built character in the course of the vicissitudes of life. There are some principles in how to overcome obstacles and how to sustain success and recover from mistakes and mishaps from the valleys of our lives. We have some common traits; character building creates a lot of spiritual foundation.

Spiritual Practice. Authenticity, courage, and the comfort to be completely genuine in the moment allow me to be *intuitively open.* In order to have antenna sharp and open, we have to be relaxed and comfortable, to be *genuine in our skin.* If we try hard to wear a mask or "tighten" our brain, or if we create tension anyplace, then we cannot hear what is already there. The capacity to relax, to *stay in the moment,* and to stay authentic and genuine only comes through spiritual practice.

And, finally, there is the principle of *not needing to own the results*—not failures and not successes, not having to own them as a coach and not needing the client to own them either. We stand together and admire the landscape. We stand together—arm in arm—looking at what we have created together in front of us and admiring the landscape. It is not anybody's; it is a phenomenon we have allowed to grow. We did not cause this. We just got out of the way; we did some things right and we look at the wonderful productivity that emerged. It is not about the ego. I do not think coaches can afford to have ego. I do not think clients need to have ego when it comes to creativity.

Bobette Reeder, Personal and Mentor Coach; ICF President 2002

Coaching with Spirit means having complete faith in the wisdom and energy of my clients, as well as that of myself, and allowing me to hear and act on that wisdom. When I touch that spiritual place while coaching, both the client and I can actually feel the energy. As a coach, I strive to experience that in every session, that is, true coaching mastery. The energy flows; I just hit it right on. It happens when I bypass my brain and connect directly from my heart/soul/wise self to my mouth. It is a powerful experience for us both, and the client has an opportunity to take a quantum leap! Celebration ensues. It requires hyperfocus and total relaxation simultaneously. I work on it all the time.

Be Selective About Clients. My recommendation for coaches who coach with Spirit is that they be extremely selective about clients. Work with clients you have more faith in than they have in themselves. Hold that faith steadfastly; become fully aware of your internal voice and know the message it brings is always true. Coaching with Spirit comes from that point of truth. Share it with no fear!

Exceptional Coaches Bring Spirit. The only way to achieve mastery is by including the spiritual realm in actual coaching. That is often what separates the well-trained coach from the exceptional coach. One can be well-versed in skills and techniques of coaching (and these are critically important), but if coaches are never able to tap into their spiritual selves, they will never reach the ultimate level of coaching. Exceptional coaches bring an added value to their clients through spiritual connection, spiritual knowing, and spiritual truth—not "woo woo"—just something greater than facts, strategizing, and method.

Marcia Reynolds, President, Covisioning; Past President, ICF

I am open to the possibility that there are other forces and sources of wisdom available to help me when I am coaching. I have to be in a space where I am comfortable, with a clear mind and no personal agenda. If I am focused on my client 100 percent, the right questions and guidance always seem to appear.

I am amazed at the significant work that can be done quickly when I coach with Spirit. We seem to move from problems to possibilities many times over in only thirty minutes.

Julie Schniewind, Business Coach

My own definition of coaching with Spirit is to have clients' best interest always at heart and to believe that they are capable of being more effective with the right support. The spirit of what I do is being someone's personal advocate. People trust me. They believe I have no agenda but their own. My own intentions are quite clear. I am not selling a product. There is no known outcome. I have a process if they need to see it, and we hardly ever stick to my process.

Emotionally I think the words coaching and Spirit have very positive connotations. Too often these days, the words coach, Spirit, and spirituality are trivialized. Deep sighs and rolling eyes greet the words, as if the topic is mystical, not practical or useful. I would like to be known as a coach with Spirit; yet I would not be surprised at being devalued because of this aspect, and that makes me sad. As a business coach, Spirit is given but not promoted by me.

Spirit is an internal thing to me. When I live my life as though I embody the Spirit in which I profess to believe, and when I approach others as though they have the Spirit in them, I am honoring Spirit.

When I can get to that preverbal part that all of us are born with, I can have a richer experience with the other being. When I come from Spirit, I trust others come from Spirit. It has been a significant learning to realize I did not have to like my clients in order to work with them. My job is to find out what value they have to add and to support that development.

John Seiffer, Owner, The SmallBusinessCoach; Past President, ICF

Coaching with Spirit means taking into account all the things we cannot hear, smell, see, taste, or touch. This includes emotions, hunches, being in flow with the universe, and wisdom—both personal and universal. I try to be open to everything out there in the world, yet detached from any explanation or doctrine. Being open helps give clients the space to be who they are while doing what they do.

I find coaching with Spirit works best as an undertone or something that informs *how* I work. If I try to make Spirit *what* I work on, then Spirit seems to disappear or lose effectiveness.

Travis Twomey, M.C.C., Coach

When I get out of my way, I allow Spirit to come in. Something happens when two people come together. If I am in the process of guiding someone and I have an attachment to a particular outcome, Spirit has a hard time overcoming my intellect. When Spirit comes in, I am able to let go and the client is able to let go. Spirit often shows up in coaching while we are on the road to creating the results we want. Many times the results we want come from some other source—for example, Mom, Dad, and other significant people in our lives. Results coming from Spirit often involve working with purpose and passion—whatever is unique to a person's way of being in the world.

Powerful Questions. Spirit first shows up with some powerful questions. I start focusing the energy present during this process. I can see body language changing, indicating the person is more than just pondering. A powerful question is one in which clients do not have a ready answer because it is a question about something to which they are not paying attention, for instance, "What about this job makes you stay?"

I develop a relationship with the client, allowing Spirit to show up. Like air, it is always there, and I may not be breathing it—I may be holding my breath. I really care about my clients and do not have attachment to their outcomes. Coming from compassion can really encourage people to let go of their defenses.

Coaching with Spirit is one of the ways I work with people, not the only way. I think it is the best way and it is only one way. Spirit is so powerful that the first time someone becomes aware of it can be scary.

How to Become Comfortable with Spirit. Find a discipline and do it. Before enlightenment: chop wood, carry water. After enlightenment: chop wood, carry water. Any discipline will work. Unless you are in tune with your own Spirit, you will not notice when Spirit shows up in your coaching. You may try to force Spirit, and Spirit will not be forced. Spirit shows up based on how you *are* in the world—not on what you do. Coaching with Spirit can become just another technique, and then we might become attached to a particular outcome. Our challenge, and we are being paid to accept it, is to let go of outcomes. Just let go.

Chris Wahl, M.A., Ed.D., M.C.C., Director, Coaching Certificate Program, Georgetown University

Coaching is getting at what really matters to people. Once you have been coached, your ability to see things in new ways benefits others—your staff, your colleagues, even your children. It is a gift that keeps on giving.

Executive coaching is about awakening the compassionate side of people and exploring ways to practice compassion in a business setting, always remembering that the person across the table is another human being. I help people remember themselves in a business setting. The wisdom is inside. I work intuitively and practically and tap into clients' intuition. The more they bring their spirit to work, the better they lead.

Spaciousness. I offer spaciousness, giving space to feel and be who you are. Clients experience the spark and joy of that space and give it to others, creating an alchemical reaction. When people allow themselves space and experience what that does inside, it gets harder and harder for them to go back to that old constricted way of being. When clients are able to create this space and relate their experiences, they say they are kinder to themselves. I help them find ways to bring more awareness into their lives, so they can make distinctions about the choices they have. I see the potential the client cannot see.

I work to be spacious. I worked with one man who was living very small, inside a narrow worldview that had two boundaries: (1) meet everyone else's expectations and (2) get ahead. He viewed himself as sick (having had a recent illness) and was also a high achiever. With a big job to do in his work, he did not feel up to it. In order to do his job differently, he needed a different worldview. How does this "living small" person begin to fill the shoes he needs to fill? He needed a partner. We started with little things—for example, letting go of reading nine newspapers per day. This created more space for him, and, after practice, he realized that he could make other similar choices about how to spend his time. I was very challenging and he took it all in, doing everything I suggested. He began to chart a new path that included speaking up, speaking out, and honoring his most essential (soul) needs. Achieving transformation and finding his wholeness again, he has been promoted twice, both times after being publicly recognized for his leadership.

Hannah Wilder, Ph.D., Principal, Wiseheart Global Leadership Coaching

Coaching with Spirit means coaching within a consciousness of an unseen web connecting everyone. When a coach is conscious of this, amazing things happen. This web has been described in Japanese Zen as Indra's Net, when a drop of water or crystal reflects (at each joining point in the net) not only all other crystals, but all reflections in all other crystals. Whatever each one of us does is seen and known by everyone else at some level. We are never alone, and how we think and act reverberates throughout the world. We are also guided by our knowledge received through this net. When we live in mindfulness, everything we think and do becomes sacred and known at some deep level.

I have had clients who were close to death or who were suddenly in a situation in which someone close to them was dying. I was the person somehow chosen to speak with them at this time. I knew if I was as mindful and open as possible I could hear them at a deep level, and truth and wisdom would come through me to them in the way needed in that situation. When I am coaching at this level, I become very quiet, grounded, focused, asking for the courage to tell the truth and hear the truth as well.

Coach as a Shadow. Working with leaders is sometimes just as sacred as experiences with ill or dying people, because they live with tremendous pressures and many people rely on their discernment. It is important that they know and trust themselves and the source of their wisdom. For them I am a shadow leader, modeling balance, discernment, the ability to make clear decisions and take courageous action when necessary, and the knowledge of when to follow. Knowing I am behind them and I stand for them allows them to be aware of the unseen web of support. They become stronger within and act from that strength.

Where clients are challenged, I am able to stand for them when it becomes difficult for them to stand for themselves; in those times, I remind them of their own spiritual strength. This may take many different forms. When I first begin with clients, I try to find out their spiritual resources so I can call on those in times when they feel challenged, afraid, or lose touch with those resources.

One leader, for example, often spent much time worrying and even lost sleep, especially after certain board meetings. I knew she was a strong Christian so I asked her if she thought the other people were protected by God as she herself was. She replied, "Yes, I do." So I reminded her that if her faith was strong, she could relax and allow God to take care of whatever was left after she had done her best. She saw how her faith and prayer could be much more powerful than worry. Worry demonstrated a lack of faith!

We coach with Spirit if we are aware both of the connection to Spirit and our responsibility to be as aware as possible of the influences flowing through us to others.

All Forms of Spirit. I am concerned when Spirit is perceived as one particular form or another—prescriptive Spirit, you might call it. I am uncomfortable when I hear people say they only want to work with people who have the same spirituality they themselves practice.

As I see it, spirituality may take many forms, and there are common principles to most of those forms. Awareness, compassion, loving kindness, doing no harm, respecting the commitments and property of others, valuing creative development, and sharing one's gifts are among the principles of most forms of spirituality.

These principles promote balance and harmony and help everyone achieve his or her potential within a context of mutual trust.

Coaching Pointers

Following are thirty-five specific suggestions and pointers from coach leaders to assist those who wish to increase their ability to coach with Spirit.

ABCs to Increase Your Coaching with Spirit

- Accept and value the differences people bring. Remember, whatever people do works for them at some level.

- Be open to different forms of spirituality, to a variety of expressions of Spirit.

- Be willing to be quiet and listen to the voice of Spirit in yourself and others.

- Communicate with fellow coaches about the spiritual side of coaching.

- Contribute and be of service where you are the best.

- Cultivate generosity and gratitude.

- Discover and own your magnificence by doing your personal work to clear the blocks to the full expression of your authentic self.

- Do not try too hard.

- Engage in follow-up coaching—the integrative phase for yourself as well as your client.

- Find a spiritual partner for sharing your own (and his or her own) spiritual concerns, experiences, and yearnings, seeking out persons you find to be profoundly spiritual and discovering how they became that way and what their callings are.

- Find your own language and style for talking about Spirit.

- Get enough rest.

- Have the communications you need to have. Give the appreciations you feel.

- Hire your own great coach.

- Ignore doctrines or programs that try to be one-size-fits-all.

- Just trust yourself.

- Keep your life clear; let go of whatever clutters your life.

- Know yourself, your intentions, and your boundaries.

- Laugh, cry, and play to find out what keeps you engaged in life in a light and fun and feeling way.

- Learn what it takes to be present and to practice "beginner's mind" when you see people and situations fresh, as if you have never seen them before.

- Make time alone with no agenda; meditate, ponder, wait, pray, listen, and so on. Take an hour a day, an entire day, a Spiritual quest retreat for several days.

- Notice what spiritual and coaching principles you live by. Teach and live those values.

- Open your heart.

- Participate in an activity-based workshop with others.

- Quest for new ways to experience peace and harmony of Spirit. Reconnect with your own spiritual traditions or seek a pluralism of spiritual paths, not one. Live a faith-based life.

- Remember every step you take is necessary for you to get where you are going, including the missteps.

- Spend a day per month in a bookstore to explore what is being written by other like-minded or spirited people. Give more credibility to authors who have been coaching with Spirit for a long time and who know what they are doing.

- Surrender to Spirit. Get your ego out of the way.

- Take some formal training by highly experienced and successful coaches with Spirit.

- Use a personal journal to access your spirit and wisdom. Write your question of the day and then, from your highest and best imagination, record your answer.

- Value yourself and share this value with others.

- Wonder. Enjoy the mystery of life.

- X-ray, recalibrate, and fine-tune your own instrument continually, in all domains—head, body, and feelings—by asking, "What is going on with me?" Be in condition to coach.

- Yes! Sport a positive outlook.

- Zero in on you. Offer yourself a space of unconditional positive regard.

Summary

The common threads for coaching with Spirit are

1. Hold the space of connection;

2. Focus on the client; and

3. Coaching is a transformational experience.

It may be that coaching with Spirit can occur at all three intelligences. First, we ask the right questions and guide clients through problem solving (cognitive). Second, as we are in touch with our emotions and those of our clients, we coach for enhancing emotional intelligence. Third, when we allow Spirit to flow and work with clients ready for deep transformational work, we are coaching spiritual intelligence—an amazing powerhouse!

[*Author's Note:* These interviews were the last material submitted for this book. To preserve impartiality, I did not share with Hetherington the three key spiritual principles I extracted from other sources (my observations, other coaches' comments, executive coaching, and international coaching). Although I should not have been surprised at the outcome, in truth, the recurrence of these three themes is quite affirming. Connection with self, the client, and the whole; being in the present; and accepting responsibility for choices seem to be the elements of coaching with Spirit.]

So far we have heard from coaches—all types of coaches, coaching at many different levels and in different settings. Now it is time to hear what clients have to say. Are clients interested in receiving coaching with Spirit? If indeed spiritual awakening is upon us, how does coaching affect the scorecard?

CHAPTER 11

Fanning the Embers of Client Transformation

SO FAR WE HAVE LOOKED AT HOW COACHES understand and experience spirituality. New coaches, as well as those considering coaching as a profession, wonder how this "spirituality stuff" is received by clients: "It is fine for *me* to be authentic, but if I am open about integrating spirituality into my coaching, will I still attract clients?" In my experience, clients openly welcome, even crave, the integration of spirituality into their coaching process. This chapter focuses on spiritual awakening from the client's point of view. With ten delightfully diverse examples collected by various coaches, we spark interest about what happened to clients, personally and professionally, and what they relay about the experience of having been coached with Spirit. The only instruction I asked coaches to give was for clients, *if* they felt they were coached with Spirit, to write down what the experience was like. In all cases, coaching with Spirit heated clients' desire to learn more about the context of self in the universe.

Ten Examples

Example: Peter D. Coppelman

The year was 1992. I was having a midlife crisis, career crisis, and spiritual crisis all rolled into one. I was fifty years old and had had a very satisfying (if not very lucrative) career as a public interest lawyer. But I had two young children to send to college someday, and I was stopped dead in my tracks by the apparent contradictions of where I was in my career—my need for meaningful work versus my need for more money; being experienced versus being too old; wanting to do what I loved versus not knowing right then what I loved to do; perhaps needing to start over versus it being too late for me to start over.

So on the recommendation of a friend, I went to a coach, and she guided me through perhaps the most important journey of my life.

It took months of struggling; wrestling with my demons; diving as deeply as I could into the innermost core of my being; searching my fifty years of living for those moments when I felt really fulfilled; distilling what it was that made those moments so rewarding; and listing, categorizing, analyzing, and prioritizing my values, skills, interests, aspirations, qualities, desires, talents, needs, strengths, hopes, and dreams.

The scope of the inquiry surprised me. I thought we were going to talk about jobs and career. Instead we talked about life in all of its aspects. Our search for meaningful moments was not confined to professional experiences. The only limits were my memory and my imagination. The list of experiences that we plumbed for remembering what I "had done or achieved that left me feeling truly fulfilled and satisfied" included the births of my two children.

Who was I and who did I want to become? In the end, under my coach's tutelage, I reduced my purpose in life to one sentence: "My purpose is to operate on all cylinders, have faith in myself, and express my uniqueness by advocating for what is right and inspiring others." What a gift! For the first time in my life I could articulate who I really was. I understood my mission in life. I knew what made me unique. I knew why God put me on this earth.

Soon after that, I received a presidential appointment as Principal Deputy Assistant Attorney General, Environment and Natural Resources Division, U.S. Department of Justice. It turned out to be the job I had trained my entire life for, a job perfectly aligned with my purpose. When that job ended with a change in political administration, I used this purpose—and continuing guidance from my coach—to make my next career decision. As my coach says: "In life, your jobs change; your purpose does not."

Example: Jordan Mitchell

An executive in a high-tech firm, I came to coaching with only one desired outcome, to access and use my intuition. Wishing to be more like a giraffe, sticking my neck above my colleagues, I asked to learn about a dormant facet of my ability, my intuition—a facet I observed was more natural for the few women in my company. This meant I had to take risks in a new way, leaving behind piles of data I typically amassed prior to making strategic decisions, my familiar work habit. I had to experience my "gut," my undocumented sense of what was appropriate. After becoming familiar with my unique intuitive physical sensations, I opened to an even bigger risk—trusting. What I learned through coaching transformed my way of leadership, my reputation among peers, and my company's fortune.

On my coaching evaluation form I wrote, "Using my intuition saves me time and makes my job easier. I had thought it to be too risky. Now I am aware I risk losing valuable information when I ignore it."

Igniting Curiosity About Spirituality

One of the common spiritual lessons clients serendipitously learn, even though not specified as a desired coaching result, is to trust patiently the timing of life. The toggle switch of timed synchronicities bounce around like flames until we appear ready. As you will read in this amazing story, Quimby Kaizer participated with her coach in an intricate dance of warm encounters for six years, periodically dipping into each other's lives as they twirled along a path of destiny beckoning them with clues validating the accuracy of their choices. And she became certified during the final proofing!

Example: Quimby Kaizer

Over the course of the past six years working and interacting with my coach, I have learned that everything has its own timing. I cannot rush something needing to take its course and pace and I cannot penalize someone for not being "ready." When one is ready, patient, and trusting—and paying attention—the lesson will be learned, the action taken, or the commitment made. This spiritual lesson was reintroduced several times before I became a coach.

Synchronistically Connecting with My Coach. In my early twenties I found myself drawn to the field of organization development and joined my local organization development chapter. Not knowing what to expect, I attended with an open and curious mind. I do not remember the details or the specific activities of that day except one—I met the person who would become my coach. What makes this interaction spiritual is I sat next to her relatively by chance—as though my only reason for being there was to meet her and be introduced to coaching.

First Step: Commitment. I knew immediately I was interested in coaching certification. As I was just out of undergraduate school, the cost of the program appeared high, given my then-precarious economic position. Could I afford it? Was it worth it? Would I benefit from this investment in myself? Was I ready? So many questions were going through my head. I finally determined I was not quite ready to begin—feeling okay about my decision, no pressure, no "right" answer. It took several months to prepare mentally and financially. When I was ready, my coach was available, without judgment, as though she knew this was exactly the right time to begin.

Purposeful Beginning. When I started the coaching program, I felt as though I had "come home." The concepts and activities were familiar and energizing. My coach and I met on a regular basis, our coaching meetings inspiring and thought-provoking. Without fully realizing the extent of my fundamental insights and personal shifts, I completed the beginning program segments feeling more centered, clear, and purposeful, personally powerful and focused.

Coaching enhanced what was already working well for me and allowed me the space, comfort, and safety to explore areas causing me trouble or confusion. At my fifth or sixth meeting, one of my key results became real. I decided to start a master's in business administration (MBA) program that fall; my life and priorities changing once again. A new demanding workload consumed all my time, so coaching meetings become infrequent during that first year. Again, this was okay; we never had assumptions about how we worked together, remaining flexible and taking coaching opportunities as they arose.

Life's Curves Bring Fortuitous Events. Almost two years passed after I began the coaching program. Finishing my MBA, I started a new job and wrote my coach goal into my career development plan. However, the timing was not right, again—being newly married, starting a new job, and buying my first home. Boy, was I not ready! Once again my coach and I were sure that the right time would present itself.

Over the course of the next three years, I experienced a few "chance" events. On one occasion I bumped into my coach's husband. A sign to restart certification? I wondered, but questions still plagued me. Was I ready? Was I capable? Could I afford it? Would the company assist with the tuition? Was the focus mainstream enough? Did I have enough time? No, not ready yet.

Another year elapsed. While shopping for a new car, I bumped into my coach in a car dealership. What a coincidence. Or was it? Just another gentle reminder from the universe asking, "Are you ready now?" This time, the answer was "yes." I was determined to integrate coaching into my work, thereby appropriately applying for tuition assistance. *I* still had to take a risk and actually ask my company: "What if they say no? Whom do I approach?" I did not act yet.

A Happy Ending—or Beginning. During a two-week vacation I fully committed to presenting my proposal the week I returned. Although I was nervous about the outcome, I felt confident in my decision to pursue this long-awaited event.

My proposal was submitted and accepted within twenty-four hours, and I began coaching two clients before the end of the month. Spirit's synchronicities and interventions taught me that when I am ready and committed the universe supports me. It just requires me to trust, be patient, and stay aware. Now I enjoy sharing this lesson with my own coaching clients.

Interpreting Synchronicities

Kaizer's story holds the combustible space for both inaction (patience and trust) and action (pursuing a master's degree and requesting financial support from work). This dichotomy resolves at the spiritual level where synergistic sparks of allowing and taking steps can coexist harmoniously. In the same way in the next story, Bren Hudson's path to coaching reminds us that synchronicities still need to be interpreted to define contextual meaning before right action can be taken. Hudson's synchronistic experiences raked her rational mind over coals, lighting the match that fired up her spiritual journey.

Example: Bren Hudson

Disillusioned with my career as a consulting senior manager in a "Big Six" accounting firm, I often swung from being frustrated and high-strung to being tired and depleted. Even though I was earning my master's degree from Johns Hopkins University, I knew there was more to becoming an executive, a partner in this firm. No real direction or clear path to partnership was identified. I knew I needed more executive presence for me to be noticed for advancement.

Finding My Coach. Returning by airplane from a conference in New York, I picked up an article about personal coaching. I did not even know that this profession existed. Being a former athlete, I certainly understood the importance of coaching, so I decided to call the coach nearest to my home and book a complimentary session. During this meeting, I felt joy and serenity. Although the program was different from what I thought I was looking for, I was intrigued by the coach's presence, the structure, and the stated results. The clear methodology for life planning appealed to the consultant in me. I signed up.

Spirituality Is Not Religion. In my first coaching meeting, my coach and I discussed in detail the coaching results I sought in different life areas. When we explored the topic of my spirituality, I said, "I've been there, done that, and I am not doing it again." I told her I grew up Baptist, but as I aged, I had became disillusioned with the church. After listening for a few minutes, she commented, "Spirituality does not have to mean religion." As simple as it sounds, it had never occurred to me that spirituality was separate from religion. That distinction opened a huge door for me.

I now felt free to explore my spirituality; my coach helped me stay open. To understand spirituality better, I pursued an intensive personal research project into various religions. Coaching continually helped me identify next steps on my spiritual path and also provided an avenue to discuss and experience the spiritual concepts I gathered.

After several months of seeking spiritual information on a mental level, I began a daily practice of meditation and yoga—starting to live the principle of mindfulness. The coaching homework helped reinforce my new patterns of behavior. I began to feel lighter and happier. Feeling direction and purpose beyond my career, I realized I was not looking to become a partner in this firm. I recognized the opportunity to use my consulting job to further my own spiritual and personal development and encourage others to do the same. Right where I was in my job, I found meaning. Enthusiastically, I shared my learning with all the young consultants I could reach, trying to open them up to a meaningful life, recommending books and tapes I had found particularly profound.

Living with Spirit Through Change. Living with Spirit has given me greater courage to make significant life changes aligned with my life purpose. At the end of our coaching arrangement, I expressed interest in becoming certified as a coach and started a new organization development job that allows me to continue my growth and use both my consulting and coaching skills to increase excellence in the workplace.

In the past five years, I have transitioned from being driven by my career to following my spiritual path. Learning to use the principles of coaching with Spirit has accelerated my spiritual growth. As I continue to deepen my knowledge and practice of mindfulness, I feel happier, lighter, and energized in all areas of my life.

Kaizer's and Hudson's stories remind us that coaching can serve to keep clients (and coaches) open to Spirit both on the intellectual and physical planes, whether they occur in car dealerships, on an airplane, or even in our own backyards. The following story by Ruth Schuler invites awareness with Spirit through nature, in this case involving the usefulness or uselessness of boundaries. Nature, being neutral in its existence, offers a spiritual opening hard to find in the human world of judgment.

Example: Ruth Schuler

 Upon beginning coaching, I was asked to write my objectives. Trusting my intuition, I wrote, "To feel less transparent and to understand what that means."

Halfway through my coaching meetings, on my evening walk, I reflected on the coaching process and the word "diplomacy" came to mind. It occurred to me that diplomacy might provide part of the answer to my interest in the question of transparency. I hurried home to consult *Webster's* for the definitions of transparency and diplomacy. *Transparency* is the property of transmitting light so that what lies beyond is visible, easily detected, and seen through. It means free from pretence or deceit—readily understood. *Diplomacy* is the skill or tact in dealing with others, a grace that results in a keen sense of what to do or say to maintain good relations. A focused sense of awareness facilitates diplomacy by knowing what to do or say without offending others, which can protect against the vulnerability of transparency.

At the next coaching meeting, my coach asked me to think of transparent things and name their positive and opposing qualities. Scanning nature and our environment for ideas and objects, I produced this table:

Transparent Items	Positive Quality	Opposing Quality
Fish	protected from predators	vulnerable
Leaves	things on other side receive light	limited, fewer options
Cellophane	can see what's inside	things are exposed
Stained glass	creates a mosaic of color	without light loses color
Crystal	focal point for light	can lose sparkle without light
Window	can see out	can see in

Boundaries Can Be Useful. I noticed that these items have barriers or boundaries, which shelter while allowing for visibility. It occurred to me that I could create boundaries in a positive way, not to shut myself away, but as a way to maintain objectivity and perspective while avoiding the confusion inherent in the problems of others. With this type of boundary, along with awareness, any vulnerability to being transparent could be moderated.

From that moment on, as I open myself to receive or give information, a heightened sense of awareness allows me to see beyond clear evidence and notice that which is not readily apparent. I have developed a deeper respect for differentiating when to share my thoughts, when to catch and reframe them before verbal expression, and when to keep them to myself.

Canadian coach Beryl Allport invited several clients to share stories revealing how coach and client can work together in Spirit.

Example: Marsha Gormley

My *Merriam Webster's* dictionary defines spirit as the "active presence of God in human life." To someone spiritual like myself, the active presence is witnessed constantly in a wide variety of ways. In my opinion, this active presence or inspiration is a key ingredient in the communication I experienced in a coaching situation.

I personally was searching (consciously or unconsciously) for a kindred spirit to support, share, and stretch me. Although I have supportive friends and family who encourage and care for me, I was looking for someone with extra skills, strategies, and even stronger belief in the "powers that be" (or should I say "the powers in me"?).

From the synchronistic way my coach and I met to the amazing creative cards I produced, my coaching experience was indeed magical. For example, one day when ready to put away my paints, I was suddenly inspired to paint a heron, the bird totem for my coach. As I had been just playing around in a relaxed, experimental way, the exquisite end product was quite a surprise! I felt "guided from above" and completed it within five minutes. My coach informs me that it hangs on her wall, matted and framed, and is much admired. I do believe when we create we model the creator and get closer to our deepest and most authentic selves.

Example: Dr. Dirk Keenan

I find that the coaching process with my coach (and Spirit) helps me get in touch with the spiritual aspects of my [chiropractic] practice and my own development and growth. By letting go and allowing myself to dream and mentally play, I am able to locate the deeper meanings and roles I have for myself. Coaching, a process that allows me to connect with the spiritual part of me, helps me understand myself better.

Example: Susan Spoke

Spirituality in coaching was revealed through these eight coaching experiences:

1. Discussing spiritual assumptions that we are, or can be, aligned with the universe working on our behalf; and if we put out an idea or intention,

the universe will support us to move in that direction. If we are conscious, we will notice all kinds of synchronicities and can have faith in that support.

2. Visualizing to clear ourselves to receive a higher wisdom to become more centered to our inner wisdom.

3. Assuming we have a purpose in life.

4. Creating space for nonmaterial, spiritual, and personal growth goals on my "Results Game," a prioritized list of what is most important to *me* (Belf & Ward, 1997, p. 63) in my designated "areas of life." In fact, my coach presented these as essential, even when I was inclined to have a long list of shoulds.

5. Choosing qualities such as harmony and balance for my well-being evaluation, qualities for my soul's good, rather than just focusing on material issues.

6. Acknowledging the way in which we are all connected and affect each other through several exercises that support my own ideas of universality and connectedness.

7. Using affirmations, certainly somewhat mystical, assuming that by asserting something it can come into being.

8. Including of lots of inspirational handouts, cards, and reading references.

Example: Bianca Desgroseilliers

Every aspect of my coaching sessions was guided by Spirit. I became open to hearing, receiving, and accepting the messages. Spirit is now ever-present in my life and living.

Coaching changed my life. I am still the same person, but now I have tools to be in control of my life. I was happy and successful before coaching, although I felt a bit too comfortable. I thought coaching would be good for my career, expand my horizons, and help me balance my life. I believe Spirit directed me to my coach.

Coaching brought me new ways of thinking and of evaluating my life. I now work toward having a balanced, happy life because I learned to put my dreams and life purpose ahead of everything else, instead of just feeling successful once in a while. I see my life as full of unlimited opportunities.

"Try," "should," and "must" have disappeared from my lexicon. If I hear myself using them, it is a sign to revisit my coaching exercises. I also learned to reward myself—Spirit encourages self-acknowledgment.

During my coaching, I gained a lot of new understanding and achievements, but the cumulative effect came after my sessions finished. I continued with the exercises and related reading materials; reshaped my attitude and my way of thinking; and started working on creating things in my mind by first visualizing the result or dream. Things become real afterward.

Instead of dreaming about what I could be living, I am living my dreams. I now plan for dreams to become a reality, no matter how impossible they may seem.

Finally, read what Jon Coppelman, principal of a consulting firm helping employers understand risk and people management, emailed his coach after just three coaching meetings.

Example: Jon Coppelman

One of the most valuable lessons of my coaching process was balance. Like most people, I tend to concentrate on my strong areas and let the others slide. When I ranked my twelve key life areas according to importance, I came to "community" and remember thinking I really wanted to do something meaningful in this area of my life. That triggered a process recently culminating in my election to my town's school committee. I am very excited about finding a way to contribute, all from that little exercise.

Summary

Clients highlight the coaching with Spirit process by mentioning life purpose and the power of making purposeful choices to enhance meaningfulness; relearning to trust and access intuition; paying attention to synchronicities; increasing our familiar three connections (with self, with another, and to the whole); emphasizing the "being" part of living; coming from a place of curiosity; having a heightened sense of awareness; trusting more; experiencing manifestation of results and well-being; and being of service. Coaches create the pool for transformation, and clients eagerly dive in.

In coaching we know that the greater the support system a client has, the more likely the results and well-being will be achieved. This is equally true for coaches. How do coaches maintain their ability to serve day after day in the highest and most meaningful way without burning out? We fan client embers, but how do we stoke our own fires? The next chapter offers some insights.

CHAPTER 12   Stoking the Fire

Coaching with Spirit
Learning Communities

ASSESSMENT

Please rate yourself on the extent to which you coach with Spirit.

0 = never; 1 = rarely; 2 = sometimes; 3 = often; 4 = most of the time;
5 = almost always

To what extent do I . . .

0 1 2 3 4 5   have adequate support to keep me in touch with my Spirit?

0 1 2 3 4 5   ask for support to keep me in touch with my Spirit?

0 1 2 3 4 5   participate in coaching events and gatherings to maintain
                    connection?

0 1 2 3 4 5   regularly seek to enhance my coaching with Spirit ability?

SPIRIT IS ALWAYS PRESENT; awareness of its presence fluctuates. So many of the coaches' stories presented in this book inform us about the necessity of remaining open to and in touch with Spirit. Our intellectual and experiential meanderings gave snapshots before, during, and after coaching meetings.

Missing from our review has been the role of support systems for those who coach with Spirit. What support do we have to keep us sourcing our creative coaching volcanoes, to enable us to be fully present in our work, to be of service in the best way possible?

Coaching Learning Communities

Coaching learning communities—supportive communities created by coaching leaders with burning desires for frequent connection—bolster and reinforce the continual presence of Spirit. Whereas a few already exist, I believe they will increase like wildfires as the coaching profession realizes the gifts offered by such communities.

People can align toward a common goal, such as running a race for a cure, without being in community. People can engage in heated discussions, as in community education programs, without being in community. Coaches can coach a group of people in an organization without being in community. Coaching learning communities need all three to be present (coaching, learning, and community) and for the supportive magic to occur.

This chapter presents descriptions by three coaching leaders who have been instrumental in fostering coaching learning communities: The Newfield Network, Professional Coaches and Mentors Association (PCMA), and Success Unlimited Network (SUN).

The Newfield Network

We as individuals and our collective civilization face enormous challenges and realize our traditional interpretations and ways of learning, knowing, and acting are insufficient to address these challenges.

Our traditional, rational, and predominantly scientific ways allow for great advances in science, medicine, our standard of living, and technology; our myopic attention on these ways of knowing brings with it a shadow we have not acknowledged because the light of advancement has been so bright.

One of the major tolls humankind pays is a progressive alienation from our biological nature—an almost epidemic questioning of life's meaning and purpose and a loss of connection with our spiritual side. This crisis will not be resolved within the context of the same vision that created it.

Our Community

The Newfield Network is a community of educators, coaches, business leaders, and other professionals in the United States, South America, and Europe carrying out the challenge of rethinking our interpretation of learning and offering programs on coaching, leadership, and organizational change. We also offer executive coaching to organizations. Our work is led by our founder, Julio Olalla, who for the past nineteen years has facilitated groups using his extraordinary ability to create environments of safety, trust, respect, and well-being that accelerate the potential for learning. The Newfield Network team has trained nearly fifty thousand people in the United States, Canada, Argentina, Australia, Chile, Mexico, Spain, and Venezuela.

Why Coaching?

"Coaching arises with postmodernism. It is a response to the turbulence of the soul," says Olalla. We believe coaching has shown up in our culture as an intuitive response to this crisis of meaning, learning, and knowing. Nothing, in fact, is more central to coaching than learning. Taking care of the coachee's learning is the coach's greatest responsibility. A coach must therefore be, above all, masterful in the domain of learning.

Traditional teaching and consulting, while still important and valuable in some arenas, have left out many of the issues and experiences of what it is to be human. Why is it that problems and issues reappear time after time? What is missing?

Redesigning Learning Practices

We are in search of new ways of creating meaning for ourselves and the relationships we find important—in our communities, families, and workplaces. We are participating in the redesign of learning practices to address the pressing demands we face that traditional interventions, learning, and consulting do not successfully address.

Our commitment is to bring forth and develop other ways of knowing and learning, integrating the wholeness of human experience with nothing left out; to be a bridge between rational, traditional, and other ways of understanding and knowing.

Our vision reflects our deep desire to reconnect with our bodies and emotions, with our imagination and intuition, with Spirit, and with our understanding of consciousness as a broader phenomenon than rationality.

A coach effecting personal and organizational transformation requires a discourse genuinely addressing the entire spectrum of human experience, instead of privileging a narrow segment. Our aesthetic experience, our intuitive experience, our spiritual and mystical experience should be as fundamental a part of our education as our logical, analytical, or material experience.

The process of learning is sometimes likened to birth—nothing can be born without learning. The great challenge and opportunity facing us as coaches is to become truly serious about elaborating a new, well-grounded, multidimensional discourse of learning—one that can address the fundamentally important questions of what it means to be a human being, how we should live, and perhaps even open up the path to achieve a higher level of consciousness, through which we may connect to our worlds in a multitude of ways.

Our learning must address not just our heads, but also our bodies, emotions, souls, and spirits—finding a balance between the conceptual on the one hand and the emotional, physical, and archetypal on the other. Thus, creating ongoing learning communities has become of central importance to our mastery in coaching.

What if we shifted our current way of learning—accumulating knowledge for the sake of producing quick answers—to a higher goal of producing wisdom for the sake of effective living? What kinds of relationships must we create? What kinds of skills do we need to create them? Where do we find this kind of learning?

The Newfield Network community is a place for such learning. More than simply taking another seminar or professional development course, the type of learning we are committed to is about expanding our awareness, living and celebrating the magic that life is, and inventing new ways of acting and problem solving in the world. We cannot do this alone. Participants who enroll in our programs come from a *variety* of professional job roles, including consultants, CEOs, entrepreneurs, educators, counselors, and managers. These participants constitute our ongoing learning community.

Learning in and as Community

A most eloquent expression of our community ideals and values is reflected in our annual gathering, held every year in the beautiful hills of southern Chile. This formal gathering of international graduates from our coaching and corporate programs has become an opportunity not only to explore the richness of our inner lives and our relationships with others, but also to experience a deep reconnection with one another, our shared concerns, nature, Spirit, and the mysteries of life.

We offer a space where we come together with leading thinkers, to explore different fields, such as health, intuition, money, body, and movement, while we expand our training in coaching and our own personal development. A magical space, it incorporates the surroundings of natural beauty with depth of purpose.

The context of this gathering and of our learning community is to allow the magic and the mystery to show up, to allow ourselves the space and time to have conversations we do not otherwise have. Our time together is spent in rich conversation, coaching, meditation, physical activities, lots of dancing, and much more. We do serious learning in a mood of lightness!

In addition to our annual community gathering, we meet throughout the year through teleconferences and in graduate programs with the same purpose—to explore and expand our ways of knowing and acting in the world and to engage in conversations not available anywhere else.

We also think of community as "the place where your gift is received," so our other community gatherings allow each individual to be part of the collective whole through the gift they are. Participants create casual friendships and strategic business alliances and design collaborative work. The diversity in age, gender, geography, culture, and expertise is part of the gift, adding so much to the richness of conversation and learning.

Our community of learners is also a space where individual declarations have a place to be held, nurtured, and supported. For us, learning is not just an individual phenomenon. Powerful learning happens in groups and can be more easily sustained in a community.

Where We Are Headed

As coaches, we must bring our discourse and learning to wider audiences. We must take it out of the hands of philosophers and psychologists and bring it to everyone. We have to take away the gravity and significance of it and show how learning can be undertaken with joy, lightness, and depth.

Contact: Terrie Lupberger, Executive Director, The Newfield Network-usa, LLC; phone: (301) 570-6680; URL: www.newfieldnetwork.com

Professional Coaches and Mentors Association (PCMA)

Headquartered in the United States (Southern California), PCMA has four chapters with four hundred members and volunteer leaders. These chapters offer more than forty-five professional development events and a multi-day international conference. Members of PCMA are usually successful professionals dedicating part or all of their lives to coaching or mentoring. PCMA members usually coach members of organizations more than they coach individuals. The association is independent of coaching certification programs and schools.

Mission

We serve business coaches and mentors and other successful professionals, expanding into these areas by offering the highest quality programs for developing professional skills and building successful practices while also connecting professional coaches and mentors with one another and with the users of their services.

Vision

- Serve professional business coaches and mentors better than any other organization, through community building, networking, and superior professional development.

- Run a financially stable, efficient operation.

- Connect coaches and mentors with those who need them.

- Promote the coaching and mentoring professions by disseminating research and conducting original research in the field.

- Meet the needs of its geographically diverse membership through multiple chapters.

Abundance-Centered Culture

PCMA is known for its abundance-centered culture. Each of our evening events includes networking, a dinner, and a focus on one or two educational segments. Special multi-day "graduate school" events help members create successful practices or businesses. Some chapter events are breakfasts; some are weekend retreats for chapter leaders. MasterMind groups, with elected PCMA leaders as volunteer facilitators, also help members grow by using the "group mind" to each person's advantage. Participants in these splinter groups (eight to ten per group) find the twelve months' membership a boost to their businesses and lives because it keeps them accountable and goal-focused.

Myriad certifying organizations and universities offering coaching certificates and degrees attend the annual PCMA conference, as do members of other coaching associations. They all seem to feel at home in this abundance-based community where "and" (inclusion) has more power than "or" (exclusion).

Giving-to-Get

Giving-to-get is what makes this community of learners unique. Sharing fee strategies, client acquisition tips, and coaching and mentoring each other one-on-one and in small groups is standard practice. So, too, is the mention of a higher purpose—even God— in our public meetings. PCMA leadership retreats are often held at spiritually centered conference centers, where everyone pays his or her own way.

Creating Community

PCMA looks for opportunities to create community learning at every turn. The "wisdom wall" technique is a unique example. In the conference community room, one entire wall is dedicated to the integration of knowledge into wisdom. Each presenter's name and topic are given space on the wall. In that space, participants post comments on what they found valuable to take away with them (called "takeaways"). Others post their thoughts on these takeaways. This growing collection of comments creates ongoing integration of the presenters' material into the attendees' lives. For example, this year's wisdom wall showed rich reaction and re-reaction to Ken Blanchard's concept of a spiritually centered life being key to wholeness. Branching out further, all of the PCMA wisdom wall becomes recorded on the association's website for all to be enriched. [*Author's note:* I have felt the PCMA spirit. It is special.]

Each chapter has an annual program on creating and maintaining abundance and assisting clients to do the same. The group's founder, Dr. Vance Caesar, facilitates these programs. "We try to maintain a culture of gratitude versus scarcity, love versus fear, and abundance versus scarcity in each chapter, on our website, at our annual conference, as well in our day-to-day dealings with each other," he says.

Contact: Vance Caesar, Ph.D., Founder, Professional Coaches and Mentors' Association; phone: (562) 799-5560; email: vance@vancecaesar.com; URL: www. PCMAONLINE.com

Success Unlimited Network (SUN)

Mission

SUN is an international community of personal and professional independent, spiritually focused coaches who inspire and coach people to demonstrate the ability to consistently produce the results they want in all areas of their lives while maintaining and enhancing their well-being.

All coaches have been trained to use the ICF-accredited Success Unlimited Network program, and we share these key values: integrity, service, spirituality, personal discovery, and fun. Our purposes for being in community include to recharge our personal batteries, to revitalize our passion for coaching, to increase coaching skills and competencies, to review coaching basics, to practice coaching, to observe others coach, to learn new techniques, to foster business collaborations, to continue our learning and growth, to share resources and business ventures, to progress toward our business goals, and to have fun.

Ways of Being Together

What do we do when we are together? When we connect we create a space for our gifts to be received. Come with me behind the scenes to see how we do this.

SUN coaches look forward to reuniting in community. It feels like coming home to be among colleagues and friends with shared purpose and vision. We honor the uniqueness of each person's knowledge, skills, expertise, style, and points of view. As a community we embrace our eight key well-being qualities: authenticity, trust, spirituality, support, challenge, fun, learning, and friendship, measuring how we experience these after each retreat.

We gather at the first of four evenings to design our ambiance and sacred center, filled with meaningful objects, personal treasures, and surprises. Throughout our time together, this center serves as a point of focus, a place to harness our collective energy as a group.

Opening our first full day with a process combining speaking circles and the Native American talking stick ritual, we reconnect first in silence, then speak each in turn from our hearts. The one holding the stick speaks; others honor by listening. Typically the content differs from the traditional introduction, with speakers honing in on the truth of the moment instead of bragging about recent achievements. This special process triggers authentic expression, communication, and trust and sets the stage for our way of relating with each other. Vulnerability grows as we move around the circle. "When vulnerability is steeped in grace, there is no vulnerability," observes Beth Hand, an active member of our community. When courage is steeped in curiosity, no courage is required. By being in community we relate with grace and curiosity.

Revisiting Our Vision and Life Purposes

Following opening circle, one of our skilled hybrid coach/organization development facilitators guides us to review the past six months and write what we feel most proud of on three different Post-it™ papers. Proud moments are placed on a three-by-five-foot SUN vision wall chart for all to see. We step back and familiarize ourselves with an overview of recent community priorities. Whether it be coaching teenagers, introducing coaching into academic settings, achieving a public relations coup, creating a new technique, assuming an identity as a new coach, or moving into international waters, pride reverberates as we recognize and acknowledge the contributions we offer to the larger coaching world.

We share our individual life purposes, a welcome way to reconnect and embrace newcomers into our space. The above pieces, now standard at each retreat, create the foundation for what happens next.

Open Space Process

We use "open space technology" (Owen, 1994) to create our agenda—never fully preordained to prevent stale topics or presentations. Open space allows people with a particular passion to claim a topic in the moment, either as a presenter or as a participant. Because we have strong commitment to continual enhancement of our coaching competencies, we always guarantee several hours each day for skills practice. Open space coordinators organize offerings and suggestions according to themes, timeframes, and overall schedules and logistics.

We pay attention to balance, with ample time for networking, quiet time, nature walks, massages, coaching one another, and so on. The natural environments we choose (retreat centers) have been selected to support our practices: meditation, exercise, and nutritionally diverse menus.

On the last day, a closing circle follows a fun celebration and recognition dinner. This circle ritual offers time to reflect and review what we have learned, how we can integrate what we have learned, what we have offered, and what we will do next—because another SUN community event is less than six months away.

Contact: Teri-E Belf, M.A., C.A.G.S., M.C.C., Executive Director, Success Unlimited Network; phone: (703) 716-8374; email: belf@erols.com; URL: www.successunlimitednet.com

Turn Down the Heat

The world is heating up, literally and figuratively. We have pushed many of Mother Earth's hot buttons to the boiling point. How can our collective coaching talent help restore equilibrium?

Into the steamy future we go. . . .

Epilogue
What's Next?
The Space for Coaching

"Like the shadow of the tree, our influence often falls where we are not."

Shakti Gawain, whose books include
Living in the Light and *Creative Visualization*

YOU HAVE JUST GLANCED AT, READ, OR SKIMMED THIS BOOK. This suggests you have some passion, interest, or curiosity regarding coaching. Please take one moment now to check inside—way down inside. Do you hear a calling to be of service as a coach or to become a better coach? If you feel goose bumps pondering this question, navigate further. How do *you* answer the call to make the greatest contribution? What is your best way of facilitating a transformation: individually, in couples, groups, a nation, a continent, a planet? Are you content to be carried along with the status quo or do you feel swept off your feet to go beyond? How might you serve the coaching profession? Better yet, how might you serve the profession to best serve our planet?

My Vision

I envision coaching continuing to grow as an inspiring, meaningful, collaborative, fun profession significantly and strategically enhancing people's lives, from young person to senior citizen. Coaching spawns reflection and sharing. Being a coach is a way of life, not just a windblown collection of skills and competencies. When in coaching mode, I am yarely in the zone, all winds in my favor, and I am the best I can be. Why not provide massive numbers of people at all ages and from all walks of life the opportunity to be coaches and to be coached as well? Participate with me in imagining a world in which there will be:

Coaching Community Circles (CCCs). People will have a circle of coaches supporting them to live more purposefully, in addition to attending CCCs with others. These circles will become models for supportive learning community environments for people to collaborate and to share visions, energy, and resources. Their purpose would be to provide forums encouraging people to talk about their learning and personal discoveries. Wherever they germinate, the turbulence of cultural chaos will be transformed.

The concept of CCCs will be windswept to all arenas of society: schools, prisons, and retirement homes to enhance the vibrant living of elders, business project teams, sports clubs, garden clubs, chambers of commerce, banks, supermarkets, plumbers' unions, singles clubs, family reunions. All arenas will have opportunities to have coaches.

CCCs will breeze around the world capturing people interested and excited in the coaching process as a way of continually clarifying and assessing choices, breathing life into their dreams and wishes. At the outset, trained coaches will be called on to facilitate CCCs, although over time the process will become so familiar to participants a transition to self-management will occur.

Service Professions. Coaches will teach other service professionals, such as trainers, guidance counselors, team facilitators, family therapists, social workers, mediators, healthcare practitioners, and so on, how to use the coaching process to complement their careers.

Schools. A cyclone of excitement will come to school systems as coaches teach teachers to apply coaching principles to facilitate CCCs of students. In these circles—part of the mandatory in-school curricula—students will experience the process of inquiry to enhance personal awareness, responsibility, self-confidence, clear expression, and presentation. A third grader will run with the wind to spend time in her CCC, knowing and feeling the respect and trust given to honoring her uniqueness.

Professional Coaching Associations. As our coaching profession continues to exemplify commitment to integrity, our professional coaching associations will have credibility, leverage, resources, and relationships to activate pilot CCCs in systems not yet engaged in coaching.

Is the Zeitgeist Ready?

When the frontier of CCCs has reached a critical number of people, dialogues about personal discovery will happen in every venue with feelings of enthusiasm, authenticity, and connection as customary experiences. Are we ready now to create this explosion of enrichment?

I have a vague memory of a grant awarded to a school system in Pennsylvania around 1965 for the creation and implementation of something called "Magic Circles." I suspect these might have been akin to coaching circles, yet the barometer of change was not ready for this type of transformation so, unfortunately, they disappeared into the fog of academic oblivion. Other attempts have probably gone out to sea due to a lack of champions to wisp them into the mainstream channel or due to sinking in the turbulence of competing priorities.

Because of the work we do, everyone will know his or her life purpose and use it to make life choices from the mundane to the significant. As the velocity of benefits increase, coaching will become a way of life—a way of relating to everyone with purposeful integrity—a highly contagious way of being!

Appendix
Coaching with Spirit
Assessment

Instructions: Take the following assessment to establish a baseline of your own thoughts and behavior relative to coaching with Spirit. Circle the number from 0 to 5 that best describes your most familiar belief or action for each of the 115 items. After you experiment with these ideas and practices for six to twelve months, retake the assessment. I have observed it takes about five or six months for people to develop new habits and truly integrate them into their daily lives. So be patient. Change (externally measured) and transition (internally measured) take time. *Please* do not forget to adopt the child's mind of wonder *and* have fun in the process.

The Relationship Between Coaching and Spirituality

Please rate yourself on the extent to which you coach with Spirit.

0 = never; 1 = rarely; 2 = sometimes; 3 = often; 4 = most of the time;
5 = almost always

To what extent do I . . .

0   1   2   3   4   5   believe spirituality is a natural part of who we are?

0   1   2   3   4   5   believe Spirit can partner with me in coaching?

0   1   2   3   4   5   believe that people can learn their life's purpose?

0 1 2 3 4 5   continually ask myself, "How can I be of service now?"

0 1 2 3 4 5   guide clients' awareness to the purposefulness
of circumstances?

0 1 2 3 4 5   believe growth can come from challenges and problems?

0 1 2 3 4 5   know what my life lessons are?

Subtotal: _____

Connection with Self

To what extent do I . . .

0 1 2 3 4 5   remember to return to my center when thrown off track?

0 1 2 3 4 5   believe I have the inherent ability to learn life lessons?

0 1 2 3 4 5   deal with the issue bigger than the one in the moment?

0 1 2 3 4 5   detach from my client's outcomes and results?

0 1 2 3 4 5   know with certainty that my clients have their own answers?

0 1 2 3 4 5   prepare myself spiritually before meeting a client?

0 1 2 3 4 5   begin meetings with a moment of silence, centering,
or stillness?

0 1 2 3 4 5   have techniques to calm my mind?

0 1 2 3 4 5   honor my own needs during a meeting?

0 1 2 3 4 5   keep perspective on the balance between doing and being?

0 1 2 3 4 5   look to see where I am negatively charged when I encounter
negativity?

0 1 2 3 4 5   check my internal physical state for information during
coaching?

0 1 2 3 4 5   check my emotional state for information during coaching?

0 1 2 3 4 5   hold up a mirror and reflect where I relate to my clients' issues?

0 1 2 3 4 5   take time afterward to assess how I experienced each client meeting?

0 1 2 3 4 5   take time to check my intuition?

0 1 2 3 4 5   recognize when I hear the voice of Spirit through my intuition?

0 1 2 3 4 5   trust my intuition?

0 1 2 3 4 5   act on my intuition?

0 1 2 3 4 5   appropriately let go of plans and expectations during a meeting?

Subtotal: _____

Connection with the Client

To what extent do I . . .

0 1 2 3 4 5   avoid seeking acceptance from my clients?

0 1 2 3 4 5   consider it unimportant to "make a difference" in my clients' lives?

0 1 2 3 4 5   automatically relate to my clients' highest potential?

0 1 2 3 4 5   allow myself to go into the void during a meeting?

0 1 2 3 4 5   trust that what emerges is perfect?

0 1 2 3 4 5   comfortably admit that I do not know something?

0 1 2 3 4 5   allow ample silence after I ask a question?

0 1 2 3 4 5   learn from my clients?

0 1 2 3 4 5   find the value in what a client says?

0 1 2 3 4 5   feel comfortable with silence?

0 1 2 3 4 5   use silence as a form of encouraging connection?

0 1 2 3 4 5   feel authentic in my expression of who I am while coaching?

0 1 2 3 4 5   listen more than I speak?

0 1 2 3 4 5   know what issues block me from being the best coach
I can be?

0 1 2 3 4 5   draw parallels between my clients' issues and my own?

0 1 2 3 4 5   acknowledge I expand my self-awareness the more I coach?

0 1 2 3 4 5   encompass my client's experience as a way of maintaining
rapport?

0 1 2 3 4 5   perceive Spirit as real?

0 1 2 3 4 5   think both coaching competence and spiritual discipline
are necessary?

0 1 2 3 4 5   habitually ask questions instead of giving answers?

0 1 2 3 4 5   knock myself off the pedestal when clients put me up?

0 1 2 3 4 5   avoid embedding recommendations within questions?

0 1 2 3 4 5   ask questions that lead to client awareness?

0 1 2 3 4 5   use questions to foster rapport with clients?

0 1 2 3 4 5   operate from a paradigm of spiritual inquisitiveness?

0 1 2 3 4 5   fully and unconditionally accept my clients?

0 1 2 3 4 5   trust that what emerges is perfect?

0 1 2 3 4 5   feel neutral in my heart instead of successful?

0 1 2 3 4 5   approach a challenging situation with neutrality?

0 1 2 3 4 5   know when my shadow side emerges?

Subtotal: _____

Connection with the Whole

To what extent do I . . .

0 1 2 3 4 5 accept the present moment as perfect?

0 1 2 3 4 5 access the morphogenetic field?

0 1 2 3 4 5 allow myself to go into the void during a meeting?

0 1 2 3 4 5 acknowledge we are part of a much larger universal force?

0 1 2 3 4 5 appropriately share my spiritual learning with clients?

0 1 2 3 4 5 note synchronicities in my life?

0 1 2 3 4 5 bring synchronicities to clients' awareness?

0 1 2 3 4 5 refer to the cycles of nature while coaching?

0 1 2 3 4 5 honor all phases of the coaching cycle, the upswings, and the dips?

0 1 2 3 4 5 use metaphors to guide clients' awareness?

0 1 2 3 4 5 mirror my spiritual values in my coaching environment?

0 1 2 3 4 5 recognize that Spirit is always around?

0 1 2 3 4 5 intentionally welcome Spirit into my coaching life?

0 1 2 3 4 5 feel myself surrender to Spirit while coaching?

Subtotal: _____

The Present Moment

To what extent do I . . .

0 1 2 3 4 5 feel present during a coaching meeting?

0 1 2 3 4 5 assess clients' well-being during a meeting?

0 1 2 3 4 5   pay attention to my feelings while coaching?

0 1 2 3 4 5   use my feelings to determine coaching strategy?

0 1 2 3 4 5   create states of expectancy to maximize learning?

0 1 2 3 4 5   honor how much I learn from my clients?

0 1 2 3 4 5   feel comfortable allowing clients to express emotions?

0 1 2 3 4 5   feel lighthearted when coaching?

0 1 2 3 4 5   use humor appropriately?

0 1 2 3 4 5   laugh with clients?

0 1 2 3 4 5   speak my intuitive insights?

0 1 2 3 4 5   regain my spiritual connection quickly when I feel I have lost it?

0 1 2 3 4 5   rely on my body to guide me in coaching?

0 1 2 3 4 5   maintain awareness of all my sensory data while coaching?

0 1 2 3 4 5   process thoughts through my heart?

Subtotal: _____

Responsibility

To what extent do I . . .

0 1 2 3 4 5   allow clients to be responsible for their own outcomes?

0 1 2 3 4 5   allow client attachments to dissolve quickly?

0 1 2 3 4 5   set boundaries and adhere to them?

0 1 2 3 4 5   avoid getting drawn into a client's plea for advice or suggestions?

0 1 2 3 4 5   use forward momentum language?

0 1 2 3 4 5   allow clients to make "mistakes"?

0 1 2 3 4 5   learn from my coaching "mistakes"?

0 1 2 3 4 5   avoid absolute language such as "always" and "never"?

0 1 2 3 4 5   keep expectations from influencing my actions?

0 1 2 3 4 5   check out my assumptions?

0 1 2 3 4 5   acknowledge the influence of my beliefs on my actions?

0 1 2 3 4 5   guide clients to uncover their spiritual beliefs?

0 1 2 3 4 5   believe motivating clients to be a disservice?

0 1 2 3 4 5   pay attention to the ecology of coaching?

0 1 2 3 4 5   accept glitches as a useful part of the journey?

0 1 2 3 4 5   experience gratitude during coaching?

0 1 2 3 4 5   remember that clients already have the knowledge and skill to succeed?

Subtotal: _____

Executive Coaching with Spirit

To what extent do I . . .

0 1 2 3 4 5   allow feelings to be discussed while coaching executives?

0 1 2 3 4 5   discuss purposefulness or life purpose with executive clients?

0 1 2 3 4 5   invite Spirit into the executive suite, overtly or covertly?

0 1 2 3 4 5   recognize the presence of Spirit?

0 1 2 3 4 5   target sustainable learning instead of what is useful right now?

0 1 2 3 4 5   release expectations and beliefs from my cultural conditioning?

0 1 2 3 4 5   connect with the Spirit of the executive?

Subtotal: _____

Stoking the Fire: Coaching with Spirit Learning Communities

To what extent do I . . .

0 1 2 3 4 5   have adequate support to keep me in touch with my Spirit?

0 1 2 3 4 5   ask for support to keep me in touch with my Spirit?

0 1 2 3 4 5   participate in coaching events and gatherings to maintain connection?

0 1 2 3 4 5   regularly seek to enhance my coaching with Spirit ability?

0 1 2 3 4 5   (Spirit invites you to add your own.)

Subtotal: _____

Scoring

To obtain your total score:

1. Add the numbers in each column for each section.

2. Add column totals together and enter on the subtotal lines.

3. Add up your subtotal scores and enter that number here.

Grand Total: _____

Interpretation

If your score is 500 to 575, you are exceptional at coaching with Spirit.

If your score is 430 to 499, you are very good at coaching with Spirit.

If your score is 345 to 429, you adequately coach with Spirit.

If your score is below 345, revisit those areas you feel need enhancement.

Your total score gives you a sense of the degree to which you consistently coach with Spirit. If you find certain areas of inconsistency or areas with lower scores, you might want to reread the chapters that address these issues and focus on the exercises and reflection questions until you feel more at ease with those parts of your coaching. Assess yourself again in a few months to see what shifts you have made. Be kind and gentle with yourself; change does not happen overnight. You would not expect that of your clients; certainly do not expect that of yourself. Remember you are respons-able to be the kind of coach you choose to be, and all the knowledge, skill, and attitudes supporting you are within you. Allow the perfection of who you are to emerge!

Bibliography

Abram, D. (1996). *The spell of the sensuous.* New York: Vintage Books.

Allen, R.C. (2001). *Guiding change journeys: A synergistic approach to organization transformation.* San Francisco, CA: Jossey-Bass/Pfeiffer.

Belf, T. (1998, November 19). The myth of the fulfilled executive: Executives are people too. *Coaching News, 50.* Available: www.coachfederation.org/generalinformation/coachingnews

Belf, T. (2001). *Facilitating life purpose: A manual for coaches.* Bethesda, MD: Purposeful Press.

Belf, T., & Ward, C. (1997). *Simply live it up: Brief solutions.* Bethesda, MD: Purposeful Press.

Bianco-Mathis, V., Nabors, L., & Roman, C. (2002). *Leading from the inside out: A coaching model.* Thousand Oaks, CA: Sage.

Blanchard, K. (March, 2001). *Coaching: Just in time wisdom.* Presented at the Professional Coaches and Mentors Association Conference, Costa Mesa, California.

Boldt, L.G. (1993). *Zen and the art of making a living* (rev. ed.). New York: Penguin.

Broom, M., & Klein, D. (1999). *Power: The infinite game.* Columbia, MD: Sea Otter Press.

Cashman, K. (1998). *Leadership from the inside out.* Provo, UT: Executive Excellence.

Dyer, W.W. (2001). *There's a spiritual solution to every problem.* New York: HarperCollins.

Escudé, V. (2000). *Getting everything you want and going for more: Coaching for mastery.* Gulf Breeze, FL: Author.

Gallwey, W.T. (1998). *The inner game of golf.* New York: Random House.

Gawain, S. (1995). *Creative visualization.* Mill Valley, CA: Entourage.

Gawain, S. (1998). *Living in the light.* Mill Valley, CA: Entourage.

Goldsmith, M., Lyons, L., & Freas, A. (2000). *Coaching for leadership: How the world's greatest coaches help leaders to learn.* San Francisco, CA: Jossey-Bass/Pfeiffer.

Green, E., & Green, A. (1977). *Beyond biofeedback.* New York: Delacorte.

John-Roger. (1984). *Passage into spirit.* Los Angeles, CA: Bakara Books.

Juster, N. (1989). *The phantom tollbooth.* New York: Random House.

King, J. (2002). *Cellular wisdom.* Santa Cruz, CA: The Crossing Press.

Kushner, H.S. (2001). *Living a life that matters: Resolving the conflict between conscience and success.* New York: Alfred A. Knopf.

Merleau-Ponty, M. (1968). *The visible and the invisible* (A. Lingis, Trans.). Evanston, IL: Northwestern University Press.

Miller, M. (1994). *Sound business bites: A common sense approach to customer service and management.* Dallas, TX: Odenwald Press.

Olalla, J. (1998a, April). *Living in the mystery of coaching* [course notes]. Coolfont Resort, Berkeley Springs, West Virginia.

Olalla, J. (1998b). *The oracle of coaching* [handout]. Berkeley Springs, WV: The Newfield Network.

Owen, H. (1994). *Open space technology.* Potomac, MD: Abbott Publishing.

Rhodes, R.E. *Emptiness.* Freeland, WA: Author.

Susan's Story. (2001, April). *Today's coach, 3*(1). Available: www.todayscoach.com/clients'stories.

Talbot, M. (1988). *Beyond the quantum: How the secrets of the new physics are bridging the chasm between science and faith.* New York: Bantam.

Thoreau, H. (1971). *Reflections at Walden.* Kansas City, MO: Hallmark.

Three Initiates. (1940). *The kybalion: A study of hermetic philosophy of ancient Egypt and Greece.* Chicago, IL: Yogi Publication Society.

Williams, K.A. (1988*). From innocence to ignorance.* Annandale, VA: Author.

Zink, N. (1991). *The structure of delight.* Taos, NM: Mind Matters.

About the Author

TERI-E BELF, M.A., C.A.G.S., M.C.C., is a coaching leader, inspiring speaker, and author. Combining fifteen years of management in human resources and training and development with another sixteen years (over 25,000 hours) of coaching experience, she is on the leading edge. Ms. Belf created the first International Coaching Symposium (1996), became an honored member of *International Who's Who of Entrepreneurs* (1999), and was appointed to the Professional Women's Advisory Board of the American Biographical Institute (2001). Since 1987, she has served as executive director of Success Unlimited Network® (SUN), an ICF-accredited coaching training school offering individualized face-to-face coaching, training, continuing education, and certification. As a board member of the Professional and Personal Coaches Association and the chair of the ICF Credentials Committee, she led the field of coaching into credentialing, competency-based training, and continuing education. Her special passion is being the founder of SUN—an international, spiritually aware, coaching learning community—radiating coaching competence, service, and integrity across the planet. Her life purpose is to inspire and guide people to go for their dreams.

Contact: Success Unlimited Network, 2016 Lakebreeze Way, Reston, Virginia 20191-4021 USA; phone: (703) 716-8374; fax: (703) 264-7867; email: belf@erols.com; URL: www.erols.com/belf; URL: www.successunlimitednet.com.

About the Contributors

LANA ACOLA is a success coach with SUN. She is also a teacher of meditation. Her background includes twenty years' experience in the entertainment industry as an actress, acting coach, and agency director. Acola has also taught personal development courses for teens and adults. She has a bachelor of arts degree in English literature from the University of Texas, Austin, lives in Arlington, Texas, and works in Arlington, Dallas, Fort Worth, and Austin. Her passion is transforming everyday life into the spiritual path.

    Contact: Acola Productions, Lakeshore Court, Arlington, Texas 76013 USA; phone: (817) 265-8862; fax: (817) 377-9133; email: acola108@aol.com

REBECCA CHAN ALLEN, Ph.D., is a consultant and coach who enjoys facilitating cultural synergy and creative transformation. She has worked with executives, managers, and professionals at Amoco, Exxon, Shell, Imperial Oil, PanCanadian, CP Rail, AEC International, HR Canada, and Calgary Native Friendship Centre. Her work integrates insights from science, cross-cultural mythologies, psychology, and wisdom traditions. Her book, *Guiding Change Journeys* (Jossey-Bass/Pfeiffer, 2001), captures her transformative change experience. Her Change Journeys programs guide people to discover their own paths of transformation. Born in China, Allen has studied and worked in Asia, Canada, the United States, and Europe.

    Contact: Delta Learning Organization Inc., 3719 Beaver Road, NW, Calgary, Alberta, Canada T2L 1W9; phone: (403) 289-3843; fax: (403) 282-8251; email: dlo@cadvision.com

BERYL ALLPORT, P.C.C., success life coach and owner of B. All Enterprises, brings a variety of life experiences and expertise to her coaching profession. She has served in three levels of government, for sixteen years in a family business, for eight years in corporate sales, and in management at a university hospital, a heritage conference center, and at several major charities. In addition to one-on-one and group success coaching since 1997, Allport facilitates workshops and seminars and is a recognized public speaker. She is also known for her wellness retreats. Allport's goal is to help others live with passion and on purpose and is "refiring versus retiring."

Contact: B-All Enterprises, 895 County Road 44, RR2, Kemptville, Ontario, Canada K0G 1J0; phone: (613) 258-6893; fax: (613) 258-6894; email: beallucanbe@ sympatico.ca; URL: www.beallucanbe.com

JULIA FERGUSON ANDRIESSEN is a love immigrant and life coach from Southern California living in The Netherlands. She coaches people who want to set dreams in motion. Andriessen listens to her clients' needs while keeping her own in mind and brings to each coaching session all the gifts she has received in her life. She motivates her clients to live their dreams, especially her expatriate clients, who often are "doing time" for a few years, waiting to return to their home countries again. Andriessen has trained with a variety of coaching approaches and has a bachelor of arts degree in psychology.

Contact: JAFA Life Coaching Services, Cape Kennedy 14, 3402 DD, Ijsselstein, The Netherlands; phone: (030) 687-8098; fax: (030) 687-8099; email: julia@jafa.nl; URL: www.jafa.nl

SUSAN BELCHAMBER is a certified personal and professional coach trained in ontological coaching (the study of being) by the Newfield Network. Also trained as a psychotherapist and small-group facilitator, Belchamber brings extensive experience in government, business, and nonprofit organizations to her coaching practice. Belchamber's work as a coach is based on her strong belief in the individual's capacity for inner knowing. Her calling is to facilitate journeys of self-discovery. She works in groups and organizations and with individuals who strive for greater clarity and meaning.

Contact: Lifespan Development, 7021 Persimmon Tree Road, Bethesda, Maryland 20817 USA; phone: (301) 767-0262; fax: (301) 767-0336; email: susanbel@erols.com

KEN BYERS, Ph.D., C.P.C.C., is a personal life coach who brings thirty years of front-line experience in business, psychology, teaching, and a wondrously diverse life to men and women who simply want more in their lives. Known worldwide, particularly for his approach to the issues of men's lives, his "Essential Self-Management Technology" crosses all gender barriers and helps businesses, groups, and individuals identify, define, and achieve their personal visions with clarity and sustainable successenergy.

Contact: The Coaching Center, 609 Shields Street, San Francisco, California 94132 USA; phone: (415) 337-9186; email: mekendar@pacbell.net; URL: www.etropolis. com/coachken

VANCE CAESAR, M.B.A., Ph.D., a premier leadership coach and mentor, focuses on helping executives have more freedom and fun by becoming successful entrepreneurs or thinking like successful entrepreneurs. His extensive background includes being a successful CEO, senior marketing and operations executive, entrepreneur, coach, professor, team builder, author, and publisher. Caesar has served on a wide variety of profit, nonprofit, and advisory boards. He has a master's degree in business administration from Florida Atlantic University, is a graduate of the Stanford University Executive Program, and has a doctorate from Walden University in organizational psychology.

Contact: Professional Coaches and Mentor's Association; phone: (562) 799-5560; email: vance@vancecaesar.com; URL: www.PCMAONLINE.com

JOHN COLLINGS, Ph.D., M.C.C., offers professional services as a life and career coach, executive coach, group process facilitator, and consultant in small business planning and development. Collings directed the corporate management development program at Scott Paper Company. He teaches business and communications at several colleges and universities and also teaches in the Anne Arundel Community College Holistic Health and Mind/Body studies program. Collings integrates his Ph.D. in organization behavior, ICF master coach certification, neurolinguistic programming, advanced Reiki, and a Jungian orientation into his coaching and consulting.

Contact: Human Resources Organization Development (HROD), 8 Silverwood Circle, Annapolis, Maryland 21403 USA; phone: (410) 263-4274; fax: (410) 275-9086; email: johncollings@comcast.net

MARCIA COLLINS is committed to having the coaching profession fully embrace the whole person's ever-expanding experience of fulfillment through conscious connection with Spirit. She has been a trainer and coach in corporate, academia, and private sectors. She is known for her fun, innovative, and experiential training style. Collins cofounded Coach For Life, where life coaches are trained in coaching the human spirit.

Contact: Coach For Life, 6343 El Cajon Boulevard, #138, San Diego, California 92115 USA; phone: (888) 262-2446; fax: (619) 287-2577; email: coaching@ coachforlife.com; URL: www.coachforlife.com

JERI COSTA combines her unique blend of expertise as a SUN coach, counselor, clinical hypnotherapist, and neurolinguistic practitioner to develop lifetime strategies for success. She is an intuitive consultant with Future Inc., a business profiling and personal development company. At the heart of her work is a strong conviction that each of us is born with an individual life purpose. Clients are coached to produce consistent results in all areas of life congruent with this purpose. In her spiritual practice as an ordained minister, she teaches others how to go within and connect to their Spirit selves.

Contact: Success Unlimited Network, 11132 Timberhead Lane, Reston, Virginia 20191 USA; phone: (703) 860-9285; fax: (703) 860-1135; email: JKC11@WebTV.net

MARILYN DABADY, Ph.D., is a personal coach with a background in social and organizational psychology and human resource management. She works with clients to identify their personal and professional goals and create strategies for achievement. Among her projects are writing a book on informal support networks among women and developing a mentor training program for a nonprofit organization. Dabady has a doctorate in psychology from Yale University and received training from Coach U and Comprehensive Coach U.

Contact: email: mdabady@aol.com

DAVE de SOUSA, "Mr. Time Management," arranges with a registered and highly experienced cowboy guide to take you on an "Extreme Cowboy Adventure," without the cows. He understands how much an experience like this can influence senior managers. If you are interested in a new approach to time management, read his book *Power Scheduling: The New Approach To Time Management.*

Contact: Power Scheduling, LLC, 64 Water Street, Meredith, New Hampshire 03253 USA; phone: (603) 279-3034; fax: (603) 279-3034; email: mstrtime@powerscheduling. com; URL: www.powerscheduling.com

VICKI ESCUDÉ, M.A., M.C.C., is a coach trainer with SUN. She has twenty-eight years' experience in executive coaching, business ownership, writing, management, and counseling. Her passion is inspiring clients to live their life purpose. Escudé wrote the book *Getting Everything You Want and Going for More! Coaching for Mastery.* She and her clients have been featured in *Healthy Living* magazine, the *Pensacola News Journal, Climate* magazine, and the *Pensacola Independent* as a successful and innovative personal life and executive coach. Escudé graduated from Vanderbilt University and received her master's degree from the University of West Florida in psychology and counseling.

Contact: e-mail: vicki@excellentcoach.com; URL: www.excellentcoach.com

BUTCH FARLEY is a professional coach living in Taos, New Mexico. Also a freelance writer and speaker, he works with individuals and organizations on a variety of issues and topics. The first executive director for the ICF and past director of community development for Coach University, Farley is also the founder of the Taos Initiative, a nonprofit organization dedicated to the spiritual growth of professional coaches and their clients.

Contact: Taos Initiatives, P.O. Box 634, Angel Fire, New Mexico 87710 USA; phone: (505) 770-0825; fax: (505) 377-3484; email: butch@cardiolifecoach.com; URL: www.cardiolifecoach.org

CAROL J. FLEISCHMAN, a human development specialist, facilitator, coach, and trainer, creates methods, procedures, and designs for organizational and personal transformation. She has worked with over two hundred organizations locally, nationally, and internationally and with businesses, institutions, communities, and individuals. Her focus is on strategic, collaborative approaches to the future, engaging people in innovative activities, and building systems that support ongoing, positive change. Her thirty-five-year affiliation with the Institute of Cultural Affairs shaped her ability to work effectively with diverse groups at various educational, cultural, and social levels. Fleischman is a professionally certified SUN coach, received the ASTD Program Award, and has associate faculty status at LSU Medical Center and Tulane University.

Contact: Fleischman Associates, 1119 Dauphine Street #1, New Orleans, Louisiana 70116 USA; phone: (504) 529-5800; email: Cjfnola@aol.com

ELAINE GAGNÉ, Ed.D., C.P.P.C., C.S.C., is a personal and executive certified coach and organizational change consultant helping successful executives get more of a life *now.* Coaching for more than ten years and working as an organizational consultant for more than twenty years, she currently works as a senior consultant with The Franklin Covey Company and with Renaissance Consulting Group. Dr. Gagné is also an author in the fields of organizational design, consulting, and coaching.

Contact: Renaissance Consulting Group, 8020 Toltec Lane, Colorado Springs, Colorado 80908 USA; phone: (719) 495-6151; email: Egagne2@worldnet.att.net

TIMI CATHERINE GLEASON is a business development consultant and executive coach in San Diego, California. Her practical background in neurolinguistic programming, creative problem solving, and emotional competency development gives structure to her unique coaching style and insights into the art of human technology. Gleason likes working with companies that have or want to develop clear strategic initiatives. She supports micro-credit lending opportunities and training for women in extreme poverty in Mexico through affiliates of Grameen Bank in Washington, DC, and Bangladesh, India. She is a certified coach, a member of the ICF, and an affiliate of B-Coach.com.

Contact: email: tgleason@san.rr.com; URL: www.executivegoals.com

BETH HAND is a master connector of people to their dreams and organizations to their goals. Her training as a SUN certified coach and her certification as a master practitioner in neurolinguistic programming defines the spirit she brings to her coaching, consulting, and speaking practice. The Internal Revenue Service, the General Directorate of Revenue in Turkey, the World Bank, the Federal Communications Commission, Bell Atlantic Corporation, and many senior executives have used Hand's abilities. She is a member of the Strategic Leadership Network and the ICF and has been a trainer and presenter for numerous national and multinational corporations.

Contact: Elizabeth E. Hand & Associates, 3322 Coryell Lane, Alexandria, Virginia 22302 USA; phone: (703) 820-8074; fax: (703) 820-8018; email: BethHand@Juno.com

DIANE HETHERINGTON, M.S., M.C.C., is a coach mentor/trainer with Success Unlimited Network and founder and principal of Diane Hetherington Associates. As a senior executive coach, organization development consultant, and educator, she specializes in developing spiritual and emotional intelligence, leadership capacity, career strategy, and bringing meaning/spirit to life and work. She is a partner with Intelligent Development Resources. Hetherington serves as adjunct faculty at Johns Hopkins University, is a former Hopkins Fellow in change management, has an M.S. in the applied behavioral sciences from Hopkins, and is a graduate of the Organization and Systems Development Program at the Gestalt Institute of Cleveland, Ohio.

Contact: Hetherington & Associates, 9612 Kentsdale Drive, Potomac, Maryland 20854 USA; phone: (301) 469-2484; fax: (301) 469-2485; email: diane.hetherington @verizon.net

TIM HODGE is a sales engineer at AltaVista Search Solutions, a CMGI company. His background includes eighteen years' experience in the software industry performing a variety of tasks, including software engineering, product training, product marketing, and direct sales. He has a bachelor of science degree in business from Bentley College and a master of science degree in computer science from Boston University. His passion is to live every day with spiritual awareness and love to achieve personal growth in all areas of life.

Contact: 175 Old Bolton Road, Stow, Massachusetts 01775 USA; phone: (978) 684-7863; email: tim_hodge16@hotmail.com

BREN HUDSON works for Wind River Systems as director of business excellence, leading the services business unit through changes to the organizational structure, culture, processes, and systems. Prior to working at Wind River, Hudson spent six years at Ernst & Young in their consulting practice. As senior manager, her focus was on ERP system implementation with an emphasis on strategy, process improvement, and change management. She has a master's degree in information and telecommunication systems from Johns Hopkins and a bachelor's degree in finance from George Mason University.

Contact: Wind River Systems, Inc., 10505 Sorrento Valley Road, San Diego, California 92130 USA; phone: (858) 509-4952; fax: (858) 509-4975; email: bren. hudson@windriver.com; URL: www.windriver.com

CARL INGRAM, M.S., founder of WayFinders Group, is a coach, speaker, consultant, and grower of minds and spirits. He applies Jungian depth psychology and ancient wisdom of indigenous people to nurture personal and leadership development. On the Center for Executive Coaching faculty in the Professional School of Psychology and John F. Kennedy University, he engages students in the process of wisdom and spiritual coaching. His master's degree is in applied psychology. His doctoral dissertation researched *Applied Wisdom Leadership*© at the California Institute of Integral Studies. He co-authored *Executive Coaching: Resource Book 2000.*

Contact: WayFinders Group, 3576 64th Avenue, Oakland, California 94605 USA; phone: (510) 632-8051; fax: (510) 632-8041; email: WayFinderG@aol.com; URL: www.executivecoachesnet.com

QUIMBY KAIZER has more than seven years' experience as a principal consultant at PricewaterhouseCoopers within the practice of Organizational and Change Strategy. She offers change management and organizational development services to commercial and government clients with leadership, business process, financial, or information technology challenges. Kaizer helps effectively emplement positive change in their organizations. Her areas of expertise include executive and business coaching, group facilitation, team building, team coaching, personal and team efficiency, training design and delivery, and Six Sigma performance improvement.

Contact: phone: (703) 633-4553; email: quimby.kaizer@us.pwcglobal.com

KATHY KELLY completed a master's degree in organization development from Marymount University while studying life purpose coaching with Success Unlimited Network. She has worked for several years as director of a vocational training program where she had the opportunity to apply a mental health model based on community, productivity, and the inherent dignity of every person. Her interest in coaching the terminally ill comes from having worked in other capacities with the aging population.

Contact: 7211 Arthur Drive, Falls Church, Virginia 22046 USA; phone: (703) 560-6445; fax: (703) 560-6595; email: kathykellyis@hotmail.com

JOAN C. KING, Ph.D., professor emeritus of Tufts University School of Medicine, founded her company, Beyond Success, upon stepping down as chair of Anatomy and Cellular Biology at Tufts in 1998. King is currently writing *Cellular Wisdom* (The Crossing Press), in which she explores the body as a teacher of how to live vibrantly. Her interest in spirit emerged early in her life. She was a member of the Dominican Sisters in New Orleans for eleven years, obtaining a bachelor's degree in chemistry and mathematics and studying theology and philosophy. After leaving the convent, Dr. King obtained her master's and Ph.D. degrees in psychology and neuroscience from the University of New Orleans and Tulane University. As a SUN coach and speaker, Dr. King assists people in evoking their greatness.

Contact: 42 Garrison Road, Brookline, Massachusetts 02445-4437 USA; phone: (617) 730-8336; fax: (617) 232-6938; email: joanking@concentric.net or joanking@ beyond-success.com; URL: www.beyond-success.com

TERRIE LUPBERGER, M.C.C., is CEO of the Newfield Network-usa, an international coaching and consulting company that delivers innovative, cutting-edge, learning programs to help individuals and organizations produce effective and meaningful results. Lupberger has been coaching executives since 1994. Prior to working at Newfield, she was a senior financial manager at the U.S. Treasury Department. Her varied work history gives her a unique perspective to help executives and organizations redesign the way they relate to others so that new results are possible.

Contact: The Newfield Network-usa, LLC; phone: (301) 570-6680; URL: www. newfieldnetwork.com

ANN McGILL, life potentials coach, shows clients how to remove the blocks that hold them back, awaken hidden potential, and release trapped genius, allowing the beautiful truth of who clients really are to break free and serve them well. McGill has been pursuing her passion for facilitating quantum-leap growth and change for more than twenty-five years.

Contact: 1983-A Villa Ridge Drive, Reston, Virginia 20191 USA; phone: (703) 262-0620; email: Iam1ur2@erols.com; URL: www.iam1ur2.com

MARGERY MILLER, a seasoned coach and business consultant, also runs a successful manufacturers' sales agency in Dallas, Texas. She devotes most of her time to working with individuals and companies interested in personal and organizational transformation. With a client base spanning from Oregon to France, Miller travels and works with people from many disciplines. Devoted to her own personal development, she continues to study and challenge herself to grow, ensuring that her work is consistently dynamic and alive.

Contact: Miller & Associates/People in Business, 2910 Merrell Road, Dallas, Texas 75229 USA; phone: (214) 353-0498; fax: (972) 720-8552; email: Margery@peoplebiz.com

PHILLIP E. NELSON, Ph.D., SUN certified success coach, is an organization development consultant, trainer, and member of Mensa. He specializes in coaching and facilitates teams implementing new information technology with organizational change principles and reengineering. His twenty-five years of training and consulting span many federal agencies. When he coaches executives, consultants, and entrepreneurs, he engages his passion of facilitating human creative synergy, transformation, and fulfillment.

Nelson holds an M.A. and Ph.D. in organization development from the University of Wisconsin.

Contact: Success Unlimited Network, Reston, Virginia 20191-4021 USA; phone: (703) 716-5511; email: penelson@comcast.net

DOTTIE PERLMAN, N.C.C., P.C.C., C.M.F., C.P.C., is principal of Insight Associates, LLP, an executive coaching and career management consulting firm. She was with Right Management Consultants and served as past Washington, DC, president of the International Association of Career Management Professionals. Perlman has more than twenty years' experience in coaching, outplacement and career transition, management, human resources, training, and organization development. She completed coaching certification at the Hudson Institute of Santa Barbara, California. She has a master's degree in counseling from The American University and a bachelor's degree in industrial psychology from Case Western Reserve University.

Contact: Insight Associates, 11611 LeHavre Drive, Potomac, Maryland 20854 USA; phone: (301) 294-0133; email: dottieperlman@erols.com; URL: www.insight1.com

PETER REDING is committed to encouraging the coaching profession to fully embrace the whole person and each person's ever-expanding experience of fulfillment through conscious connection with Spirit. He has been a trainer and coach in international, corporate, and private sectors. He is known for his fun, innovative, and experiential training style. He co-founded Coach for Life, where life coaches are trained in coaching the human spirit.

Contact: Coach for Life, 6343 El Cajon Boulevard, #138, San Diego, California 92115 USA; phone: (888) 262–2446; fax: (619) 287-2577; email: coaching@ coachforlife.com; URL: www.coachforlife.com

MARY ANN ROBBAT is a SUN coach and director of strategic initiatives at Viant, a business solutions consulting firm. Robbat has been coaching for more than ten years privately and in her corporate role. She has focused primarily on helping high achieving women live the lives they desire. Robbat brings a diversity of experience, tools, and processes to her coaching work to burst through barriers and limiting beliefs clients may hold about themselves. She incorporates energy work, healing, spiritual guides, and intuitive processes when working with clients.

Contact: Viant; phone: (781) 259-8767; email: mrobbat@earthlink.net

ANGIE ROOTE, with her background in psychology and communication as well as her specialized training in coaching and neurolinguistic programming, assists clients in making their dreams come true and living their ideal lives by participating in any of her WorldWin Coaching programs.

Contact: WorldWin Coaching, 1801 N. Craig Street, Sterling, Virginia 20164-3534 USA; phone: (703) 450-7867; fax: (703) 450-8901; email: aroote@erols.com; URL: www.erols.com/aroote

G. LEE SALMON is an executive coach and president of Learning for Living. He works with senior executives in the federal government and private sector on leadership development and the management of organizational change. He is also an executive consultant with the Federal Consulting Group and is practice leader for coaching and mentoring programs. Using his years of experience as a health physicist with the U.S. Environmental Protection Agency, he works with executives and managers in science and technology-based organizations to develop leadership talent at all levels and create humane and alive learning organizations.

Contact: Learning for Living; phone: (703) 323-8845; email: glsalmon@aol.com

RUTH SCHULER is a SUN coach and coaches clients in the greater New Haven, Connecticut, area. Her professional experience includes work with the community services department of Hamden, Connecticut, and Infoline, Connecticut's statewide resource and referral agency. She created and directed programs, engaged in consumer education, and participated with area human services networks. Schuler is also trained in spiritual psychology, which she incorporates into her daily living and her work as a coach.

Contact: Success Unlimited Network, P.O. Box 4049, Hamden, Connecticut 06514 USA; phone: (203) 281-7656; email: ralschuler@aol.com

ABOODI SHABY is one of the United Kingdom's best-known personal coaches. He is a Coach University graduate and president of the ICF in the UK. He specializes in supporting people who want to get more joy from life and is writing a book on happiness, based in part on his coaching experiences.

Contact: Aboodi Shaby & Associates, 50 Upper Regents Park, Bradford on Avon, Wiltshire BA1I1EB, UK; phone: 44-1225-862005, fax: 44-870-126-9913; email: aboodi@aboodi.net; URL: www.wonderful-life.com

ED SHULKIN is a certified SUN coach and founder of Meant2B Unlimited, an organization of coaches and trainers dedicated to the organizational philosophies of values-driven cultures and the ongoing professional and personal growth potential of coaching. Prior to becoming a coach, his career was a combination of "serial entrepreneurship" and corporate leadership. He coaches senior executives and top-level managers as well as entrepreneurs whose organizations have outgrown their unique skills and are ready to create an enduring culture-based community.

Contact: Meant2B Unlimited, The Adventure of Success, 15 Foster Circle, Enfield, New Hampshire 03748 USA; phone: (888) 440-9664; email: meant2bunltd@aol.com

ALAN SHUSTERMAN, J.D., C.S.C., is principal of Insight Associates, LLP, an executive coaching and career management consulting firm. Leaving the practice of law for coaching was the best career move he says he ever made. As a coach, he has had the pleasure of working with a wide variety of top executives committed to professional growth and excellence. A graduate of the University of Pennsylvania (B.A. in economics, *summa cum laude*) and Harvard Law School (J.D., *cum laude*), Shusterman successfully completed the Success Unlimited Network Coaching Certification Program. An active member of the ICF, Shusterman serves as chapter host for the Metro Washington, DC, chapter.

Contact: Insight Associates, 8211 Larry Place, Chevy Chase, Maryland 20815 USA; phone: (301) 562-8807; email: alan@insight1.com; URL: www.insight1.com

TRAVIS TWOMEY, M.C.C., has more than thirty years' experience coaching, facilitating, and mentoring attained over a professional career in the U.S. Federal Prison System and a volunteer career in youth sports. He is a coach trainer with Success Unlimited Network and completed the New Ventures West coach certification. He has served the ICF as a co-chair of several committees. Holding an undergraduate degree in government and two postgraduate degrees in criminal justice and public administration, he blends experience, training, and education into a diversified array of coaching and Coach Approach training services for individuals, professional coaches, teams, and organizations. Twomey has created coaching programs in a variety of private and public sector organizations.

Contact: Twomey Coaching Services, Austin, Texas USA; phone: (512) 330-9877; email: travistwomey@juno.com; URL: www. successunlimitednet.com

PETER G. VAJDA, Ph.D., is a professional, personal, and executive coach, consultant, and facilitator. His work focuses on life purpose and on the benefit of reflecting on one's belief systems and thought processes, knowing that one's thoughts, beliefs, and attitudes result in behaviors, limiting and productive, that affect results. Vajda's work is founded on the principle that circumstances happen *for* us, not *to* us. This spiritual perspective toward self-fulfillment allows one to focus on the truth and honesty of one's relationship with self and others and, thus, balance becomes a harmony of the internal and external. Vajda serves clients throughout the United States and Europe.

Contact: SpiritHeart, People-Tech Solutions, 6851 Roswell Road NE, Suite E-8, Atlanta, Georgia 30328 USA; phone: (770) 804-9125; fax: (770) 804-9179; email: Pvajda@pipeline.com

JULIA WALZ, P.C.C, balances and fine-tunes the direction of her own life, fulfills her dreams, experiences life fully, and, most of all, integrates spiritual principles into her day-to-day life. She believes Spirit unifies and appreciates uniqueness, while coaching enhances the selection of life's treasures of experiences. She works with individual clients and corporations that are searching for more depth, clarity, and cooperative spirit while feeling drawn to know more and to explore their own energy and wisdom with guidance.

Contact: Success International, 4584 Lake Village Drive, Atlanta, Georgia 30338 USA; phone: (770) 451-4475; fax: (770) 451-4985; email: successintl@mindspring. com

CHARLOTTE WARD assists clients with editing and rewriting books and composing ad copy; she excels at analyzing for logic, transitions, and flow. Ward facilitates meetings and speaks to groups. Through the PhotoReading™ Whole Mind System, she leads people to read at a blistering pace with pinpoint comprehension. Ward administers the Myers-Briggs Type Indicator® and teaches the quiet practice of yoga and meditation. She also supports clients with finding brief solutions through neurolinguistic programming for business strategy and personal achievement. In addition, she coaches people to go for their dreams.

Contact: Accelerated Coaching and Learning, 7106 Saunders Court, Bethesda, Maryland 20817 USA; phone: (301) 365-8112; fax: (301) 983-3980; email: charlotteward1@yahoo.com

KIM A. WILLIAMS, M. M., has been managing teams toward the goals of producing educational CD-ROMs, DVDs, and websites. As a producer and manager, Kim has developed over thirty educational titles for some of the largest educational publishers in the country such as McGraw-Hill, Prentice Hall, Thomson Learning, and Houghton Mifflin. His bachelor of science in performing arts was obtained from Emerson College and his master's degree in management, with a concentration in negotiation and conflict resolution, was obtained from Cambridge College. His passion is bringing together and focusing people's disparate talents into a clear and concise vision.

Contact: 58 Gregory Street, Marblehead, Massachusetts 01945 USA; phone: (781) 631-0597; email: kimwilliams@attbi.net

SHARON WILSON serves as a certified spiritual counselor and is the spiritual officer of Coaching From Spirit, an evolving community of coaches who assist in transforming the world one person, one organization at a time. She has coached hundreds of individuals and coaches in a proven process that provides a foundation to partner and trust one's "inner coach." Wilson creates and guides transformational business programs in marketing, intuitional management, and income building that blend science, spirituality, and personal success principles in an integrative and practical way. Her background includes executive positions in sales, marketing, human resources, and consulting.

Contact: Coaching From Spirit, P.O. Box 836, Saxonburg, Pennsylvania 16056 USA; URL: www.coachingfromspirit.com

Index

A

ABCs for coaching with Spirit, 227–229
Abram, D., 68
The Absolute Continuum, 131–133, 132*fig*
Accelerating evolution, 2
Acknowledgment, 175–176
Acknowledgment marketing step, 167–168
Acola, L., 145
Action marketing step, 164–166
Actions: from resistance to commitment to, 145–148; from tension to attention and, 144–145; generated from thoughts/beliefs, 142–148; progression from thoughts/beliefs and, 130–131
Agnes Mura, Inc., 219
Aida, 210–211
Allen, R. C., 190
Allport, B., 166, 201
Alma, 132
Andriessen, J. F., 199
Androgynous power, 9–10
Anita, 50
Assessment. *See* Coaching with spirit assessment

Attraction principle, 152–153
"An Awakening of Inner Knowing" (Belchamber), 60–61
Awareness: of embodied Spirit, 113–116; of the moment, 34–35; of spiritual, physical, and emotional space, 42

B

Balance, 241, 252
Be Quite, Get Connected, Take Action, and Celebrate model, 171–173
Beginnings, 235
Behavior. *See* Actions
Belchamber, S., 60
Belf, T.-E., 103, 145, 156, 170, 240, 252
Beliefs. *See* Thoughts/beliefs
Beryl, 161
Bettina, 139–140
Bianco-Mathis, V., 17
"Bigger than the issue of the moment," 34–35
Blanchard, K., 40
Bottom Line: Personal, 163
Boundaries, 238

Bourget, L., 218–219
Brew, J., 128–129
Broom, M., 58
Buber, M., 50
Byers, K., 46

C

Caddy, E., 78
Caesar, V., 250
Call, D., 20
Carlos, 37
Cashman, K., 59
CCCs (Coaching Community Circles), 254
Cellular Wisdom (King), 53
Centering, 31–32
Change. See Client transformation
Chinese proverb, 66
Choice, 130–131
Christopher, 19
Client transformation: desire for, 127–128;
    guiding process for, 128–129; living Spirit
    through, 237; ten examples of, 231–241;
    Three Turns of, 190–195
Clients: assuming personal responsibility,
    122; being selective about, 158–160, 222;
    centering, 31–32; confidentiality of, 157;
    desire for relief by, 134–137; from resis-
    tance to commitment by, 145–148; going
    through the dip, 84; guiding to internal/
    external connections, 37–38; handling
    diametrically opposed beliefs by, 137–141;
    making different difference with, 99–102;
    negatively energetic, 42; the "perfect,"
    162; seven magic words to say to, 29–30;
    uncovering understanding of Spirit by,
    126–127; unfolding for highest good
    of, 42; why is that important? question
    for, 36. See also Connection with clients;
    Executive coaching with Spirit

Coach leader perspectives: by Agnes Mura,
    219–221; by Bobette Reeder, 221–222; by
    Chris Wahl, 224–225; coaching pointers
    from, 227–229; by D.J. Mitsch, 217–218;
    by Fran Fisher, 217; by Frderic Hudson,
    216–217; by Hannah Wilder, 225–227;
    by John Seiffer, 223; by Julie Schniewind,
    222–223; by Julio Ollala, 214–216; by
    Linne Bourget, 218–219; by Marcia
    Reynolds, 222; by Rich Fettke, 219; by
    Travis Twomey, 223–224
Coach training metaphors, 91
"Coach You, Heal Me" (Lupberger), 54–55
Coach-client relationship: coach's authenticity
    and, 59; connection with clients through,
    53–55; ending of coaching and, 79–
    80; energy field building and, 60;
    establishing caring, 207; importance
    of intention in, 58; safety net constructed
    in, 58–59; synchronistical connection
    in, 234; transformational listing and,
    59–60
Coaches: authenticity of, 59; being selective
    about clients, 158–160, 222; dip experi-
    enced by, 85–86; handling diametrically
    opposed beliefs by clients, 137–141; per-
    sonal integrity of, 141–142; professional
    ethics and, 157; seeking deeply trained,
    219; as shadow, 50, 226; Spirit as super
    trainer of, 29–30; synchronistically
    connecting with, 234; teaching other
    service professionals/schools, 254; third
    ear of, 216–217; thoughts and beliefs
    of effective, 123–126; Three Turns of
    Transformation experience by, 194–195.
    See also Wizard Coach
Coaching cycle: circles and, 77–83; dip and,
    83–86; ending of, 79–80
Coaching with the flow, 105
Coaching From Spirit, 116

"Coaching From Spirit-An Emerging Form of Coaching" (Wilson), 117–119

"Coaching the Human Spirit" (Reding and Collins), 125–126

Coaching learning communities: assessment related to, 243, 264; benefits of, 244; Newfield Network as, 214, 244–247; PCMA (Professional Coaches and Mentors Association) as, 248–250; SUN (Success Unlimited Network) as, 1, 251–252; vision of CCCs as, 254. *See also* Learning

"Coaching the Nature of Spirit and the Spirit of Nature" (Ingram), 185–190

Coaching space, 92–94

Coaching with Spirit: ABCs for, 227–229; addressing topic of Spirit and, 2–3; being selective about taking clients for, 158–160, 222; defining relationship between spirituality and, 4, 5; difference between therapy and, 13; ecology and, 147–148; ending of, 79–80; examples of, 17–21; helping clients to assume responsibility function of, 122; life purpose and, 16–17; official definition of, 12, 13, 29; only where clear, 218–219; path to, 22–25; perspectives of 14 coach leaders on, 214–230; Piggyback Principle of, 32–33; pointers from perspective of coach leaders, 227–229; preparing to, 15–16; questions to ask self when, 16; shadow side and, 50, 226; Spirit expanding through, 94–95; Spirit as partner in, 17–21; spirituality and, 16; spirituality role in, 41; three grounded principles of, 25; unconditional acceptance for, 14–15; in the wild, 179–195. *See also* Executive coaching with Spirit; International coaching with Spirit; Marketing coaching

Coaching with spirit assessment: interpreting your score, 265; related to coaching learning communities, 243, 264; related to connection with clients, 51–52, 259–260; related to connection with self, 27–28, 258–259; related to connection with the whole, 73–74, 261; related to executive coaching with Spirit, 169–170, 263–264; related to responsibility, 121–122, 262–263; related to spirituality, 11, 257–258; scoring your, 264

Coaching with Spirit path: patterns of, 22; pits and problems of, 22; polarization, paradoxes, preparation for, 23–24

"Coaching and Transformational Listening" (Salmon), 58–60

Coaching vision: author's, 253–254; PCMA (Professional Coaches and Mentors Association), 248; SUN (Success Unlimited Network), 251

Collings, J., 140

Collins, M., 123, 124, 125

Columbo Persona, 70–71

Commitment, 234

Competencies, 195–197

Completion marketing step, 166–167

Confidentiality, 157

Connection: CPR combining responsibility, present moment and, 25; creating synchronistical, 234; executive coaching with Spirit and, 177–179

Connection with clients: assessment related to, 51–52, 259–260; Columbo Persona used in, 70–71; encompassment and, 55–62; partnership as part of, 53–55; the question/questions templates for, 62–67; questions used for, 67–70. *See also* Clients

Connection marketing step, 163–164

Connection principle, 155–157

Connection with self: assessment related to, 27–28, 258–259; awareness of the moment

Connection with self (*continued*)
and, 34–35; being and doing for, 30–38; centering and, 31–32; emcompassing me and my shadow and, 49–50; intuition and, 41, 42–49; letting go of attachment and, 37–38; Piggyback Principle of Coaching and, 32–33; practice for, 39–40; three-step approach to, 38–42; why is that important question for, 36; Wizard Coach and, 29–30

Connection with the whole: assessment related to, 73–74, 261; coaching space and, 92–94; cycles, circles, dip and, 77–83; ending of coaching and, 79–80; Game of Spirit and, 86–89, 87*fig*; metaphors facilitating, 86–91; Spirit in the environment and, 91–92; synchronicity is purpose behind circumstances and, 74–77

Coppelman, J., 241

Coppelman, P. D., 231–232

"Cosmic triplets" pattern, 75

Costa, J., 146

CPR: C=Connection, P=Present moment, and R=Responsibility, 25

Creation marketing step, 162–163

Creative Visualization (Gawain), 253

Crew, S. B., 20

Curtis, 177–178

Cycles, circles, and dip, 77–86

D

Dabady, M., 104

Daniel, 33

"Dan's Canyon" (de Sousa), 179–181

de Sousa, D., 179

Debbie, 117–119

Desgroseilliers, B., 240–241

The dip, 83–86

Diplomacy, 238

Duncan, 153–154

Dyer, W., 75

Dylan, 100–101, 110

E

Ecology and coaching, 147–148

"Effective Spirit Coaches' Beliefs and Intensions" (Wilson), 123–124

Ego and Self, 191

Embodied Spirit, 113–116

Emily, 135

Emotions: blocking success, 110–113; as coaching motivation, 12; connection with self and, 39; Spirit role in mobilizing, 108–109

Empowering prospects, 164–165

Emptiness (Rhodes), 37

Encompassing me and my shadow, 49–50

Encompassment: in context of marketing, 156; described, 55–56; power of silent speech exercise and, 56–62; spirit/inquiry partnership and, 62

Energy field building, 60

Enlarging the frame, 215–216

"Entitlement" (Ward), 127–129

E's (envision, examine, experiment, expand, evaluate, engage, and evolve), 8–9

Escudé, V., 94, 139

Ethan, 14–15

"Executive Coaching: Antidote for the Seduction of the Times" (Gagné), 171–175

Executive coaching with Spirit: acknowledgment and, 175–176; assessment related to, 169–170, 263–264; competencies used in, 195–197; connection and, 177–179; as emotional risk takers, 176–177; expression of Spirit in, 173–175; myths of, 170; personal purposefulness and, 170–175; Three Turns of Transformation and, 190–194; in the wild, 179–195. *See also* Managers

Expectancy, 106–107

Expectancy paradox, 107–108

"Exposing the `S' Word" (Shulkin),
    183–185

F

Farley, B., 81

Fatimah, 211

Felicia, 78

Fettke, R., 219

Fifth Hermetic Principle, 77

"Finish the Floor" (Roote), 89–90

"A Fish in Water" (Escudé), 94–95

Fisher, F., 217

For Managers Only, 148–149

Franci, 109

Freedom from "shoulds," 194

"From Canada" (Allport), 201–202

"From France" (Miller), 202–204

"From Indonesia" (Fleischman), 206–212

"From Innocence to Ignorance" (Williams),
    69

"From The Netherlands" (Andriessen),
    199–201

"From the United Kingdom" (Shaby),
    204–206

G

Gagné, E., 42–43, 171, 175

Gallwey, W. T., 31

Game of Spirit, 86–89, 87fig

Gawain, S., 30, 253

Genève, 203–204

Georgetown University, Certificate Program,
    224

Gerda, 155, 161

Gift of Spirit, 194–195

Giving-to-get approach (PCMA), 249

Gleason, T., 176

Glen, 129, 130–131

Goethe, J. W. Von, 19

Golf analogy, 39, 40

Gormley, M., 239

Greatest good principle, 157–158

Green, A., 38

Green, E., 38

Gregor, 99

"Guideline for Winning" (Belf and Ward),
    145

H

Hand, B., 181, 251

Happy endings, 235

Harmonic Convergence (1988), 15–16

Henrietta, 140–141

Hetherington, D., 212, 213

Hodge, T., 84

"Honoring the Voice of Spirit" (Robbat),
    44–46

Hudson, B., 236–237

Hudson, F. M., 216–217

The Hudson Institute of Santa Barbara,
    216–217

Humor, 108–110

I

Ibu Rukiah, 209–210

ICF-accredited Success Unlimited Network
    program, 250

Ida, 136–137

Indra's Net, 225–226

Information Age, 2, 3

Ingram, C., 185

Inner Games series (Gallwey), 31

Inquiry-Spirit partnership, 62

Integrity, 141–142

Intellect: coaching and, 12; connection with self and, 38

Intention, 58

International coaching with Spirit: from Canada, 201–202; from France, 202–204; from Indonesia, 206–212; from the Netherlands, 199–201; from United Kingdom, 204–206; honoring culture when, 207

Intuition: The Newfield Network use of, 215; spiritual preparation for, 41; voice of Spirit as, 42–49

J

Jan, 62

Janey, 112

Jean, 174–175

Jim, 187–189

Joe, 34–35

John-Roger, 108

Jones, T (TJ), 190–195

Juster, N., 140

K

Kaizer, Q., 233–235

Keenan, D., 239

Kelly, K., 133

Ken, 47–49

Ken Blanchard Companies, 40

King, J. C., 53, 162

Klein, D., 58

Kubler-Ross, E., 83

Kushner, H., 50

The Kybalion (Three Initiates), 77

Kyle, 138

L

Laiya, 206

"Lasting Revolution" (Farley), 81–82

Layah, 211

"Leaders as Emotional Risk Takers" (Gleason), 176–177

"Leading Is a Courageous Act" (Hand), 181–183

Learning: in and as community, 246–247; exercise to encourage continuum, 132; micro vs. macro, 34; PCMA creation of communities for, 249; redesigning practices of, 245–246. *See also* Coaching learning communities

Learning from the Inside Out (Bianco-Mathis, Nabors, and Roman), 17

Learning mirrors principle, 153–154

Learning theory, 106

Letting go of attachment, 37–38

Life choices, 103–105

Life purpose: coaching to find, 16–17; for each individual, 207; as spiritual tool, 201–202; SUN's approach to revisiting, 251

Life's curves as fortuitous, 235

Living a Life That Matters (Kushner), 50

Living in the Light (Gawain), 253

Living in the Mystery of Coaching (Olalla), 59

"Living Your Dreams" (magazine headline), 166

Living Your Vision (Coach Training Academy), 217

Loughran, C., 34

Luigi, 143

Lupberger, T., 54, 247

M

McGill, A., 112

"Magic Circles," 255

Mahalia, 159–160

Malcolm Baldrige Quality Award Criteria, 173

Managers: responsibilities of, 148; scenarios for, 148–149. *See also* Executive coaching with Spirit
Manifesting Spirit, 193
Manuel, 103
Marcy, 34
Margaret, 139–140
Marketing coaching: acknowledgment step in, 167–168; action step in, 164–165; completion step in, 166–167; connection step in, 163–165; creation step in, 162–163; difficult coaching choices regarding, 158–160; four ways spirituality enhances, 152–158; principle of attraction and, 152–153; principle of connection and, 155–157; principle of greatest good and, 157–158; principle of learning mirrors and, 153–154; six steps to fluidly marketing with Spirit, 161–168; with spiritual fluidity, 151–152; stillness step in, 161–162
Merci, 211
Meredith, 144
Metaphors: used during coach training, 91; dip, 83–86; facilitating connection using, 86–91; marketing coaching with spiritual fluidity, 151–152; Spirit as running horse, 201; spiritual journey, 185, 188–189
Milena, 14
Miller, M., 202
Mitchell, J., 233
Mitsch, D. J., 217–218
Morphogenetic field, 140
Motion, 80–81
Motivation theory, 134
"Moving Spirit" (Dabady), 104–105
Mura, A., 219–221
"My Journey to Coaching" (Allport), 166–167
"My Path Is Perfect" (Hodge), 84–85
Myron, 152–153

Mystery, 215
Myths of Coaching Executives, 170

N

Nabors, L., 17
Nancy, 111
Natasha, 31–32
Negative clients, 42
Negative expectations, 139–141
Nelson, P., 2
Neurons in culture dish, 53*fig*
Neutrality, 110–113
New beginnings, 235
Newfield Network, 214, 244–247
The Newfield Network, 214–216
NLP (neuro-linguistic programming), 128

O

Observation of observing, 215
Olalla, J., 59, 214–216, 245
Olivia, 108–109
Open space technology, 251–252
"The Other Side of Judgment" (Kelly), 133–134
Others, 193
Owen, H., 251

P

Paradoxes, 23
Parry, C., 102
Partnership, 24–25, 207. *See also* Coach-client relationship
Passion, 215
Pattern development, 22
PCMA (Professional Coaches and Mentors Association): abundance-centered culture of, 248–249; community learning created

PCMA (*continued*)

by, 249; contacting, 250; giving-to-get approach by, 249; mission/vision of, 248

The "perfect client," 162

Perlman, D., 177

Personal integrity, 141–142

Physical place of purpose: connection with self and, 39; described, 102–103; making a choice using, 103–105. *See also* Purpose

The Piggyback Principle of Coaching, 32–33

Polarization, 23

Possibilities of learning, 24

Power: accepting Spirit's, 191–193; androgynous, 9–10

Power of silent speech exercise, 56–57

"The Power of Spirit" (Shusterman), 195–197

Practicality principle, 220

Preparation: described, 23–24; spiritual, 41–42

The present moment: assessment related to, 97–99, 261–262; coaching from Spirit and, 117–119; CPR combining responsibility, connection and, 146; embodied Spirit and, 113–116; expectancy and, 106–108; humor and, 108–110; making different difference and, 99–102; neutrality and, 110–113; Spirit's physiological presence and, 102–105

Principle of attraction, 152–153

Principle of connection, 155–157

Principle of greatest good, 157–158

Principle of learning mirrors, 153–154

Principle of Rhythm, 77

Principle of Vibration, 80

Professional Coaches and Mentors Association conference (Costa Mesa), 40

Professional coaching associations, 254

Professional ethics, 157

Professional Speaker's Club of Toastmasters, 168

Profound trust, 215

Purpose: executive coaching with Spirit and, 170–175; physical place of, 102–105; synchronicity and, 74–77. *See also* Physical place of purpose

Purposeful beginning, 234

Purposefulness, 24

PWP (Parents Without Partners), 47

The Pyramid Resource Group, 217–218

Q

Questions: as best evidence of wisdom, 3; on coaching with Spirit, 16; used for connecting with clients, 67–70; during ending of coaching, 80; followed with silence, 67–68; Game of Spirit, 88–89; templates for connecting with clients, 62–67; timing and sequencing of, 69; the ultimate "why," 68–69; to uncover client's relationship with Spirit, 126; why is that important?, 36

Quimby, 161, 233–235

R

Randy, 18–19

Reding, P., 123, 124, 125

Reeder, B., 221–222

Relief, 134–137

Resistance, 145–148

Responsibility: action generated from beliefs and, 142–148; assessment related to, 121–122, 262–263; CPR combining present moment, connection and, 146; ecological, 147–148; For Managers Only, 148–149; as key function of coaching, 122; thoughts and beliefs used to reach, 122–142; of "whole" person, 124

Reynolds, M., 222

Rhodes, R. E., 37–38
Rituals (ending coaching), 79
Robbat, M.-A., 44, 44–46
Roman, C., 17
Roote, A., 89
Running horse metaphor, 201

S

Safety net, 58–59
Saint-Exupéry, A. de, 98
Salmon, L. G., 57, 58
Samantha, 115–116
Schniewind, J., 222–223
Schuler, R., 237–239
Sean, 204–206
Seiffer, J., 223
Self: ego and the, 191; shadow and, 49–50.
    See also Connection with self
Selina, 44–46
Sensory Awareness Day exercise, 116
Shaby, A., 204
Shadow, 49–50, 226
Sharma, 160
Sheryl, 158–159
Shulkin, E., 183
Shusterman, A., 195
Silence, 67–68
Silent speech exercise, 56–57
"Sometimes Spirit Withdraws. . .for Good
    Reason" (McGill), 112–113
Spaciousness, 225
The Spell of the Sensuous (Abram), 68
Spinning, 80–81
Spirit: accepting power of, 191–193; all forms
    of, 227; embodied, 113–116; executive
    coaching and, 173–175; expanded
    through coaching, 94–95; gift of,
    194–195; intuition as voice of, 42–49;
    lessons to learn about, 3–4; living through

transformation, 237; manifesting, 193; as
    partner in coaching, 17–21; partnership
    of inquiry and, 62; physiological presence
    of, 102–105; preparing to coach with,
    15–16; recognizing presence of, 196–
    197; role in mobilizing emotions,
    108–109; running horse metaphor for,
    201; six steps to fluidly marketing with,
    161–168; as super coach trainer, 29–30;
    uncovering client's understanding of,
    126–127; when it withdraws/when it
    takes over, 112–113
"Spirit at Work" (Collings), 140–141
Spirit in the environment, 91–92
"Spirit Is in Fleas" (Costa), 146–147
Spirit of service, 216
Spiritual Age, 2, 3, 4
Spiritual conversation, 218
Spiritual intelligence, 213–214
Spiritual journey: as metaphor, 185,
    188–189; sharing, 82
Spiritual meaningfulness, 12–13
Spiritual practice, 221
Spiritual preparation, 41–42
"Spiritual Preparation" (Walz), 41–42
Spirituality: assessment related to, 11,
    257–258; coaching with Spirit and, 16;
    defining relationship between coaching
    and, 4, 5; Harmonic Convergence experi-
    ence and, 15–16; igniting curiosity about,
    233–235; as not being religion, 236–237;
    preparing for, 41–42
Spoke, S., 239–240
Stillness marketing step, 161–162
SUN (Success Unlimited Network): contact-
    ing, 252; mission of, 250; open space
    process by, 251–252; revising vision/life
    purposes by, 251; setting the stage for
    approach by, 1; ways of being together
    approach by, 250–251

Sutiah, 206, 211–212

Synchronicities: as coach-client connection, 234; interpreting, 235–241

Synchronicities Worksheet, 76e, 152

Synchronicity, 74–77

T

Talbot, M., 74

Tension, 144–145

Therapy vs. coaching, 13

Third ear, 216–217

Third Hermetic Principle, 80

Thoughts/beliefs: absolute continuum of, 131–133; action generated from, 142–148; of effective Spirit coaches, 123–126; eight key, 123–124; field of possibilities in, 122–123; on free from/free to motivation, 134–137; generating advice using client's, 127–131; handling diametrically opposed, 137–141; personal integrity and, 141–142; progression to action from, 130–131; uncovering client's, 126–128. See also Values

Three Turns of Transformation: accepting power of Spirit, 191–193; coach's turn with, 194–195; connecting with Spirit in others, 193; manifesting Spirit, 193–194; success using, 190

Timothy, 114–115

TJ, 190–195

Tomlin, L., 28

Transformation. See Client transformation

Transformational listing, 59–60

"The Transformed Attorney," 177–178

Transparency, 238

"Trial and trial," 24

Trust, 215

Twomey, T., 223–224

U

Unconditional acceptance, 14–15

V

Vajda, P., 20–21

Values: following professional ethics and, 157; SUN use of, 250; taking a stand on, 220. See also Thoughts/beliefs

"Victory in the Void" (Byers), 46–49

Vision: acknowledging that every individual has a, 207–208; author's, 253–254; PCMA (Professional Coaches and Mentors Association), 248; SUN (Success Unlimited Network), 251

W

Wahl, C., 224–225

Walz, J., 40, 41

Ward, C., 123, 127, 145, 240

Why is that important?, 36

Wilder, H., 225–227

William, 199–201

Williams, K. A., 69

Wilson, S., 116, 123

Wisdom: being receptive to, 146; questions as best evidence of, 3

Wiseheart Global Leadership Coaching, 225

Witherspoon, R., 170–171

Wizard Coach: adopting the role of, 30; seven magic words of, 29–30. See also Coaches

"Working with Spirit: Coaching Executive Leadership" (Allen), 190–195

X

"X" spot of the spiral, 21fig

"The 'X' Spot of the Spiral" (Vajda), 20–21

Y

Yugin, 110

Z

Zeitgeist (spirit of the times), 2, 255
Zink, N., 67, 83